LIVING OUT OF BOUNDS: THE MALE ATHLETE'S EVERYDAY LIFE

STEVEN J. OVERMAN

Westport, Connecticut
London

Library of Congress Cataloging-in-Publication Data

Overman, Steven J.
  Living out of bounds : the male athlete's everyday life / Steven J. Overman.
    p. cm.
  Includes bibliographical references and index.
  ISBN 978-0-313-34668-2 (alk. paper)
1. Sports—Sociological aspects. 2. Athletes—Social life and customs. 3. Athletes. I. Title.
GV706.5.O88   2009
796.01—dc22   2008028210

British Library Cataloguing in Publication Data is available.

Library of Congress Catalog Card Number: 2008028210
ISBN: 978-0-313-34668-2

First published in 2009

Praeger Publishers, 88 Post Road West, Westport, CT 06881
An imprint of Greenwood Publishing Group, Inc.
www.praeger.com

Printed in the United States of America

The paper used in this book complies with the
Permanent Paper Standard issued by the National
Information Standards Organization (Z39.48–1984).

10 9 8 7 6 5 4 3 2 1

For the "Jackson Tennis Bums" Dick, Steve B., Duane, Maurice, and three generations of Spongs: Rich, Brian, and Bryce; native Mississippians and transplanted Yankees, dear friends and fellow weekend athletes over two decades.

CONTENTS

Contents

PREFACE

My two consuming passions growing up were reading and sports. Typically, I could be found either propped up on my bed with my nose in a book or on the school playground with a leather ball in my grasp. Given that I grew up in Indiana, the object in hand was usually a basketball, but we also played hours of touch football in the streets and softball in backyards. When I turned 13, my family moved to a neighborhood near the city park and zoo. The animal house was located next to the baseball stadium. Sitting on our front porch on a summer evening, you could hear the lions roar when they were hungry and the baseball fans roar when someone knocked a ball over the outfield fence. This sound carried heroic overtones as local legend had it that future New York Yankee slugger "Moose" Skowron once hit a ball over the center field scoreboard and clear across Main Street onto the schoolyard where I routinely played basketball.

My love of sports came from my father. He occasionally took me in tow on Bowling Night where I watched him attempt to break 200 through a thick haze of cigarette smoke. But he wasn't so much an athlete as a fan. My most cogent memories are of him stretched out in front of the television with the sound turned down, watching the televised game while listening to another game simultaneously on the old wooden radio. This meant the Chicago Bears and Purdue Boilermaker football in the fall, high school basketball all winter, followed by a summer of the St. Louis Cardinals on radio, and the Game of the Week on TV. Even now, to hear a vocal rendition of "The Wabash Cannonball" brings back vivid memories of commentator Dizzy Dean's voice from the CBS broadcast booth.

My love for books was nourished by the public library, a good bike ride to the edge of downtown. A favorite haunt was the library's juvenile room on whose far wall nested a shelf of orange-covered biographies written for young readers. My reading interests, like that of many boys, included the lives of famous people. I read of presidents, founders, and frontiersmen—Andrew

Jackson, Ben Franklin, and Daniel Boone. I also read the lives of famous athletes, mostly men, given the times. The biography of tennis's Althea Gibson
was the rare exception. In my teens and college years, I began to digest more
meaty offerings: American classics like *Walden* and *Two Years before the Mast,*
as well as the autobiographical fiction of Jack London and Thomas Wolfe.
But reading was routinely interrupted by the clank of an errant jump shot
against the front of a rim outside my bedroom window, as virtually every other
Hoosier driveway offered a basketball goal.

Despite the distraction of basketball, I was a more serious reader than athlete. For me, sports were about enjoyment, and I resented anyone—especially
authoritarian coaches—who attempted to gainsay that prejudice. To be an outstanding athlete requires a single-minded pursuit of finely wrought skills and a
devotion to arduous training that I generally disdained. I was not a specialist; I
was a generalist. I preferred a variety of recreational activities to the two-hour
sessions of repetitive drills doled out on the high school practice field. My
model was Tom Sawyer not Rocky Balboa.

I had the physical characteristics to be a good athlete. My frame combined
the qualities that coaches look for in a middle-distance runner or tight end,
but alas I was not particularly swift of foot. I reached somewhat over six feet
in height with unusually long arms that led to my perfecting the hook shot as
compensation against taller opponents under the basketball goal. But basketball was evolving beyond the choreographed style of offense that my boyhood
hero Goose Tatum practiced with the Harlem Globetrotters. Though my left-
handed hook shot had a well-deserved reputation on the city courts, I never
made the varsity squad.

A knack for wrestling had won me the grade school championship. So I tried
out for the wrestling squad in junior high school, but my impatience with the
dull routine of practice soon gave in to the siren call of the sandlot. Subsequent
forays into school sports met with mediocre results in football and tennis. Less
demanding intramural and church league basketball offered greater appeal.
But most of my leisure was spent on the public courts. We would play ball till
supper time and then carry on the ritual until darkness intervened. We played
in the heat of the Midwest summer and through the winter, even if it meant
donning gloves. We played on blacktop, concrete, and dirt both muddy and
frozen. Pickup basketball supplanted Methodism as my true religion.

Though I was not cut out to be a star athlete, I was witness to a fair amount
of athletic brilliance. I shared vicariously in the triumphs of some great names
in sports. I had observed a young Oscar Robertson dazzle the crowd in my high
school gym; watched an ancient Satchel Paige befuddle the local hitters one
memorable summer night at the ballpark where I hawked cokes and peanuts
in the stands. In Purdue University's football stadium, I admired quarterback
Len Dawson's long passes deposited into the lanky arms of Lamar Lundy, a
future member of the LA Rams "Fearsome Foursome." And I once played in
a church league game against a former Indiana Mr. Basketball, an icon whose

status among Hoosiers rivaled that of the state's governor. Howard Cosell conceded he "never played the game"; at least I brushed shoulders with greatness on the basketball court.

As the first in the family to go to college, my two passions steered me toward a dual concentration in physical education and English. At Purdue in the 1960s, I was to rub elbows with several great athletes in my classes at Lambert Field House. I sat behind future Detroit Lion and Pro Bowler Ed Flanagan whose impressive neck and shoulders blocked my view of the lecturer. An ill-advised pickup game of water polo with members of the football team motivated me to enroll in lifeguard training as a matter of self-defense. I could readily identify with the overmatched George Plimpton whose best-selling book, *Paper Lion,* had just been published.

Following graduation, I moved to the Southwest and a brief stint in public school coaching. My induction into this profession revealed more about school principals' desperation to find coaches than anything on my résumé. Once again, I met with surprising, if brief, success. My football coaching career debuted with a flawlessly executed onside kick at the opening kickoff followed by a completed "Hail Mary" pass for a touchdown. Any allusions of becoming a future Vince Lombardi were tempered, however, by the ultimate outcome of the game, an 8–6 loss via an ignominious safety. Undeterred by a spotty record on the gridiron, I tried my hand at coaching basketball. The first season climaxed with the only sports trophy I ever won. Mentoring a group of oversized Anglo kids against a league replete with diminutive Hispanics, we outlasted the State School for the Deaf in a double overtime for the tournament championship.

Again, I found myself pinned against the hall bulletin board by principal Ed Spence, the desperate recruiter of coaches. He explained that it was only an *assistant* track coach position that he needed to fill. I told him, without false modesty, that I was one of the slowest athletes in Indiana sports history which is why I never went out for track, and that I knew virtually nothing about coaching the sport. "Buy a book and read up on it," he countered. I did, and it was an auspicious decision as this was the year the nation's best track athletes would appropriate our facility in the Jemez Mountains at 7,000 feet above sea level to train for the Mexico City Olympics. I watched some great runners train; it was more informative than the coaching book I had purchased. If I were a failed athlete, maybe I would become a successful coach after all.

However, the gods that intervene in career choices spirited me off to other venues where I would stand in the shadows of more sports greats. I left the mountains and public school coaching for the Palouse Hills of Eastern Washington and graduate study at a PAC-10 school, where Coach John Wooden (another transplanted Hoosier) and his UCLA basketball team once graced our college gym. After graduation, I escaped the brutal Northern winters by heading to Jackson, Mississippi, to teach at a historically black college that rivaled the legendary Grambling in its penchant for producing football players.

Here, I would meet the incomparable Walter Payton and teach his brother Eddie along with dozens of other future NFL stars. During one year in the 1970s, 16 of my former Jackson State students graced the rosters of professional football franchises.

Ensconced in the hinterlands of the American South, an unlikely meeting took place that would underscore my role as acolyte to the pantheon of sports immortals. On a Friday afternoon as the day was winding down and I sat alone at my desk, Joe Louis—*the* Joe Louis—appeared in my office doorway. He was introduced by his companion, a front man for some now-forgotten political candidate. This was no apparition but the ex-champ himself dutifully playing his assigned role as hired celebrity. I shook the hand that knocked out Max Schmeling with a sense of overwhelming awe blunted by a shred of sadness. I pondered what it was like to be Joe Louis past and present.

I could claim personal acquaintance with the great Walter Payton and Joe Louis. Within "two degrees of separation" (I know someone who knows someone), I could even claim a connection to the venerable Jim Thorpe. During a visit with my children's maternal great grandfather, he reminisced from his Indiana nursing home bed how he had played football with the Olympic champion back in 1915 on Pine Village's semipro team. Thus, like Boswell standing in the shadow of Johnson, I have been fated to bask in the penumbra of greatness, but in the arena of Mars not Minerva. Lacking the talents of these two literati, I have opted not to write biography but to excavate the extant narratives to capture the athlete's life written large.

Fortunately, athletes are inclined to tell stories of their exploits and talk about their everyday lives. Some of these tales are little more than boasting or "war stories," but often their accounts are reflective and insightful. While most athletes limit their audience to teammates, friends, and fans, a few are literate enough to put their thoughts to pen and paper or share their life stories with professional writers. Mining these books has reacquainted me with some of the outstanding sports writers of the 20th century: Nat Fleischer, Frank Graham, Al Hirshberg, and Frank DeFord among others. The project also introduced me to some surprisingly good autobiographical writing by athletes who defy the stereotype of "illiterate jock."

In writing this book, I plead guilty to H. L. Mencken's characterization of a college professor as "a man devoted to diluting and retailing the ideas of his superiors." In my defense, I believe that I have recovered some long-forgotten gems gathering dust on library shelves, buried in auto/biographies that were avidly consumed when their subjects were in the limelight but now lie dormant. By implication, I am suggesting that this distillation offers insights into the athletic experience beyond what is obtainable from reading the life of any solitary individual.

I'll leave it to the reader to determine if the retail item is worth the price.

INTRODUCTION

What is it like to live the life of an athlete? The question implies more than what occurs in the stadium on the field of play. It encompasses events that take place before and after competition, between games, and in the off-season. How does the athlete handle everyday life punctuated with grueling workouts, a relentless travel schedule, and the constant pressure to perform? How does the competitor balance these responsibilities with obligations to family and friends? What is it like in the locker room, at training camp, and holed up in hotel rooms in strange cities? This book attempts to answer these questions through a collection of personal narratives written by and about athletes, reaching across sports and across time. We follow the athlete from childhood, through adolescence; his ascent into the limelight, during the twilight of his career, and into retirement. The goal is to provide the reader with an alternative to the two-dimensional image on a box of breakfast cereal or trading cards. The athlete is presented as a multidimensional human being, a real person with a life beyond the sports arena.

Many of us have been athletes in the sense that sport once provided an aspect of our identity. We may have played on school teams and in local youth leagues. As adults, we hit a golf ball or tennis ball on weekends. But we are mere amateurs, dilettantes, compared to the athletes in this book. Our victories and defeats are given little regard beyond the club bulletin board or the local sports page. However, our interest in sport surpasses this level. We are sports fans, connoisseurs of the performances of highly skilled athletes. We admire the grace and mastery with which the truly gifted exhibit their talents in the public arena. We identify with them; try to imagine ourselves in their shoes. Occasionally, we catch a glimpse of the actual person behind the performer. Such revelations occur when intense competition triggers emotions or during those brief intermissions when the athlete's game persona recedes. But these occurrences are just that, brief glimpses.

Increasingly, our image of the athlete is filtered. The electronic media provide an intimate and yet detached view. While radio broadcasts allow us to project our own visual perceptions, television imposes an image both scripted and choreographed. Newspapers and magazines, for their part, offer little more than photos and short descriptions of athletic feats along with occasional anecdotes about the athlete. Commercial films depicting the lives of athletes rely on actors, constructed scenes, and invented dialogue—all of which alter reality for dramatic effect. The overall view of athletes we acquire through the news and entertainment media is both circumscribed and enhanced.[1]

Together, the above sources of information constitute an album of impressions, frozen in time and framed by context. They provide interesting snapshots but reveal less than the whole picture, the events leading up to the recorded episode and its aftermath. The conception of the individual athlete assembled from these images is more of a caricature than an evolving character. To really know a subject means becoming familiar with the person's history. A point-in-time impression is unable to fulfill this requirement. We need a better window to perceive the human essence of the athlete in the context of his everyday experiences. The premise of this book is that biographical writing provides such a window. Book-length narratives, in particular, enable us to interpret sport in ways that reach beneath the veneer of performance data. This medium provides a context in which the athlete isn't typecast by chance events or colored by fleeting impressions.

Life stories offer valuable insights. They increase our sensitivity to the particular details in the lives of unfamiliar sorts of people. These narratives make it more difficult for us to marginalize or idealize people different from ourselves. In the process of describing what unfamiliar people are like, we are provided a lens into our own lives. This allows us to see others as "one of us." The power of the life story to create empathy is vital in the case of "exemplary people" who have achieved public prominence. A tendency persists to view such individuals as fundamentally different. Books about athletes have the potential to breach this barrier. Duncan suggests that the sharing of experiences is most likely when the accounts are about the body, since bodies have both private and social dimensions. Stories about the body connect our private experiences with the social norms of our society.[2] If Duncan is correct, then we should find something especially revealing and meaningful in the life stories of athletes. Indeed, the physicality of these subjects may explain why sports biographies are so popular.

The late anthropologist Clifford Geertz proclaimed, "When I tell myself a story about myself, I imagine who I am and create myself in the act of imagination."[3] The point of storytelling is the imaginative ability to position oneself as the "other." In doing so, voices to which the reader (or listener) would have only superficial access are experienced in greater depth. Storytelling simultaneously becomes a sharing of experience and an account of meaning.[4] When boxer Jack Johnson wrote his autobiography *In the Ring and Out* (1927), he not only told his life story, he created a character that was himself and stamped his meaning on the relationship between race and sport in early 20th-century America.[5]

Jack Johnson's book illustrates the narrative's power to present different voices. It would be a mistake to assume that the athletic experience is uniform. Diverse experiences occur even within particular sports. NFL lineman Michael Oriard[6] remarks on the multifarious impact of football, the range of possible incidents, the diversity of players, and how they adapt to the game. If personal experiences vary within a sport, they can be expected to differ across sports. The following chapters illustrate this point. At the same time, all athletes share in the common elements of their craft: training, competition, victory and defeat, injury and recovery, the capriciousness of fame, the gradual decline of physical ability, and adjustment to life after sport. Thus, while each individual sports narrative is distinct in its own way, the genre of sport auto/biography evokes a shared experience.

Champion bowler Carmen Salvino's autobiography features a photograph portraying two dozen men and women honored by the National Italian American Sports Hall of Fame on its 10th anniversary.[7] Among those pictured with Salvino are baseball's Joe DiMaggio, football's Dan Marino, boxing's Jake LaMotta, hockey's Tony Esposito, and golf's Donna Caponi. Members of this distinguished group are linked by two themes. While their ethnic identity was an accident of birth, they all chose to become athletes. The gathering reflects a basic premise of this book: that a common element runs through sport. Whether a bowler, golfer, boxer, or ballplayer, the essence of the athlete's life is a shared experience. And, this experience can be narrated and understood.

The written accounts of athletes' lives offer a sense of authenticity but this medium is not without its limitations. Reading about sports—or any life events for that matter—is distinct from experiencing or observing them first hand. A written account is a *representation* of the actual event, not the thing itself. There remains what novelist Don DeLillo refers to as "that other world unsyllabled." All life stories are mediated. They are filtered through memory, censored due to sensitivity, and embellished by their retelling to oneself and to others. These limitations apply to both autobiography and biography. Short story writer Damon Runyon addressed this problem in his preface to Jack Johnson's autobiography. As to whether the colorful boxer could give an honest account of his life, Runyon comments: "If he tells the truth, which is doubtful, his will be a most enthralling tale. I say it is doubtful if he tells the truth because John Arthur [*i.e.,* Jack] isn't old enough [at age 49] to tell the truth in an autobiography. A man has to be just about ready to die before he has the courage of unburdening himself completely."[8]

In point of fact, few athletes delay the writing of their memoirs to satisfy Runyon's criterion. If all this is not troublesome enough, critics would have us believe that athletes are not the most articulate individuals when it comes to verbalizing their experiences or converting them to ink and paper. Despite these limitations, I am persuaded that the following chapters offer valuable insights into the unique everyday experiences of athletes. The individuals selected for inclusion in this book have led exceptional lives, and they have left a compelling record for our enjoyment and edification. Those who have written about their sports careers speak for themselves.

Constructing a sports *biography* involves two participants, the athlete and the writer, while *autobiography* obligates the subject to don both hats. Aside from the shared roles of author and subject, the two forms of narrative each present their own peculiar problems. The biographer generally doesn't know enough and must extract information from the athlete. This requires a fertile dialogue, or a prodigious amount of research if the athlete is deceased. The athlete/autobiographer, on the other hand, knows too much and must decide what to include and what to leave out of the story. Given that most athletes are not professional writers, they must work closely with an editor or collaborator to accomplish a well-crafted narrative. Thus, whether the form chosen is biography, autobiography, or memoir, a crucial element is teamwork. Cooperating on a successful book can prove as challenging as winning the Kentucky Derby. Neither the horse nor rider can do it alone.

The athlete who wants his story told by a biographer must submit to extensive in-depth interrogation. Athletes are no strangers to interviews. They are routinely accosted by journalists looking for a story. Some are more cooperative than others. In preparing his comprehensive biography of Muhammad Ali, Thomas Hauser traveled with the former champ and interviewed him on several occasions including a five-day visit at his home. A mature Ali showed a willingness to be interviewed that had not been characteristic of the boxer in his youth. In 1976, Random House published the Ali "autobiography" actually written by Richard Durham. The young boxer was uninterested in the project and spent relatively little time with Durham. Indeed, he never looked at the book until after it was published. Subsequently, more than three dozen books would be written on Ali's life, with and without his cooperation. Ali freely admitted, "I haven't read ten pages in all the books written about me."[9]

Biographers are aware that there can be problems extracting information from sports figures. The veterans have built up defenses against intrusive questions. A successful interviewer must breach any barriers to openness, honesty, and trust. Chuck Knox, who played Division III college football prior to his illustrious NFL coaching career, was approached by several writers who wanted to do a book on him. He rejected all of them before agreeing to do a cowritten autobiography with Los Angeles sportswriter Bill Plaschke. Knox explained his reluctance, "You can buy and sell whatever a man wears, but there is no price on what he has inside. So I turned them down."[10] Fortunately he relented, as he had an engrossing story to share.

Longtime *Herald Tribune* editor Stanley Woodward observed, "It is one thing to interview [a sports personality] on the bench before a game and another to get him on his night out with his hair down."[11] Fortunately, there are athletes willing to submit to extensive interviews. A busy Ted Turner agreed to sit down in his living room for over four hours to go over his yachting scrapbooks and memorabilia with biographer Roger Vaughan, as he reminisced about his 10 years as a racing skipper.[12] Writer Perry Young spent four to six hours a day for three months doing interviews with football player Dave Kopay in preparing *The Dave Kopay Story.* The book was written by the two men working in tandem. Kopay wrote his part in first person. Young wrote his part in third person.[13] A critically ill Brian Piccolo taped an incomplete monologue with the goal of publishing his life story. He met on several occasions with biographer Jeannie Morris during his hospitalization for cancer. The Chicago Bear running back's wife Joy was left to complete the task upon her husband's untimely death.[14]

Even when the athlete makes himself available to the biographer, this may not necessarily unveil the "inner man." Al Stump was invited to live with the elderly Ty Cobb for several months in 1960 for the purpose of cowriting Cobb's autobiography. However, Stump's efforts to reveal his subject were repeatedly sabotaged by the defensive, image-conscious curmudgeon. Stump actually kept two sets of notes: one for the book that Cobb wanted written (the highly sanitized *My Life in Baseball*) and covert notes that generated the biography that Stump would write later under the subtitle, "The Life and Times of the Meanest Man Who Ever Played Baseball."[15] His encounter with Cobb provides a lesson in how the biographer's purpose can be stymied by a guarded or uncooperative subject.

Then there are the athletes who are all too eager to reveal themselves in print. I purposely circumvented the autobiography of flamboyant NBA star Dennis Rodman, titled *Bad as I Want to Be,* in favor of an "unauthorized" biography of the former NBA star written by Chicago journalist Dan Bickley.[16] I made a different decision for Deion Sanders, whose sobriquet "Neon Deion" suggests the tenor of his persona. Once one gets past the title of his autobiography, *Power, Money & Sex: How Success Almost Ruined My Life* and makes allowances for self-promotion, the reader discovers an interesting and reflective subject.[17] I found Deion more likable and intelligible after reading his life story. The same cannot be said for NFL linebacker Bill Romanowski, whose recent book *Romo: Life on the Edge,* comes across as a hyperbolic indulgence in self-justification and self-aggrandizement.[18] Yet, the book is indispensable as a statement on the role of drugs and violence in contemporary sport. While these three colorful athletes' stories add a vibrant dimension to the present book, I sought to balance these panegyrics with more prosaic narratives.

Diaries, given their composition in the present tense, provide a distinct perspective on sport. Their value resides in the fact that they tend to be less reflective and more experiential than biographies and memoirs, which are written with a conscious regard for the subject's image and place in history. When 30-year-old Arthur Ashe chronicled his daily impressions of playing on the tennis circuit from Wimbledon 1973 to Wimbledon 1974, he wrote at first in longhand but then switched to a tape machine. He would record every night, or occasionally in the middle of the day. Ashe comments on a week's gap in the record: "It's easy to keep a daily diary if a lot of interesting things are happening all around you, and it's even easier if you are pleased with yourself. But if things are dull . . . ." Ashe's efforts culminated in an insightful book with writer Frank Deford whom he had known since the early 1960s.[19]

In *Instant Replay* (1968), Green Bay Packer guard Jerry Kramer shares his diary from the start of training camp to the end of the 1967 football season. Each night he would speak into a tape recorder or take notes and record them later. He then mailed the tapes to Dick Schaap at the *Herald Tribune* on a weekly basis. The transcripts reached over 100,000 words. Schaap edited Kramer's material, condensing it and adding background and explanation to produce the book.[20] Pitcher Jim Bouton interviewed himself in preparing his account of the 1969 baseball season, *Ball Four.* He talked into a tape recorder for seven months, beginning autumn 1968, resulting in a 1,500-page manuscript, eventually cut to 500 pages.[21]

The diary is self-limited in perspective. Biography incorporates the impressions of many others beside the athlete. Thomas Hauser interviewed over 100 people for his book on Muhammad Ali, as did Michael Sokolove for his biography of controversial baseball player/manager Pete Rose. Some of Sokolove's sources asked to be quoted anonymously, and there were those who refused to be interviewed at all. Biographers rely on more than interviews for their material. Other sources of information include informal conversations, direct question-and-answer sessions, press conferences, and off-the-record private exchanges of information. In addition, biographers resort to the same sources that historians employ: diaries, letters, public papers. Nick Tosches' account of the crime-ridden life of boxer Sonny Liston involved delving into police files, court records, and even the transcripts of congressional investigations.[22] Newspapers provide a secondary source for writers. Much of the material for George DeGregario's biography of Joe DiMaggio came from newspaper accounts. Indeed, there's no indication that DeGregario interviewed his subject at all—and given DiMaggio's legendary inaccessibility, he probably didn't.[23] Neither did Richard Ben Cramer get any help from DiMaggio in writing his unsympathetic biography.[24]

Recently, another actor has intruded into the delicate relationship between the athlete and writer. Sports management agencies wish to mediate the writing of biographies of their clients. The International Management Group which represented Tiger Woods didn't like the fact that Tim Rosaforte was writing a biography of the then 20-year-old golfer, as they weren't going to get their 20 percent commission. IMG had been taking bids on Tiger's book contracts with offers reputedly as high as $1.5 million. Rosaforte wrote the book anyway. He countered, "Maybe Tiger didn't sit down one-on-one, but I was around enough, and talked to enough people, that I ended up with too much material."[25] In spite of commercial interests, the hype of agents and publishers, intrusive sportswriters, and the ego needs of sports celebrities, a majority of sports books are successful ventures that offer a window into the athlete's life.

The author commenced research on this book with the commonly held prejudice against sports *auto*biographies. One major "rap" on this genre is that athletes don't write (and occasionally don't even read) their autobiographies. Typically, these books have been ghost written or by a credited coauthor. Sportswriter Leonard Schecter once sneered about a book "authored" by New York Yankee catcher Yogi Berra: "It was a typical baseball autobiography, all shiny and bright for the kiddies, naturally written by somebody else."[26] Indeed, many sports autobiographies are directed at the juvenile reader. Even adult sports fans seem quite willing to forgive athletes for seeking assistance in putting their words onto paper. Former NFL coach and television commentator John Madden traded on the perception of sports personalities being less than authorial with his title, *Hey, Wait a Minute I Wrote a Book!*—predictably cowritten with a sports columnist. Its fair to say that the great majority of athletes lack the writing skills, sense of reflection, or personal insights to create first-rate autobiographies or memoirs. Employing a professional coauthor usually results in a higher-quality narrative. Books authored by athletes often have two names on the title pages; Bill Romanowski's features three.

The other major criticism of sports autobiographies—as well as some biographies—is equally damning: that they are boilerplate productions written according to formula and published prematurely, about subjects still in their formative years. These books are motivated by the author's (or publisher's) desire to exploit temporary notoriety. Such efforts constitute little more than "puff pieces" to be consumed by loyal fans. Forewarned of these limitations, I was pleasantly surprised to find several autobiographies of merit. Deion Sanders' is one of the better known; but those by football's Michael Oriard and Dave Meggyesy, and hockey's Ken Dryden are equally insightful.

The memoir, distinct from the autobiography, focuses on a time in the subject's life that was unusually vivid or framed by circumstance. The occasion may be triumph or tragedy. Notable sports memoirs include Olympic champion Don Schollander's *Deep Water* and Arthur Ashe's *Days of Grace,* penned in the shadow of an HIV infection that ended his life. Minor league pitcher Pat Jordan, NFL lineman Tim Green, and NBA forward Bill Bradley also wrote literate memoirs; the first two went on to become professional writers; Bradley went into politics.

While professional biographers generally produce more polished books than athlete/authors, no sweeping judgment can be made about the superiority of "as-told-to" books versus the self-written. I was determined that the present book should include a variety of sports narratives. My goal in writing the book was to reveal the athlete's life primarily through books written by them or about them. This involved several key decisions. Selection of source material was the initial task. I had to decide on which sports to include to represent the broad athletic experience. I then chose a representative sample of athletes, considering such factors as gender, ethnicity, and nationality, and what time frame to cover. The other major question was how many and what kind of books by and about athletes should be included to capture their experiences. The following remarks explain how these decisions were made.

The span of time covered by the book is roughly coterminous with the 20th century. I made the assumption that despite changes in sports rules, technology, training methods, and media coverage, the kernel of athletic experience has retained its coherence over time. Beginning with horse racing's "Yankee Doodle Dandy" Tod Sloan (born in 1874) and boxing's post-Victorian *parvenu* Jack Johnson, the narrative extends to the new-millennium *Wunderkind* Tiger Woods. This scope allows for comparison and contrast across the decades.

Athletes in this book who competed in the first half of the 20th century along with Johnson and Sloan include: Gene Tunney, Jack Dempsey, and Joe Louis (boxing), Christy Mathewson, Ty Cobb, Babe Ruth, Joe DiMaggio, Lou Gehrig, Josh Gibson, and Satchel Paige (baseball), Red Pollard (horse racing), Jim Thorpe (track and field; football), Jesse Owens (track and field), Bill Tilden (tennis), C. L. R. James (cricket), and Ben Hogan (golf). Jackie Robinson appropriately appears at the century's midpoint; a harbinger of things to come. The remainder of the athletes competed in the second half of the century, and a couple are still active.

One limitation presented itself early on in the reading. I had intended to include the lives of both men and women athletes, but it became apparent that differences based on gender rendered this approach ill-advised. It's true that young men and women often relate similar stories about their initiation into sport. Champion figure skater Michelle Kwan was introduced to the ice rink at age five; the same age that Tiger Woods began hitting golf balls on the back nine with sawed-off clubs.[27] Jackie Joyner-Kersee's account of how she found her niche in track and field through a chance event at an East St. Louis recreation center is not that dissimilar from young Cassius Clay's story about his stolen bike that led him to the boxing gym in Louisville.[28]

However, women athletes experience sports and relate to their bodies quite differently than men. A representative comment illustrates the point. Distance swimmer Sally Friedman describes the pleasures and pain of her sport with references to childbirth and the body's production of endorphins. She exclaims, "I am absolutely energized after a workout, my body glows through the aches, the blissful fatigue washes my cares away."[29] Male athletes simply do not make these kinds of observations, based on the nearly six dozen book-length auto/biographies that I read in preparing for this book. Joan Ryan's description of the stilted life of young gymnasts in *Little Girls in Pretty Boxes* (1995) reinforced my impression of the gender-specific aspects of the athletic experience. She found that many of the girls struggled with eating disorders and arrested puberty; these issues don't appear in the life stories of young male athletes.[30]

Although men and women athletes in some ways have become more alike in our increasingly androgynous culture, they continue to be distinct in their responses to sport. The collective experience of women athletes merits a separate book. Such an effort may have to wait awhile, for the number of sports biographies currently published continues to reflect the gender bias of professional sport. Books written by or about women athletes remain underrepresented. For these reasons the present effort was limited to male athletes, notwithstanding the inclusion of transgendered tennis player Renée Richards, who grew up male as Richard Raskind.[31] On a stylistic note, given this limitation, the writer has employed exclusive male pronouns more freely than the normal convention of gender neutrality would dictate.

I have generally limited my sample to American athletes but bent the rule on occasion. British soccer player Paul Merson's memoir was included on the assumption that American soccer had not yet become popular enough to spawn a representative book.[32] Later, I found NASL goalie Shep Messing's autobiography.[33] I kept Merson anyway because I found his story compelling and not that different from those of the Americans. The same rationale applied to the sport of hockey. I discovered the autobiography of Canadian hockey player Ken Dryden, one of the most reflective and literate athletes I came across in my reading. He provides valuable insights into the athlete's life regardless of nationality.[34] I also borrow from Michael Smith's *Life after Hockey* (1987), a series of interviews with retired Canadian and American hockey players. Also included is Canadian-born jockey Red Pollard—the costar of Laura Hillenbrand's book *Seabiscuit* (2002)—who rode for an American stable. Although cricket is not an American sport, I reference the memoir of renowned Caribbean-born scholar and cricket player C. L. R. James for reasons explained below.[35]

The book's focus is on athletes as distinct from "sportsmen." The latter term refers to those who may dabble in sports or pursue them seriously as avocations, but don't make sport their primary occupation. An exemplary case is British-born Nobel laureate in chemistry Francis W. Aston (1877–1945), a superb sportsman who skied, built and raced motorcycles, became devoted to surfing in his 30s, and hit a golf ball on weekends throughout much of his life.[36] Despite these accomplishments, Aston's vocation was in the laboratory not the athletic arena. Sports remained his avocation.

I made exceptions to what constitutes a career athlete in several instances for what I considered sufficient reasons. A few individuals who are writers foremost but also athletes are found in the book, including the above-mentioned C. L. R. James. He straddles the line between career athlete and sportsman in his lifelong devotion to cricket. James ultimately turned down an offer to play professionally; instead opting for a job as cricket reporter for the *Manchester Guardian*. His classic autobiography, *Beyond a Boundary* includes material on his own amateur career and that of a few professional cricket players.[37] I also reference writer George Plimpton's *Paper Lion* (1966), about the former Ivy League quarterback's experience "trying out" with the 1963 Detroit Lions. Likewise, I included author Pat Conroy, a talented basketball player in high

school and college. Conroy wisely directed his talents at becoming an outstanding novelist not a professional ballplayer. His memoir *My Losing Season* (2002)
about his college basketball career offers a unique glimpse into relationships
with an authoritarian coach and a tyrannical father. Writer Mark Edmundson
didn't play football beyond high school, but I borrowed a couple of paragraphs
from his book *Teacher* (2002) for their insights into his personal transformation on the athletic field. Another sort of exception is anthropologist Robert
Sands, whose participant observation study, *Gutcheck!* (1999) offers an insid-
er's view of a junior college football team.

Most people would label the young Ted Turner a sportsman. However, I
include his yachting biography, *The Grand Gesture* because this surprisingly
athletic sport remains unappreciated by the typical sports fan. Turner's obsession with boats waned as he explored other vocations and avocations, but
yachting remains a competitive sport.[38] Others included in the book straddle
the line between full-time and part-time athletes. At the opposite end of the economic spectrum from yachtsmen, one finds the athlete whose sports career is
compromised by the realities of making a living. Michael Oriard played Canadian professional football in the 1970s, following a brief career in the NFL.
He writes about teammates who required second jobs during the season. Their
day was free of football until 4 p.m. when they had a brief meeting and short
practice. Weekends were "game time."[39] Shep Messing describes a similar situation among professional soccer players during the early years of the sport
in the United States. His teammates were part-time athletes, but serious athletes
nonetheless.[40]

The book also includes athletes in sports where professional opportunities
are limited or nonexistent. Track and field has been one such sport; swimming
is another. Olympic swimmer Don Schollander refers to athletes like himself as
"professional amateurs." Following actor Johnny Weissmuller's victory in the
1924 Olympics, American swimming evolved into the equivalent of a professional sport based on the time and effort devoted to it by serious competitors.
Schollander reminds us that these "amateurs" not only practice for hours on a
daily basis and make great personal sacrifices for their sport, but they often
compete against athletes from other nations who *are* professionals.[41] The stories of amateurs provide a point of comparison with athletes who are paid to
compete. Also, athletes in some sports become famous as amateurs and then
turn pro. The first half of Tiger Woods' biography by Rosaforte covers the
young golfer's notable amateur accomplishments; the last half, his budding professional career. Given the above exceptions, the great majority of athletes
included in this study are men who have competed for money under some type
of contractual relationship. Their sport is their job.[42]

Hundreds of books have been written by and about athletes, and I made no
attempt to read an exhaustive or even proportional sample. Nor did I make an

effort to identify the definitive biography for each athlete. I read more than one book on several athletes, notably Joe DiMaggio, Arthur Ashe, and Muhammad Ali. In addition to autobiographies, diaries, and memoirs, I read both scholarly and popular biographies including a couple written for juvenile readers. I also read several feature-length articles on athletes such as Richard Ben Cramer's 1986 in-depth profile of Ted Williams in *Esquire* magazine.[43] And there are a few newspaper accounts of current events. My intent was to sample the entire genre of biographical literature that covered the major sports. I arbitrarily excluded motor sports (engineering) and professional wrestling (choreography). Having set out on this scheme, I found it relatively easy to determine when I had read enough for my purposes. At a distinct juncture, I began to share Yogi Berra's sense of "déjà vu all over again."

Some sports have received more coverage than others. In defense of this bias, I reference an article in *The New Yorker* about eccentric chess champion Bobby Fischer. The writer Louis Menand opens with the statement, "Chess is not friendly to prose."[44] This observation applies to several games and sports, but clearly baseball and boxing aren't among them. The athletes included in this book reflect the fact that these two sports have dominated sportswriting and biography throughout much of the 20th century. (Football has come on strong in the second half of the century.) For whatever reasons, some sports do lend themselves more than others to compelling narratives. Baseball and boxing may be overrepresented—and I admit a fan's bias toward the former— but I did make an effort to be representative of the entire range of Anglo-American sport.

A conscious attempt was made to strike a balance between individual and team sports in selecting athletes for inclusion, but the latter category clearly tipped the balance. In a few cases, the distinction is blurred. Track, swimming, and gymnastics combine aspects of team and individual effort. Scoring is often calculated by team but based upon individual performances. World champion shot putter Randy Matson was a member of various track teams—high school, college, and Olympic—but set national and world records as an individual. Bowling offers a special case. Into the 1960s, the sport was mostly a team event where the five members had their scores totaled and shared prize money. By the 1980s it had become a distinctly individual sport on the professional circuit.[45] The distinction between individual and team sports is coherent but not always definitive. C. L. R. James captures the ambiguity between the individual and team in his following description of cricket. He observes

> two individuals are pitted against each other in a conflict that is strictly personal but no less strictly representative of a social group. One individual batsman faces one individual bowler. Each represents his side. The batsman facing the ball does not merely represent his side. For that moment to all intents and purposes, he is his side. The part and the whole are strategically imposed on the players.[46]

During my survey of books on sport, I came across what might be labeled "team biographies." I have included Chris Lear's *Running with the Buffaloes* (2000) about cross-country distance runners. I also reference John Feinstein's *A Season on the Brink* (1989) about Indiana University's basketball team and coach Bobby Knight. David Halberstam's *Playing for Keeps* (1999) offers a dual focus on ballplayer Michael Jordan and his team, the Chicago Bulls. Books about teams provide a distinct perspective on the lives of athletes; however, the best narratives focus preeminently on the individual. This seems true whether the athlete is competing against dozens in a cross-country event or as one component of a highly synchronized basketball squad. In regard to the latter, Pat Conroy's memoir bridges the gap between the individual ballplayer and his team as well as any.

In addition, I made it a point to read books by and about those who are close to athletes for their insights into the athlete's life. I've included anecdotal material from Jerome Holtzman's *No Cheering in the Press Box* (1995), a lively account of sportswriters who not only wrote about, but traveled and socialized with athletes. Neil Isaacs' *Batboys and the World of Baseball* (1995) provides an intimate view of baseball's dugouts and clubhouses. Jeanne Parr's *The Superwives* (1976) offers 28 interviews of women married to athletes. I read Chuck Knox's autobiography *Hard Knox: The Life of an NFL Coach* for a coach's view of athletes. Chuck served as both an assistant and head coach with experience at the high school, college, and professional levels. He was the quintessential "players coach," the type of mentor who would put on a helmet and join his charges in a scrimmage.

The main focus of this book is on life beyond the field of play; an account of what it's like to be an athlete when not performing. The fact is that athletes spend most of their time outside the sports arena. While the following pages include occasional accounts of practice sessions and competition, what the reader will not find are depictions such as: "McEnroe served deep to his opponent's backhand," "Ortiz hit a sinking line drive to center field," or "Michael Jordan stopped short and fired a jump shot from the top of the key." Most sports fans have witnessed dozens of home runs, touchdowns, and birdies dropping into cups, if only on television. We are less familiar with the everyday life of the athlete, and there are compelling reasons to redirect our focus outside the arena. The noted British literary scholar Samuel Johnson suggested that biographers should seek out their subjects in "domestic privacies" as this is where little known facts or anecdotes reveal character.[47] More and more authors of books about athletes are following Johnson's advice. Their efforts provide valuable insights into the private lives and personalities of their subjects.

However, the great majority of sports books continue to focus on the athlete's performance on the field. Descriptions of ball games, competitive matches and tournaments are exploited repetitively, even gratuitously. At a certain point, reading about one more triumph of a champion or the come-from-behind victory of a dark horse adds little to our knowledge of sport—or, more to the point, our understanding of the individuals who compete. The unique contribution of the present book is its conscious choice to forgo the narration of events on the fields of competition in favor of what takes place during the everyday lives of athletes. The author's thesis is that what transpires when the athlete hangs up his uniform can prove much more revealing.

The reader will learn more about father-son relationships through Earl Woods' dreams for his son and the regimen he created to develop his young prodigy than from a description of Tiger sinking a 30-foot putt. Racism is revealed through the accounts of Roberto Clemente, Josh Gibson, and their teammates negotiating life in restaurants, hotels, on planes and busses, as well as from racist taunts on the playing fields. Our insights into the reclusive Joe DiMaggio are gained through his relationships with wife Marilyn Monroe, buddy "Toots" Shor, and son Joe Jr. His teammates barely knew him. We follow Babe Ruth into brothels, Aaron Pryor into crack houses, Sonny Liston into prison, and Jim Piersall into a mental hospital. These are the venues that reveal character. The book accompanies athletes into their retired years beyond the roar of the crowd. Jim Thorpe's descent into alcoholism and Arthur Ashe's battle with AIDS unfold far in time and distance from football stadiums and the courts at Wimbledon. This is the athlete's life lived "out of bounds."

The book is organized topically and chronologically. The chapter titles reflect the topical focus, while the order of chapters roughly follows the life course of the athlete. Chapter One looks at childhood, family upbringing, and what initially draws young men into sport. Following chapters address the influence of coaches, teammates, and significant others during the athlete's formative years, away from home. The middle of the book chronicles the athlete's public and private life during the course of his professional (or amateur) career. The final two chapters focus on the veteran athlete as he ages and struggles with physical limitations and infirmities, leading to termination of the sports career and life as an ex-athlete.

A broader chronological perspective is the historical one, most evident in Chapters Five and Six. The former briefly traces gender issues beginning with the rise of American sport in the 19th century, as preface to a discussion of sex roles and gender relations among today's athletes. The latter chronicles race relations in sport through the course of the 20th century. Elsewhere in the book, such topics as life on the road and the treatment of athletic injuries are presented historically for the purpose of comparison and contrast. Thus, the reader is offered a depiction of the individual athlete over the course of his life time and a chronicle of the everyday lives of athletes over the course of a century.

The reader may ask, "Is this book necessary?" Why not simply read the originals? The present undertaking is based on the idea that broad insights will emerge that cannot be gleaned from simply reading a couple of sports biographies—in short, that the whole is greater than the sum of the parts. Moreover, I have revived cogent passages from books no longer in print. An unexpected bonus has been the subjects' comments about fellow athletes, those in the second tier who'll never merit their own biographies. NBA star Bill Bradley brings to life several teammates with unusual insight and empathy.[48] Biographer William Brashler does the same for Josh Gibson's Negro League colleagues.[49] Soccer's Shep Messing provides some wonderful anecdotes about colorful teammate Hubert Eusebio.[50] Together these varied accounts meld into a compelling picture of the athlete's life across sports and across time. What follows is a window into the everyday lives of some of the great—and not so great—athletes of the last 100 years.

1

THE ATHLETE'S FAMILY AND YOUTH

I lost myself in the beauty of sport and made my family proud while passing
through the silent eye of the storm that was my childhood.

—Pat Conroy

ROOTS

"The child is father to the man," observed the poet William Wordsworth. Sports
biographers have taken these words to heart. Narratives of precocity are their
stock and trade. Former Red Sox outfielder Jim Piersall's cowritten autobiography informs us that he was throwing a ball in the backyard before he learned
the alphabet.[1] We read that four-year-old Pete Rose grabbed a baseball bat as
tall as he was and with a prodigious swing sent a baseball through a first-floor
window of the family home. Pete's father Harry took it as an omen.[2] Parents of
athletes have been known to embellish childhood events for the consumption
of biographers. Cassius Marcellus Clay Sr. would recall that his son Cassius
Jr. (aka Muhammad Ali) came into the world, "with a good body and a big head
that was the image of Joe Louis." The elder Clay liked to point out the significance of junior's first words, "Gee Gee" as a sign that he was destined to win
the Golden Gloves.[3]

Such anecdotes, though compelling, provide cautionary tales. Lincoln biographer Richard Carwardine warns against the writer who "too easily detects in
every footstep" the "making out of a course to greatness."[4] This advice seems
particularly apropos for a subject who was born only "one score and two years
ago" when his biography was published, as was the case with Tiger Woods.
We are introduced to the infant Tiger sitting in his high chair avidly watching
his father Earl hit golf balls into a net, and then swinging his own putter as soon
as he could stand up. The book informs us that Tiger was playing the course at
Los Alamitos when he was still in Pampers. Two months shy of his third

birthday, the diminutive golfer putted with comedian Bob Hope before a national audience on the televised *Mike Douglas Show*. At age three, he won a Pitch, Putt, and Drive competition. Before his fourth birthday, Tiger turned in a score of 48 on the back nine on a Navy course, shooting from the red tees.[5]

Tiger Woods is a glaring exception to the cautionary rule. His early footsteps, like those of Jim Piersall and Pete Rose, prefaced an outstanding sports career. But not all child prodigies go on to become champions. Pat Jordan's autobiography illustrates Carwardine's caveat. Jordan was a teenage pitching phenomenon. He had discovered his talent for throwing a baseball at age eight and honed it with single-mindedness. In high school he was a superstar. During one game in his sophomore year, he struck out 19 batters. The following year, he won 12 consecutive games. In his first semiprofessional game playing against ex-minor leaguers, he pitched a one-hit shutout. Pat soon attracted the attention of major league scouts and was signed by the Milwaukee Braves upon graduation. He looked to be the next major league rookie of the year. However, after three downhill seasons in the minor leagues, his career as a professional baseball player ended.[6] Unlike Tiger, Pat never made "The Show."

Sport also has its share of late bloomers. Michael Jordan first blossomed as a basketball player in college. Likewise, Dennis Rodman was relegated to the bench on his high school basketball team. Following an amazing growth spurt near his 20th birthday, he became a small-college standout and went on to play in the NBA.[7] Manny Sanguillen who grew up in a *barrio* in Colon, Panama, "never touched a baseball until he was nineteen when he heard a pastor preaching sermons on a street corner, joined the Evangelical Baptist Church, and became a member of the church team." Two years later he signed a professional baseball contract. Playing on the Pittsburgh Pirates with Roberto Clemente, Manny developed into one of the finest catchers in the major leagues.[8]

The norm, as one might imagine, falls somewhere between Tiger and Manny. Most athletes are beyond nursery school and shy of college when they discover their athletic talent. In this regard, future Olympian Jesse Owens was right on track, although there were few indications during his early childhood that he would become an athlete. Jesse was a small, sickly child whose family had to nurse him through the cold winters in Northern Alabama. As the drafty Owens cabin rattled with every blast of icy wind, Jesse, wrapped in cotton feed sacks, would cough and sweat with pneumonia for weeks at a time. Somehow he survived these near brushes with death, and by the age of six he was well enough to walk the nine miles to school. As for play, Jesse recalls, "I always loved running [but] I wasn't very good at it." His family moved to Cleveland, Ohio, around 1920, where a junior high school coach saw potential in the young Owens. Coach Charles Riley changed Jesse's regimen from walking nine miles to running 100 yards, and the once sickly child went on to become an Olympic champion.[9] Jesse Owens' story provides a classic instance of the child *not* being father to the man.

The above anecdotes do share one common message. Significant others and early life experiences shape a young athlete's destiny prior to his initial appearance in the sports arena. What occurs beyond the boundaries of the playing fields can be just as crucial as what happens within those lines. This chapter looks behind the myths and caricatures that frame the athlete's childhood. We shall examine family structure and the influence of environment; consider the merits of natural ability and habit. The narrative analyzes the influence of siblings, fathers, mothers, surrogate parents, mentors, and coaches. The following paragraphs will explore the norms and departures from the norm.

Stereotypes dominate the childhoods of highly accomplished people. The Goertzels' 1978 study of 300 eminent personalities concluded that such individuals were more likely to be the first born or only child in a middle-class family where the father is a businessman or professional, that parental expectations for the children were high, that the family had strongly held values, and that the eminent child resembled the rest of the family. Their model implied that prominent people come from a distinct type of family setting. The study included nine auto/biographies of athletes. Based on this small sample, they concluded that athletic talent revealed itself early in life, that athletes typically came from working-class homes, disliked school and were almost always poor students, and that athletes' fathers often were athletically inclined.[10]

In truth, no one set of family circumstances produces future athletes. They emerge from a variety of backgrounds. A disproportionate number of athletes may indeed come from working-class homes. Notable examples include Jim Piersall, Steve Howe, and Lou Gehrig among others. Dave Meggyesy grew up in the 1940s in a farm house with no indoor plumbing. Sonny Liston, Joe Louis, and Jackie Robinson were the sons of tenant farmers and sharecroppers. Jim Thorpe was born on an Indian reservation in Oklahoma. Boxers Mike Tyson and Aaron Pryor spent their childhoods in economically deprived circumstances in America's inner cities. At the same time, NBA star Kareem Abdul-Jabbar (born Lew Alcindor) came from a middle-class class family in Harlem; soccer's Shep Messing from a professional family in the Bronx. Randy Matson and Bill Bradley were raised in middle-class families in small towns; Don Schollander grew up in an upscale suburb. Tennis champion Bill Tilden and yachtsman Ted Turner were the scions of wealthy families.

The above examples tend to reinforce the conventional wisdom that athletes in contact sports tend to come from lower-class families, while the so-called club sports like tennis, golf, and yacht racing recruit from the ranks of the affluent.[11] But there are exceptions here, as well. While Ted Turner was born into the country club set, his yachting rival Dennis Conner was the son of a commercial fisherman. As a young man, Conner spent his free time at the yacht club, five blocks from his house in San Diego because that's where all the other kids hung out. He began sailing competitively as a boy and went on to become an America's Cup champion.[12] Arthur Ashe grew up in a working-class home, raised by his father after his mother died. The young African American learned tennis on the segregated public courts of Richmond, Virginia, but played his way onto the courts of the All England Lawn Tennis and Croquet Club at Wimbledon.[13] Ben Hogan was raised by his mother following his father's death. He had a paper route and caddied at the local golf course to make ends meet. Ben's golf scorecard would be his admission ticket to the country clubs. Most athletes from working-class families pursue their sport in public venues.[14] Lance Armstrong, raised by a single mother, notes that he didn't have the option to swim at the country club. Instead, he was on his bike everyday after school, putting in the miles. This was his chance to succeed at sports.[15]

Social mobility is an article of faith among Americans, and sport has been touted as the great equalizer. Gene Tunney's life exemplifies the American dream realized through sport. Tunney was the son of a dock worker who spent his youth on the lower West Side of New York, fighting on the streets and playing on the docks. He joined the Marines during the Great War where he spent most of his tour of duty fighting in the ring. The "Fighting Marine" from Greenwich Village went on to become the light heavyweight title holder and the successor to heavyweight champion Jack Dempsey. Tunney was that rare boxer who knew when to quit. He was the only heavyweight champion at that time to resign his title undefeated. Hardly had the sports world recovered from his dramatic retirement than Tunney announced his engagement to a member of New England's social set. The newlywed couple's circle of intimates was made up of the socially prominent and intellectuals not the sporting crowd.[16]

In contrast, the life of Johnny "Red" Pollard illustrates the vicissitude of fate and circumstance upon social status. The Canadian-born jockey's father had made his fortune as the owner of a brick factory during the turn-of-the-century construction boom in Alberta. Pollard grew up on the family estate amidst culture and luxury, but life changed drastically when his family lost everything in a flood. John Sr. found himself bankrupt with a wife and seven children to feed. John Jr. sought diversions from the penury through boxing and riding horses. The restless would-be jockey left home at age 16 with his father's guarded blessing and his mother's swallowed fears. On the road, he had to earn his own keep. He began haunting carnivals and racetracks, talking his way onto the backs of race horses. Pollard drifted around the American West from Montana to California, until he found his place in history riding the great thoroughbred Seabiscuit.[17]

Athletes emerge from virtually every level of the social hierarchy. The structure of families that produce athletes appears to be equally diverse. Bill Bradley, Mickey Mantle, Brett Favre, and Randy Matson represent the norm by being raised in nuclear families. Cricket player C.L.R. James grew up in an extended family. Lance Armstrong, Dennis Rodman, Aaron Pryor, Mike Tyson, and Jackie Robinson all came from one-parent families. Bill Tilden was raised by his maiden aunts after his parents died. Deion Sanders often lived with his grandmother. Dave Kopay and Dave Meggyesy both fled troubled families; Kopay to a seminary while Meggyesy moved in with the family of a friend.

Babe Ruth and Jim Thorpe both were institutionalized as young men. Ruth spent a decade of his adolescence at St. Mary's Industrial School for Boys. The Babe always looked back at St. Mary's with warmth and nostalgia. It was, in effect, his home.[18] Jim Thorpe hated institutional life. He was taken away from his parents and placed in a mission boarding school when he was six years old. The school was modeled on the rigid manual labor concept that the government had decided was the only way to educate Indians. The regimen was one of tight discipline, enforced work details, and part-time study. School uniforms were required. The students got up by bells, ate by bells, and went to class by bells, a routine much different than the free life on the Oklahoma reservation. No ball playing was allowed, only pitching horseshoes. Jim acquired a reputation for being restive and obstreperous. He rebelled against the enforced discipline and ran away the 20 miles to his home, only to be sent back by his father Hiram. There was a positive side to his institutionalization. It prepared him for his later matriculation at Carlisle College in far-off Pennsylvania where he would become an outstanding athlete under the tutelage of Coach "Pop" Warner.[19]

Contrary to social theories, birth order and family size don't seem to explain much either. Mickey Mantle and Steve Howe were the oldest child. Carmen Salvino was the middle child. Bo Jackson was the eighth of ten children; Roberto Clemente, the youngest of seven. Bill Bradley was an only child, as was cyclist Lance Armstrong. There does appear to be value in having siblings who share an interest in sport. Steve Howe and his three brothers were all crazy about baseball and contact sports like football and hockey. Gymnast Bart Conner and his two brothers participated in soccer, speed skating, baseball, swimming, and diving. Don Schollander played football with his older brother, and Brian Piccolo grew up playing ball with his two older brothers. Indeed, several athletes credit siblings for their careers in sport. It was Roberto Clemente's older brothers who took him to play baseball at the kid's league at the Barrio San Antón School when he was 10 years old. Tod Sloan's brother Cash was instrumental in his becoming a jockey. Ken Dryden began playing hockey in his driveway as a six-year-old boy. He was pulled into the game by his older brother and his friends—the archetypical little brother tolerated by the older boys. Michael Jordan's fierce competitiveness came from his rivalry with older brother Larry, a formidable athlete in his own right. Dennis Rodman had no brothers; he learned basketball from his older sisters. Boxer Jack Johnson had three sisters and one brother. He credits his sister Lucy with teaching him to fight.[20]

The three DiMaggios arguably were the most famous brothers in professional sport. Their family included nine children with Joseph and Dominic the two youngest. The oldest brother Tom dabbled in baseball and may have been good enough to play professionally, but the first son in an Italian-American family carried the obligation to follow his father into the family business. Guiseppe (Joseph Sr.) was a fisherman, but his namesake came to hate the fishing trade. Joe Jr. made his escape to the baseball diamonds following older brother Vince, who was a skilled semipro player. Vince later signed with the minor league San Francisco Seals (to be followed by brother Joe) and then with the major league Boston Braves. By 1940, there were three DiMaggios playing in the major leagues. Joe was with the Yankees when younger brother Dom signed with the Boston Red Sox, where he would enjoy an 11-year career.[21]

Athletes hail from both established and immigrant families. Tennis champion Bill Tilden's forefathers had come to America in the 1630s. Sonny Liston's African American ancestors go back to the 1840s. Jim Thorpe could claim Sac and Fox ancestors who were in North America long before any African Americans or European Americans arrived, but Thorpe also had French and Irish roots. Joe DiMaggio and Lou Gehrig were the sons of immigrants; Carmen Salvino, a second-generation American. Roberto Clemente grew up in Puerto Rico and came to the States as a young man to play baseball. Despite an elitist and racist past, sport was becoming a melting pot of hyphenated Americans.

Many Latino immigrants had discovered the American sport of baseball prior to arriving in the United States. Puerto Ricans had been playing baseball since the early 20th century. Roberto Clemente and his boyhood friends had no official baseball equipment or uniforms. They would bat empty tomato sauce cans with sticks; Roberto could hit them farther than anyone. At age 14, he was given a T-shirt with the letters of the local softball team that had been organized to compete in a big tournament in San Juan. While still a teenager, Roberto and his father Melchor signed a contract with Dodger scout Pedrin Zorilla for a bonus of $400, and the young Puerto Rican began playing Winter League ball for the Santurce Crabbers for $40/week. Then in 1954 while still in high school, Roberto signed a huge bonus contract to play for the Brooklyn Dodgers' farm team in Montreal. The 17-year old ballplayer who could speak only halting English said goodbye to his father at the San Juan airport and flew North to begin his remarkable baseball career.[22]

OPENING ROUNDS

The above examples underline the role that family and environment play in steering boys toward sports careers; but there's also something to be said for natural ability and habit. Deion Sanders recounts, "When you're still just a kid and you find out you're gifted at something. When you discover you can do things that other kids can't do at that age.... That's the awakening I experienced when I was six, seven, eight years old." Young Deion played baseball, football, basketball, and excelled in all of them.[23] Bo Jackson, like Sanders, was a multitalented athlete. On his high school track team in Alabama, he was a sprinter and also competed in the high jump, the long jump, and the triple jump. He played basketball in gym class but claimed he never liked the sport.

His former high school coach recalls that one day after class when all the other students had left, Bo picked up one of the basketballs and looked around to see if anyone was watching. The coach relates what followed: "He put his books down and walked slowly over to the hoop. I watched him standing flat-footed under the basket. Suddenly he just jumped straight up and dunked the ball, two hands over the head. Then he calmly picked up his books and walked out."[24] Bo went on to become a professional athlete and was featured on the cover of *Sports Illustrated*—not in a track or basketball uniform but in his football and baseball uniforms!

Other athletes focus on one sport. For Bill Tilden it was tennis. Biographer Frank Deford ponders how the young Tilden "became so good so fast." He concludes that Tilden "was a natural athlete composed of valuable raw material that only needed mining." Tilden mined his talent relentlessly; he practically lived on the tennis courts.[25] Likewise, Mickey Mantle lived on the baseball fields. He recalls of his Oklahoma childhood: "...that's all I did: play, play, play. I had no other enjoyment."[26] For some young men sport is more than a preoccupation; it becomes an obsession. Pete Rose's biographer renders a scene from the Cincinnati-born ballplayer's youth:

> A woman from Rose's neighborhood remembers driving every Sunday past Shultes Fish House, down the road from the Rose home, on her way to visit family in Indiana. Each time she would see little Pete Rose, maybe six or seven years old, pounding a ball against the wall of the restaurant. On her way back five or six hours later she would see him in the same spot, still tossing the ball.[27]

At first the woman thought the young boy must be hopelessly bored. Then she suspected that perhaps he was unbalanced. Finally, she concluded that he was simply determined.

Not all youngsters are as single-minded as Rose. Some initially fail at a sport but keep shopping around for something they are good at. Randy Matson, despite his size, had an uneven start in athletics. Nearsighted and wearing glasses, he grew so fast that his joints ached. He was a baseball player with bad eyes; a football player with bad knees. Putting the shot became his sport almost by process of elimination.[28] Lance Armstrong tried to play football but was no good at it. Determined to find something he was good at, he became a competitive swimmer at 12 years old. Lance rode his bike through the streets in the early mornings to the pool where he would swim 4,000 meters before school. He combined the two sports and became a competitive triathlete in his teens. When he was recognized as national rookie of the year in the sprint triathlons, he realized he had a future as a cyclist.[29]

Once athletes experience success in their sport they are swept along by their own excitement and ambitions, and by the encouragement of parents or coaches. Many young men compete in organized sports in elementary school or in public recreation programs, and then in high school and college. Deion Sanders was typical. He began playing T-ball at age five and was on a Pop Warner League national championship team when he was eight years old. He also played city-league football. Deion played ball whenever and wherever he could: Little League, YMCA. But the talented young athlete would make his mark in school sports, first in junior high school then at North Fort Myers High School. He then enrolled at Florida State University where he played baseball and football, setting school records for interceptions and punt return yards. Deion, like Bo Jackson, went on to play these two sports on the professional level.[30]

Two generations earlier, Lou Gehrig also played sports in and out of school. Lou's father Henry like many German Americans belonged to the local *Turnverein,* a private club devoted to the anomalous mix of gymnastics and politics. On winter afternoons, Lou would exercise with his father and soon became an accomplished gymnast. When Henry became a temporary invalid, Lou's mother had to work and run the household. But they kept Lou in school where he excelled at baseball, football, and soccer. Later, his parents found jobs as cook and handyman at nearby Columbia University. Young Lou was indulged by the local fraternity men and allowed to play ball with them. He became one of the fortunate sons of working-class parents who was able to attend college when Columbia offered him a football scholarship. Ironically, the future New York Yankee was ineligible to play college baseball because he had played in a summer semipro league. However, he continued to play amateur ball until he caught the eye of a Yankee scout. Lou joined the major league team as a pinch hitter when he was 20 years old.[31]

These vignettes chronicle the diverse patterns of initiation into sport by young men across time, social class, and culture. Clearly, there are many paths that lead to the arena.

Carmen Salvino gravitated to the working-class sport of bowling. His parents had insisted that he find a job after school to help support the family. This prevented him from playing high school sports. So he combined bowling with his after-school job. He had been setting pins at a local bowling alley since he was 12 years old. The pin setters were allowed to use the alleys when they weren't on the job. Carmen could hardly wait till school was out so he could spend the rest of the day rolling bowling balls. He always hung around the older guys at the alleys and was bowling in adult leagues when only 17. A local league bowler gave Carmen his first ball. Then a teacher at his high school started a school bowling team, and Carmen jumped at the opportunity. The future champion was still in high school when he turned professional.[32]

For kids like Josh Gibson growing up in the rural South, there wasn't time for much else other than work and going to church on Sunday, but they found the occasion to play baseball at picnics in the late afternoon sun. All it took in the country was a ball and a bat. Rocks deposited on the local field would serve as bases. Most of the games were pickup, but occasionally organized teams would be formed. The women sewed uniforms out of work shirts. In the spring or late fall, a touring team of black professionals might come through the area and put on an exhibition game. When Josh Gibson was 11 years old, his family moved to Pittsburgh, Pennsylvania, where his father Mark had found a job in the steel mills. There Josh roller skated up and down the hills of North Pittsburgh, established his swimming skills at the neighborhood pool, and his batting prowess on the local playgrounds. Many of the steel workers played semipro ball, some on Negro League teams like the Homestead Grays. Gibson made his mark as a sandlot ballplayer then on organized teams, going on to play for the Grays and the Crawford Giants.[33]

Boxing is known for stories of initiation. One of the most famous surrounds how Muhammad Ali got into the sport. Born Cassius Clay, he grew up in Louisville, Kentucky. His introduction to boxing revolves around a stolen bicycle. On a Fall day in 1954, 12-year-old Cassius and his friend Johnny Willis stopped by the local recreation center. Cassius parked his brand-new red, white and chrome Schwinn and went inside for the afternoon. When the two exited the center at about seven, Cassius realized his bike had been stolen and he burst into tears. A passerby told the boys that there was a police officer at a nearby gym and they should report the theft. The officer Joe Martin recalls that Cassius "was having a fit, half crying because someone stole his bike. . . . He was gonna whup whoever stole it." Martin suggested that the young victim had better learn how to fight before challenging the thief and handed him an application to join. A few days later, a determined Clay showed up at the gym and threw himself into the sport. Within six weeks he had his first amateur bout, defeating his opponent in a three-round split decision. This initial success was preview to an amateur career in which he fought 106 times with only six losses. It would reach its zenith with an Olympic gold medal prior to his turning pro.[34]

Many young men have been taken off the streets and initiated into the sport of boxing by social workers, policemen, and priests. Charles "Sonny" Liston's story is a variation on that theme. Sonny was a rough kid who fell in with the wrong crowd. He spent much of his rural Arkansas childhood working and had gotten very little in the way of education. When he moved to St. Louis, he became a street thug. It wasn't long before Sonny ran afoul of the law and was sentenced to Missouri State Prison for first-degree robbery and larceny. There the big husky 20-year-old was always getting into fights with other inmates, so the prison chaplain Father Edward Schlattmann, who was also director of athletics, put Liston into the main-yard ring to fight. After four weeks of dominating the competition, nobody would get into the ring with him. Boxing promoters in St. Louis got word of the promising young fighter and pressured the parole board for his release. In July of 1952, Sonny moved from the state pen to the St. Louis YMCA. With the aid of a manufactured birth certificate, he began dominating the southern Golden Gloves circuit on his way to the professional heavyweight crown.[35]

While Sonny Liston learned to box in prison, Jack Johnson was once thrown in jail for boxing. It was against the law in Texas at the time. Jack had grown up in Galveston in the late 19th century, the son of a school custodian and part-time preacher. He had barely finished grammar school when at age 12 he ran away to New York City to seek out his idol Steve Brodie, a man who had achieved fame by leaping from the Brooklyn Bridge. Jack eventually met Brodie but soon ended up in the Bowery. A year later he found himself working the docks in Boston harbor. His coworkers were a rough lot to whom fighting was a function of existence. As the youngest of the group, Johnson suffered his share of beatings. He took up the sport of boxing out of self-defense. He quickly developed a reputation as an accomplished fighter. Back in Texas a year later, he pursued a career as an amateur boxer, often fighting bare-knuckled. By the time he was 17, he was fighting for money in Chicago. He would go on to become the first black heavyweight champion.[36]

There are as many different stories about how young men get into sports as there are ways to win a ball game. However, family remains at the center of these narratives. Auto/biographies are grounded in family history, the presence and absence of fathers and mothers, as well as the influence of step parents and "father figures." Athletes acknowledge this influence. Jack Johnson's autobiography is dedicated to the memory of his mother. Deion Sanders dedicates his autobiography to his biological father Mims Sanders and his step dad Will Knight—overlooking their peripheral roles in his upbringing.[37] Michael Oriard comments in his memoir that he made a connection with his father through football that was sustained throughout his childhood and youth.[38] Pat Conroy remarks, half seriously, that if it were not for sports, his father would have never spoken to him.[39] Parents may be a strong or a weak factor in an athlete's upbringing, a positive influence or a negative one, but the role they play can't be ignored.

THE INFLUENCE OF PARENTS

Youth sports are notorious for "huddle fathers" and "soccer moms" who push their children into competition at an early age and orchestrate their prodigies' athletic careers. Don Schollander once commented, "Swimming parents are like stage mothers."[40] He was referring to parents who buy their young son (less often their daughter) all the requisite sports equipment and paraphernalia, tutor him to refine his skills, drive him to tryouts and practice sessions, nag his coaches, cheer him on from the sidelines, cut his clippings from the local sports page, and bask in the reflected glory when he becomes a star. For many boys, it is the father who plays the pivotal role in shaping their interest in sports, but not all fathers match the above stereotype. Messner interviewed 30 former athletes about their upbringing. From their responses, he identified four types of sports fathers: the pushy father, the gently goading father, the father who offers conditional love, and the role model. He also noted that six of the athletes interviewed grew up without fathers.[41] While Messner's model focuses on fathers, we shall examine the role of both parents in shaping young athletes. Based on the auto/biographies incorporated in this book, parents can be controlling, supportive, uninterested, ambivalent, or even hostile to their son's sports career.

If one were looking for an exemplary childhood of an athlete, that of Brett Favre could serve as a Hollywood script for the All American boy. Favre grew up in the small town of Kiln (pronounced "Kill"), Mississippi. The family home was on a county road named after his father Irvin to honor his almost 30 years as a high school baseball and football coach. Bret was the second of four children. The three Favre brothers were active boys who fished for crawfish, climbed tress, and shot BB guns. Brett's parents were both teachers with sports backgrounds. Irvin had pitched for USM (University of Southern Mississippi). Mom had been a softball player. Their three sons began playing baseball, football, and basketball when they were quite young. The Favres became a typical sports family with parents and kids running from game to game. However, the children were expected to take their schoolwork just as seriously. Brett never missed a day from the third grade through high school, setting a record for perfect attendance. He also played quarterback on the school team coached by his father. He went on to play college ball at USM and to an illustrious career with the Green Bay Packers.[42]

Olympic gymnast Bart Conner had a similar storybook upbringing. He was an active child who participated in soccer, baseball, swimming, and diving with his two brothers Bruce and Michael, who were nationally ranked speed skaters. Bart began gymnastics when he was 10 years old and competed in his first meet when he was 11. His parents bought him his own set of parallel bars and a pommel horse. They would drive all three boys to practice, and Mom would sit in the lobby of the YMCA while Bart was in class. His early success led to his competing in meets all over the United States and overseas before graduating from high school. The Conners might spend as much as $3,500 to accompany their son to foreign meets. Bart went on to become an NCAA champion and Olympic gold medal winner on the parallel bars. He later commented, "My parents encouraged us to participate in sports, but they never dictated which ones or to what degree. We were always told, 'You must decide. If you want to go to the game, we will take you. If you don't want to go, we'll stay at home.'"[43]

Harry Rose was one of those parents who did the deciding for his son. As soon as Pete Rose could sit up, Harry began rolling balls at him. At the age of two, Pete got his first baseball glove. Both of the Rose parents were athletes. Harry played semipro football and Pete's mother LaVerne had quite a reputation in Cincinnati as an outstanding softball player. The family dinner table became a classroom, a never-ending sports seminar. When nine-year-old Pete joined his first youth team, Harry gave the coach an ultimatum: let my son switch-hit or he'll play on some other team. Harry never let up on Pete. If he got four hits and came home from a game with a smile on his face, Harry would want to know about the one at bat he didn't get a hit. Playing ball was all that

was expected of Pete. When he was advised to go to summer school after failing 10th grade, his father wouldn't allow it because it would interfere with
American Legion baseball. Pete couldn't play varsity ball his senior year of high
school because failing grades rendered him ineligible; so he played semipro
ball in Dayton. On the Saturday morning after Pete graduated from high
school, his father and uncle took him to the Cincinnati Redlegs' executive office
to sign a professional contract to play with their minor league Geneva team.
It didn't take long for Pete to make it back to Cincinnati.[44]

No father set out more single-mindedly to groom his son to become a professional athlete than Earl Woods. He had played his first round of golf at Brooklyn's Fort Hamilton course at age 42 just before his retirement from the
military. Earl confessed to a reporter, "if I ever have another son I'm starting
him out at a young age." After retirement, Earl and his wife Tida moved to
California. There in 1975, Earl got his son whom Tida named Eldrick but Earl
would always call "Tiger." Earl didn't wait long to put young Tiger through his
version of "basic training." At age six, he had him listening to subliminal tapes
to improve his concentration. Father and son would then go out on a par-three
course and Earl would play mind games with the kid, trying to distract him when
he was swinging a club. Earl says he pulled every dirty trick he could think of.
After two months of this intimidation, Earl told Tiger he was ready. At age eight,
Tiger won his first Junior World's Championship, shooting five under par at
Presidio Hills. Encouraged by his son's success, Earl employed a professional
golf coach to work with Tiger.[45]

Training Tiger became Earl's avocation. He floated five credit cards and two
mortgages on their house to support a rigorous golf schedule which took father
and son across the United States and to Mexico, Canada, and Thailand. Earl quit
his job with McDonnell Douglas to travel the country with his son when Tiger
turned 12. This was when he introduced Tiger to sports psychologist Jay Brunza
to bolster his mental game, which included hypnotizing the young golfer. Biographer Tim Rosaforte would write of the father-son relationship, somewhat implau-
sibly: "There was never any pressure on him [Tiger] to play golf. All Earl cared
about was raising a 'meaningful, articulate citizen.' They didn't care if Tiger grew
up to be a professional golfer.... If tomorrow he said, 'Pop, I'm tired of golf,' I'd
say, 'that's fine with me,' Earl would say. 'You make your own decisions.'"[46]

Despite Earls Woods' protestations about imposing his agenda on his son,
golf preempted Tiger's opportunities to do the things that most teenagers do.
When he arrived at the Wollaston Golf Club in Massachusetts for the U.S.
Junior Championship, "He had no time for a Red Sox Game at Fenway Park,
or a tour of Boston Garden or a trip to historic Faneuil Hall. This was not a
sightseeing visit, this was strictly business." At home, Tiger never had much
time to check out a movie, to date girls, or hang out with friends at the mall.
The golf and the traveling often left him exhausted.[47]

Earl Woods occasionally let his enthusiasm get the best of him, belying his
claims of neutrality about his son's golfing career. He showed all the signs of

a father living vicariously in his son's achievements. Shortly after Tiger turned pro, Earl would boast, "There is no comprehension by anyone on the impact this kid is going to have, not only on the game of golf, but on the world itself." He once told a banquet audience that he was personally selected by God to nurture his son to "make a contribution to humanity." Not content with these pronouncements, the proud African American father proclaimed, "You don't want to tangle with Tiger on a golf course. He's what I visualize in the Old West as a black gunslinger. He'll cut your heart out in a heartbeat and think nothing of it." Earl might have been conjuring up memories of the prejudice his generation faced on the football fields and the golf courses. When asked about his pretentious father, Tiger's standard line was, "My father's my best friend."[48]

Tiger Woods seemed able to adjust to his father's relentless agenda with remarkable equanimity. However, not all young athletes survive unscathed when fathers insistently push them into sports and demand perfection. Mickey Mantle's father Mutt was a semipro baseball player who, like Harry Rose, made a conscious decision to train his son to be a major league ballplayer. Mickey's mother Lovell shared her husband's passion for baseball. She made Mickey's first baseball uniform at his father's request when he was three years old. By the time Mickey started school, his father had bought him a miniature bat and would pitch balls to him until darkness intervened. Mickey excelled in baseball from grade-school age, but the effects of his father's expectations were mixed. On the up side, interest in baseball was something father and son could share. They would occasionally travel to St. Louis for a Cardinals game. However, Mickey felt incredible pressure to please his father. From the time he was five, he felt he couldn't face his father if he failed on the baseball field. He wet the bed until he was 16 years old. Later, during his early professional career with the New York Yankees, Mick struggled and was sent down to the minor leagues. Hanging his head in defeat, he was confronted by Mutt, who charged, "I thought I raised a man. You ain't a man. You're a coward." Both men ended up in tears with Mick begging his father to give him one more chance. Mick made it back to the major leagues, where he often coped with the pressure to achieve by drinking too much.[49]

Jim Piersall was another boy placed on a program by his father. Jim was the late child of a mother who would be repeatedly institutionalized for mental problems. The Piersall household was dominated by father John, a frequently unemployed house painter. The elder Piersall began honing his prodigy into a baseball player when he was still a toddler. Often angry and demanding, Jim's father was not above planting a shoe in his son's backside or using the strap on him. The strict regimen imposed by his father caused Jim to suffer severe headaches beginning when he was 15 years old. John Piersall was intent on his son becoming a major league baseball player and refused to let Jim play football (although he would play on the sly). In high school, Jim starred in baseball and eventually signed a professional contract with the Boston Red Sox, the team his father had insisted that he play for. John continued to orchestrate his son's career from the sidelines when he became an outfielder for the Boston club. Jim was always aware of his father's critical eye in the crowd of fans. Following a series of highly publicized incidents of bizarre behavior on the baseball field, Jim suffered a mental collapse and had to be institutionalized. He continued to struggle with emotional problems throughout early adulthood.[50]

A fine line separates parents who force their agenda on a son and those who support a child's natural talents and interests in sport. Wendell Schollander had been a star football player in high school and college; his wife Martha had been a swimmer. Clearly, the Schollanders were sports-oriented parents. Wendell felt he had been denied his chance as a football player and he would spend hours with his two boys teaching them complicated plays. Son Don craved recognition from his father for being a good athlete. He recalls that at age nine that swimming wasn't considered a very important sport to him; football, baseball, and basketball were the "real sports." They were so important that when he was in the first grade and the teachers wanted to push him ahead a grade, his parents wouldn't let them because they thought it would hurt his athletic career. At one point after experiencing failure Don wanted to quit sports, but his parents told him that he couldn't. Then in his freshman year of high school, Don had to make a decision whether to try out for the football or swimming team. His father steered him to swimming. Don showed such promise in this sport that at age 15 his parents persuaded him to leave home in Oregon and move to California to train under a noted coach. With Don now living in a foster home, both of his parents continued to promote his swimming career. He went on to set 22 world records and win four Olympic Gold medals. Don was able to handle the pressure from his parents and coaches, and to cope with his Olympic success and the accompanying publicity better than most young athletes.[51]

Other parents are ambivalent about their sons making a career of sport. They may steer them in another direction. Lew Alcindor grew up in New York City in the 1950s. His parents were interested in their son pursuing a career in the arts. Ferdinand Alcindor, a graduate of Juilliard School of Music, would take his son on jaunts in the city, often winding up at jam sessions where the elder Alcindor would play trombone. Lew was given dance and piano lessons, but he shirked practicing. He preferred going to baseball games with his Dad and playing football with the older boys on the river bank. However, when Ferdinand heard about the broken bones and teeth among some of Lew's playmates, "pick-up" football was outlawed. Lew's father was an avid reader who filled their home with books, and he passed his love of reading on to his son. Lew became an outstanding student, and his father encouraged his son's scholarly interests. But his prodigious height (6'7" at age 13) predestined him to achieve on the basketball court, and his father gave in to the inevitable. Lew became a star player in high school and then at UCLA under coach John Wooden. As a young man, he was known for his seriousness and social conscience. He converted to Islam, and as Kareem Abdul-Jabbar went on to win the National Basketball Association's most-valuable-player honor six times and set an all-time record for points scored.[52]

Another New Yorker Shep Messing grew up in a family with a similar set of values. His father Elias, a lawyer, had been an outstanding college athlete, and the entire Messing family played sports. However, the prevailing ethic in this Jewish family with doctors and lawyers on both sides was to make a living with your head. Their plans for son Shep didn't include his becoming a professional athlete, and Elias paid scant attention to his son's athletic achievements which stood low on the list of priorities with homework and music lessons. However, the Messing backyard on Long Island was routinely filled with neighbor kids playing ball. Shep's older brother, an outstanding high school athlete, would become his role model. Shep competed in school at wrestling, baseball, and pole vaulting as well as soccer. He found his niche as a goalkeeper in the 10th grade. He went on to play goalie for the New York Cosmos professional club where he had the opportunity to play a season with Brazilian soccer great Pelé. Shep was always something of a rebel who questioned authority and flaunted his unconventional lifestyle. His family came to accept his independence and choice of a soccer career.[53]

Athletes from working-class families may receive little or no encouragement from parents. Dave Kopay grew up in an ethnic Catholic family in Chicago. His father Anton was a grade-school dropout and ex-Marine who worked in the stockyards and for the Chicago Transit Authority. Dave recalls his father as aloof and silent when not angry, never calling him by his first name but referring to him as "son." Anton had not played sports and didn't have the time or inclination to teach them to his boys. After Dave suffered a bout of Osgood-Schlatter's disease, a knee inflammation, both of his parents discouraged him from playing ball. Only when Dave and brother Tony became successful football players, was their father content to share in their success. While in high school, Dave left home for a Catholic seminary in California. The move was in part a way to get away from parents who fought. He went on to star at the University of Washington and then played for several National Football League teams.[54]

Brian Piccolo also grew up in an ethnic Catholic family. His father Joseph worked long hours running the family delicatessen in Fort Lauderdale, Florida. Preoccupied with work, Joe Sr. didn't seem to enjoy being with his children and was inclined to toss the kids a nickel and say, "get lost." It was Brian's older brother, Joe Jr., who took him hunting and played ball with him. Brian began playing football when he was eight. His memories of childhood didn't include much about his father. It was his indulgent mother Irene who ran the household, rode herd on three rambunctious boys, and encouraged Brian in his athletic career. Irene commented about her boys, "So whatever they wanted I was one hundred percent in back of them, and I wouldn't hesitate to do everything I could . . . I went to games all the time. I was the boys' chauffeur." Brian went on to play with the Chicago Bears as backup for the brilliant running back Gale Sayers.[55]

Brian Piccolo's upbringing illustrates the point that in some families the mother is the significant parent. Where the father is weak, distant, or absent, the mother's role is one of substitute and compensator. In families where a father's behavior is in some way inappropriate (e.g., abusive, alcoholic), the mother often acts as moderator and protector. Even in intact, functional families, mothers can be just as instrumental as fathers in promoting their sons' athletic careers, as was the case with the Roses, Mantles, Conners, and Schollanders.[56]

Not all mothers of athletes exert their influence in a conventional sense. Richard Raskind grew up with a passive father and an overbearing psychiatrist mother. Indeed the Raskind household was dominated by women: mom, sister, and aunts. Richard's sister "Mike" taught him how to ride a bike and play ball. His father David, also a physician, spent much of his time at the office. When Richard would appeal to his father for support against female tyranny, he recalled that his father would always buckle. He has strong memories of seeing his father lose at tennis. Commenting that he had seen his father falter so many times, it was almost as if his own victories on the court helped to vindicate some of the weaknesses that he perceived in the elder Raskind. The tennis courts also provided sanctuary from his mother's dominance. Richard began cross-dressing at an early age. His gender ambiguity eventually led to sex reassignment surgery and adoption of the name Renée Richards. As Renée, the trans-gendered six footer pursued a brief professional tennis career amidst objections from some of the players on the women's circuit. Richards went on to coach Martina Navratilova to a triumph at Wimbledon. Off the courts, the talented tennis player and coach completed medical school and built a success-ful practice as an ophthalmologist. In this regard, both parents were models.[57]

Athletes from one-parent families typically are raised by their mothers. Examples include Dennis Rodman, Aaron Pryor, and Lance Armstrong. (Arthur Ashe was the exception.) Several athletes attribute their athletic success to their mothers. Lance Armstrong's autobiography *It's Not About the Bike* is a paean to his mother. Linda Armstrong was not only a good provider but strongly supportive of her son's athletic endeavors. Lance idolized his mother. He paints her efforts to provide for him as heroic. When quoted in the book, both Lance and his mother employ the pronoun "we" in contexts where "I" or "you" would be more fitting. The message is clear: they were a team.[58] Deion Sanders' mother Connie steered her son into Pee Wee baseball and Pop Warner football in order to shield him from undesirable elements in a crime-ridden neighbor-hood, after Deion's father left.[59] Ben Hogan's mother supported her son's ambi-tions to become a golfer after father Chester took his life when Ben was nine.[60]

Dennis Rodman's father left when he was barely old enough to walk. He grew up as a passive youngster who matured slowly. Often labeled a momma's boy by the other kids, he retreated to the Rodman household managed by his resolute mother Shirley. Dennis remained a sickly child, skinny and frail, who had few friends and preferred to hang around his two sisters who were developing into good athletes. He would tag along to the local recreational center where they played basketball. Later, Dennis tried out for the high school football team but was "cut" because he was too small. Shirley demanded a meeting with the coach to argue her son's case, but to no avail. The protective mother once commented,

"I interfered in my children's lives quite a bit." At age 19, Dennis' life turned around, as he grew almost a foot in one year. No longer would he occupy the bench on the basketball team. His mother's faith in him had finally paid off.[61]

When Jackie Robinson's father, a share cropper in Georgia, deserted his family, his indomitable wife Mallie held things together. She moved the family to Southern California where she worked long hours as a domestic to provide for her sons. Jackie's older brother Mack, who became an outstanding Olympic athlete, was Jackie's role model. Mack probably spoke for both boys when he said of his father, "We didn't know him, and we did not recognize him being a part of the family."[62] Young Jackie would deny having had the slightest interest in knowing his father but later in life admitted that he thought of him in bitterness. As a youth, Jackie starred on the playgrounds and went on to "letter" in four sports in college before becoming the first African American in the 20th century to play major league baseball. Robinson's close relationship with the patriarchal team manager Branch Rickey provided him the support he needed to battle the racial prejudice he would encounter in an all-white sport. In many ways, Rickey was like a father to him.[63]

COACHES AND FATHER FIGURES

For young athletes who don't have a father at home, coaches or other men in the community often act as surrogate fathers. After Deion Sanders' father left when he was six, he was shuttled back and forth between his mom and grandmother. Moreover, his Pop Warner coach Dave Capel often took him into his home. Coach Capel's interest in Deion went beyond the young man's potential on the athletic field. Capel would sit down with him in the locker room and help him with his homework, whether Deion wanted to or not. He would coach Deion for some 10 years on various Fort Myers youth sports teams. Deion commented, "Coach Capel has a daughter and two sons of his own, but he always treated me like a third son.... If it wasn't for Coach Capel I don't know where I'd be today."[64]

Lance Armstrong commented in his autobiography, "The main thing you need to know about my childhood is that I never had a real father, but I never sat around wishing for one either." Lance initiated himself into the sport of cycling with his mother's strong support. However, there was a significant male who helped to shape his athletic career. Across the street from Armstrong's suburban Dallas apartment was a bike shop. Its owner Jim Holt liked to sponsor bike racers out of his store and was always looking to get kids started in the sport. Holt made Lance a deal on his first bike and became something of a father to the headstrong youngster. Holt wasn't above taking Lance's bike away if he felt the young cyclist had behaved inappropriately. Young Armstrong often bridled at the imposed discipline but later acknowledged Holt's pivotal influence on him.[65]

Mike Tyson grew up on the mean streets of Brooklyn. His father Jimmy never got around to marrying his mother. When Mike was just two years old, Jimmy developed a heart condition and could no longer work; so he left. Lorna Tyson was forced to move with her two sons into a tenement in the notorious Brownsville District, a place where the strong preyed on the weak. Mike soon began carrying a gun and running with a street gang that engaged in petty crimes. By age 12 he had a rap sheet. His mother reluctantly accepted the decision of the authorities to send Mike to the Tyron School for Boys in upstate New York. It turned out to be a fortuitous decision. There Mike met Golden Gloves champion Bobby Stewart who introduced him to Cus D'Amato, the trainer of former heavyweight champ Floyd Patterson. Cus took young Mike into his home, put him into school, and initiated a serious regimen of training with the goal of turning Mike into an accomplished boxer. Mike spent most of his adolescence with the D'Amato's who filled their rambling frame house in the Catskills with young boxing prodigies. It would be a stormy relationship. Cus was convinced he had another heavyweight champion in Mike and was inclined to bend the house rules for him, and excuse his chronic misbehavior. In truth, Cus was at times as much an enabler as mentor. Mike developed precociously in the ring. D'Amato should be given credit for turning a street fighter into a talented boxer. Unfortunately, he didn't impose the same level of discipline on Mike outside the gymnasium. Tyson became a menace in the ring and out.[66]

Babe Ruth's father George Sr. was a saloon keeper in Baltimore at the turn of the 20th century. Little George ran the streets, throwing apples and eggs at inappropriate targets and dodging the cops. The elder Ruth kept long hours and had little time to deal with a budding juvenile delinquent. When Babe was about eight years old, his father had him committed to St. Mary's Industrial School for Boys. St. Mary's was half orphanage and half reform school, and Babe was its youngest inmate. He shuttled back and forth between St. Mary's and home, but over the years he saw his parents less frequently. At the school he fell under the tutelage of Brother Matthias. Matthias (his Xaverian name) was a huge man, nearly six feet six and probably 250 pounds. He carried a calm expression that could turn icy cold when the occasion called. He never ranted or shouted but was always consistent and fair. The boys at St. Mary's called him "Boss." Characteristically, when a fight broke out Matthias would pick up each boy under his arm like sacks of laundry and separate them until tempers cooled.[67]

Brother Matthias' job was to make boys behave, and Babe was an accomplished misbehaver. The good brother quickly imposed discipline on the rowdy Ruth while cultivating his athletic abilities. He hit ground balls to his young prodigy by the hour and found him to be a natural hitter. Babe's throwing talents were redirected from eggs to baseballs, and he soon developed into a superb pitcher. Babe left St. Mary's at age 20 and signed a professional contract to pitch for the Boston Red Sox, prior to his legendary career as a home run hitter for the New York Yankees. The adult Ruth would occasionally visit his father but his real affection was for St. Mary's. He revered Brother Matthias, referring to him as "the greatest man I ever met."[68]

Detroit Pistons' coach Chuck Daly was a father figure to the emotionally mercuric Dennis Rodman. Dennis had grown up without a man in the house. When he arrived to play with the Pistons in the NBA, he was still a naïve kid in many ways, overwhelmed by his new surroundings but full of adolescent enthusiasm. Daly understood how vulnerable Dennis was. He also recognized the rookie's exceptional talent. Daly would repeatedly challenge the young forward, and Dennis would respond positively. Whenever Dennis was around Chuck, he felt good. Later when Daly resigned as coach of the Pistons, Dennis changed dramatically. He had never known his real father, and now the most instrumental man in his life was gone. It was like what a child goes through in a divorce.[69]

One of the prevailing narratives in sports literature has been that of the "failed black family." According to this scenario, young African Americans do not receive support from parents in their athletic endeavors but rely on the encouragement of an adult friend or coach who represents the surrogate father.[70] The relationship between Dennis Rodman and Chuck Daly reinforces this theme, as does that of Deion Sanders and Dave Capel. However, the experiences of other African American athletes belie the stereotype of the failed family. Michael Jordan, Tiger Woods, Lew Alcindor, Jesse Owens, and Josh Gibson all grew up in functional families with supporting parents. Moreover, one can identify failed families among white athletes. The fact is that most athletes are influenced by coaches and mentors; some of them supplement parents' efforts, others act as substitutes for missing or apathetic parents. Here again, no single pattern prevails.

LOOKING BACKWARD

Family and early environment combine with natural ability and habit to shape a young man's future in sport. At the same time, the patterns of behavior that a budding athlete adopts and the challenges he faces form his character. Athletes' lives may not be predetermined by early events, but to a great extent childhood does father the man.

Biographical narratives reveal that athletes come from a wide variety of family backgrounds, from sharecropper's cabin to manor house. Ted Turner and Bill Tilden were born into the country club set. Don Schollander's upscale family had money for private coaching and expensive travel required for their son's swimming career. On the other end of the economic spectrum, Ben Hogan and Carmen Salvino were compelled to combine the pursuit of sport with part-time jobs. Jockey Red Pollard was alone on the road as a young men. He either found a mount or he didn't eat.

There's no such a thing as an archetypal family for producing future sports stars. Athletes emerge from extended families, intact nuclear families, one-parent families, dysfunctional families, foster families—as well as those expelled from families to a boarding school. While Don Schollander and Bart Conner were born into a nurturing climate that groomed them to become sport stars, others like Aaron Pryor and Dave Kopay have had to overcome hostile or indifferent family circumstances to pursue their careers. Some athletes are distinguished by overcoming adversity. Ambition, perseverance, compensation, and social mobility are familiar elements in successful sports careers.

Childhood experiences of athletes have changed over the decades. Most of the stories of adverse circumstances and indifferent parents come from an earlier era when fathers and mothers worked long hours and had little time to indulge their children. Jack Johnson is an example of a young athlete at the turn of the century who said goodbye to his family and "struck out on his own." The immigrant experience stands out as distinct. The fathers of Brian Piccolo, Carmen Salvino, and Dave Kopay all saw themselves as hardworking providers; they had little time for or interest in their children's recreational activities. Sons were expected to follow traditional roles. Giuseppe DiMaggio had a difficult time understanding why young men would want to occupy themselves playing children's games, until his sons began making money at it.

It's impossible to distill the relationship between male athletes and their parents into one model. Fathers of athletes may be distant or close, menacing or benign, supportive or apathetic. The ones like Mutt Mantle who obsessively manipulate their athletic sons often succeed at a severe emotional cost to their progenies. The ambivalent or indifferent father seems preferable, if and when he accepts his son's choice of a sports career. With all the attention on fathers, the mother's role in nurturing young athletes remains largely unappreciated. Connie Sanders recognized that sports were a way for her son Deion to escape the ghetto. However, Aaron Pryor's mother Sara was dead set against her son becoming a boxer. She couldn't see that this was his ticket out of Cincinnati's slums. Lance Armstrong's mother Linda, like Connie Sanders, realized that sport offered a golden opportunity for her talented son. Mallie Robinson stands out among working-class mothers as someone who labored long hours to feed and clothe two athletic sons. One of them would change the image of professional baseball.

No matter what type of family spawns athletes, they ultimately find a surrogate family within the culture of sport at school, college, the country club, or the local gym. They "cut the parental cord" to join like-minded young men in pursuit of their passion. The locker room becomes their second home, teammates their siblings, and the athletic coach both father and mother, for better or worse.

2

THE NARROW WORLD OF SPORTS

The Saturday heroes strut on a stage that is also their cage.

—Robert Lipsyte

PART I: SPORT AS SANCTUARY

The metaphor "world of sports" underscores the separateness and autonomy of the athletic province. Sports are indeed a world apart. Athletes as a breed harbor a sense of the "other." Former NBA forward Bill Bradley claims that the human closeness of a basketball team cannot be reconstructed on a large scale in the real world. This may be true, but the uniqueness of the sports experience carries beyond team cohesion. Athletes perform within a peculiar frame of reference. Their feats make little sense outside the arena. Arguably, running around in circles carries no rational meaning beyond the 400-meter track. In the broadest sense, the very culture and mind-set of sport appear to be discrete. Sportswriter Leonard Koppett sketches out several fundamental differences between the world of sports and everyday life:

- *Sports* have few and simple rules with no serious dispute about interpretation, and which must be observed if the game is to continue, and there is always a referee present and completely in charge.
  Life has many, complex rules which aren't explicit; interpretation is open to doubt, and can be ignored at some risk.
- *Sports* end at a definite point with the final score defining the outcome, and a new game always starts even. Only "affordable" stakes are agreed to.
  Life is open-ended with the no score and the outcome vague; activity continues out of preceding results, and the stakes can be high.
- *Sports* have a few, well defined choices where the parameters are known, the matchups are fairly equal, and "us" versus "them" is clearly defined.

Life has many hard-to-define choices where parameters are indefinite, with an
unknown future, frequent mismatches, and competing interests often unclear.[1]

The above distinctions may be lost upon the ardent participant. As athletes
separate themselves from the world outside gymnasiums and stadiums, they
begin to believe that their special realm is legitimate and lasting. The world of
sports takes on its own reality. Dave Kopay declares, "football was never just a
game" to him; "football was life itself."[2] Bill Romanowski proclaims that he "ate,
drank, and slept nothing but football" since he was a 12-year-old boy with a
dream.[3] This state of mind is not uncharacteristic of those who immerse themselves in sport. It can be instructive to examine what draws athletes into this separate reality and how they function within its unique frame of reference.

This chapter explores the influences and circumstances that pull young men
into the world of sports and their resulting transformation. It focuses on the
attractions of games and physical competition: the compensations of the athletic
life. The following account examines the order, the regimen, and the rituals of
sport; considers the realm of sport as sacred space. In the second part of the
chapter, the discussion turns to the phenomenon of retarded maturity common
among athletes and how sport contributes to this condition. The paternalistic
coach is singled out for his role in promoting arrested development. The chapter
ends with a discussion of the athlete's adjustment to life outside the arena.

Home Away from Home

Why do young men become so absorbed in sport? Lance Armstrong claims,
"There's probably some truth to the idea that all world-class athletes are
actually running away from something."[4] It's not difficult to find examples.
Joe DiMaggio fled to the baseball diamond to avoid duty on his father's fishing
boat. For Dave Meggyesy, football provided escape from a brutal life on the
farm and an alcoholic father. Jim Thorpe was always running away; from his
father, from school. He found asylum running around quarter-mile tracks and
up and down football fields. Sport provides a place to run to; it can offer refuge
from unwanted responsibilities, consolation for uncomfortable feelings, sanctuary from troubled surroundings.

More than a few athletes have turned to sport as a way to get away from their
families. Transgendered tennis player Renée Richards, growing up as Richard
Raskind, sought to avoid a domineering mother. Reflecting on her youth, the
adult Richards comments that she would have liked to live at camp all year round
and see her family once a month. Since this arrangement was not possible,
Richards retreated to the tennis courts. The budding tennis star recalls, "I spent
approximately four hours per day on the courts, either in competition or in practice or in just hanging around. It was an ideal way to keep out of the house."[5]

Boxer Aaron Pryor grew up in a troubled family in Cincinnati's inner city. His
no-nonsense mother Sarah (who banished Aaron's errant brother from the

house at the barrel of a gun) made it clear that she disapproved of boxing. To avoid his mother's displeasure, Aaron roomed with a buddy but virtually lived at the gym. One day, gym manager Phil Smith confronted the young boxer at the door: "I'm not letting you in here today, Aaron. Go home for a few days. You gotta go home every once in awhile kid." Aaron protested, "I don't wanna go home. This is my home! Don't you understand? I ain't got no home life."[6]

If sport offers sanctuary from the athlete's family of origin, this habit once engrained can carry over into married life. Pryor observed that as a professional fighter in training he was away from his family for months at a time. He reflects, "In my tunnel vision, I had my eye on the championship belt, not on my son or, for that matter, my wife."[7] Rocky Marciano was noted for his consummate devotion to training. He would routinely isolate himself from his family for as long as three months to prepare for a fight.[8] The obligation to train or compete isn't the only reason that athletes stay away from home. There are those who simply prefer the golf course, the gym, or hanging out with teammates to being with wife and family. Michael Oriard describes his short stint in Canadian football at the end of his professional career as a refreshing diversion from his more orderly married life.[9]

Carried to an extreme, sport insulates the athlete not just from family but from the larger world. A classic case is Bill Tilden, the great tennis champion of the 1920s and '30s. His upbringing is relevant. Tilden's protective mother Linie tutored him at her skirts while projecting her hypochondria onto her progeny. Among the communicable ills she feared that her son might contract included what were then called venereal diseases. Women were presented to young Bill as a source of infection. The son inherited the neurotic fears of the mother. Tilden's biographer notes, "Physically, he simply never was able to accept another body, male or female, and, in extension that made it so difficult for him to get close in any way to people, especially to his peers." Bill Tilden diverted his sex drive to a "clean, bright place," the tennis arena.[10]

Tilden was more comfortable dealing with people across a net or a card table. Five sets of tennis a day were not uncommon for him. His other preoccupation was playing bridge in the clubhouse. Labeling Tilden a "tennis bum" would understate the case. This was his life: the club locker room, his bedroom; the bridge table, his living room. He hung around the club all day and never looked beyond. He existed only as an athlete. The sanctuary of his mother's skirt was supplanted by the fenced enclosure of the tennis courts.[11]

What athletes are escaping *from* is only half the picture. Human motivation is a combination of "push" and "pull" factors. While the vicissitudes of life may drive young men to sport, the draw of sport can be quite seductive in itself. Pat Conroy gives expression to the dialectic of forces that drew him to the basketball court. Reflecting on his life as a military brat, he recounts, "What strange joy is felt as you leave the flatness of your daily life, the fatigue of routine, and the killing sameness of jobs to move among thousands toward a brightly lit field house at night."[12] Likewise, Aaron Pryor was pushed *and* pulled into his sport. Upon discovering boxing he exclaimed, "Oh yes, I can do this!" He recalls, "When I walked inside the gym, I noticed the pungent aroma of sweat and the constant sound of leather gloves hitting pads, speed bags, and flesh. It was love at first sight."[13]

Aaron Pryor became a "gym rat." Like the tennis bum, the gym rat is a type: someone who hangs out for hour after hour at his chosen arena. Bill Bradley was a self-proclaimed gym rat. From age 14 to 21 he would spend hours a day on the basketball court. He recounts, "Basketball was my only passion in life. I was immune to the normal profusion of interests that accompany adolescence. I pressed my physical and emotional life into basketball alone."[14] Dennis Rodman was someone else who found comfort in the gym. He haunted the weight room when not on the basketball court. While playing for the San Antonio Spurs, he would spend half his waking hours there—another gym rat! [15]

Linebacker Bill Romanowski, like Pryor, would camp out in gyms. He notes that after practice when all the other players had left the weight room, he would still be hard at bench presses, leg squats, or bicep curls. It got to the point where the trainers couldn't get rid of him. He recalls the head trainer imploring him, "Time to go home, Romo." The assistant trainer and strength coach would pipe in, "'Please Romo, enough already,' they'd say." He admits that his passion for training was to a great extent the pure escapism of it. "When I was on the track, in the weight room, or in the cold and hot tubs, I was able to shut out everything in my life. Every problem, every concern."[16]

Feelings of control and escape from life are common among athletes during training and competition. Aaron Pryor explains, "It seemed as if there was no problem once I got inside the ring. Once outside of it, however, it seemed as if my personal life was always out of control."[17] Pryor wasn't alone among boxers in harboring this feeling of sanctuary. Mike Tyson, whose personal troubles continued to mount over the course of his career, once commented during a prefight interview, "When I'm in the ring, I don't have no more problems [*sic*]. It's easy to forget problems when people are throwing punches at your head."[18] Life outside the ring proved more complicated.

Joe DiMaggio was different than the stereotypical boxer or linebacker. He grew up a rather shy, awkward kid; a poor student who never raised his hand in class for fear of embarrassing himself. But all the anxiety subsided when he stepped onto the ball field. Here he felt that he was in charge of everything he did. Here he could do everything right.[19] The baseball diamond like the boxing ring could provide a sense of order for wayward young men. Dizzy Dean was a case in point. St. Louis sportswriter Ray Gillespie remembers the Cardinal pitcher: "I always had one saying for him: He never did anything wrong on the field and he never did anything right off the field."[20] The same could be said of Pete Rose. He seemed to do the right thing instinctively on the baseball diamond, but outside the stadium it was as if he were operating in the total absence of any social norms.

Control was Steve Howe's hallmark on the pitching mound, but it was totally absent in his life outside the ballpark. He recounts, "Through the worst of times, baseball had been my safe harbor.... 'I was lucky to have baseball, because it was my only source of self-worth when my addiction raged out of control....' It was when I stepped off the mound, took off my uniform...and reentered the real world that I got into trouble." Steve's nemesis was cocaine; it eventually destroyed his career. Following one of his suspensions, he admitted, "I wasn't ready to live without baseball. My life didn't feel normal or complete without it. It's my gift and my greatest obsession." On the mound, Howe was master; off the mound, the drugs took over. He would eventually beat the habit, but it would be a long struggle.[21]

Sport itself can be habit forming. Athletes experience a kind of withdrawal. Former Chicago Bears linebacker Mike Ditka acknowledged that it is the off-season that is a time of anxiety for football players.[22] British soccer star Paul Merson was a classic case of off-season angst. Between seasons he was aimless, restless, depressed. Merson once commented: "It is such a relief to be playing football [*i.e.,* soccer] again. No matter what your problems, you can really lose yourself in it for 90 minutes. Nothing gets in the way. All you have to do is react spontaneously to the events going on around you."[23] This emotional dependence on sport perseveres over the course of an athlete's career and often carries into retirement. Ten years after Pat Jordan's stint in professional baseball had ended, he still missed it. Jordan confesses, "I often go to the small park near home and, when the field is deserted, take the mound and begin to pitch baseballs into the screen behind home plate. It relaxes me."[24]

Athletes describe the places where they train and compete with a sense of reverence. Lance Armstrong remembers the back roads of North Carolina where he prepared for his comeback as feeling like a Holy Land, a place he had come to on a pilgrimage.[25] These deep feelings are reinforced by the customs and ceremonies of sport. Pat Conroy recounts a pregame ritual of his college basketball team, one repeated by coaches and athletes in countless sports arenas: "We said the Lord's Prayer and then gathered in the center of the room, placing our hands over the hand of our fiery-eyed coach."[26] Team ceremony reinforces the feeling that sport is sacred space; its effect on the athlete is quasi-religious. Michael Oriard found football to be less of a group celebration than a private communion. He proclaims, "The sport in all its phases...meant things to me that I did not share with all those I played with...those private pleasures and pains were not the ones we talked about."[27] Anthropologist *cum* wide receiver Robert Sands frames his personal relationship with college football in the context of spirituality and transformation. He writes, "I experienced the ordinary while I bumped along on a daily road of the mundane...but once I stepped onto the field, I stepped into a sacred and altered state of reality. My focus changed, my personality was subsumed by something greater than myself."[28]

The donning of a uniform and the feel of the equipment can have transforming effects. Bill Romanowski declares, "From the time I strapped on my first football helmet...I found a purpose to living."[29] Writer Mark Edmundson, a self-proclaimed "high school jock," recalls the internal change that accompanied his stepping onto the high school football field in his battle gear. The adolescent Edmundson proclaims, "I feel that when I pull on my helmet, I am completely transformed; the great cage, three bars horizontal, one down the middle—designed come to think of it, much in line with the helmets that they wore at Troy—confers a new identity."[30] He continues:

> I love the feel of the shoulder pads and the thigh and knee protectors and the smell of the harsh shirt—like rotting leather, really, but appealing to me. Suddenly, within the armor, I—who am usually a human incoherence, ready to fly off in every adolescent direction—pull almost completely together. I am now all of a piece, unified, self-contained. And am also blissfully, beautifully, isolated. No one can get in; no one can get at me.[31]

This feeling of moving from incoherence to sense of purpose is reinforced by the regimen of sport. Dave Meggyesy recalls a time when he felt at odds with the world, and that football was what gave his life structure. He observes, "At times, I felt I was really flipping out, and that I'd be in the loony bin if it wasn't for the simple regularity of training camp. I could always depend on how practice would go and how stable the football routine was. It was the only time I was ever grateful for the game's authoritarianism."[32] Sands describes college football practice, "structured around the daily repetition of drills, scrimmages...sprints, bleachers, push-ups and sit-ups," and notes that both tedium and comfort are present in these routines, as well as meaning.[33]

The athletic arena epitomizes a realm of order and simplicity. Texas Rangers' fan Tim Morris is an academic who writes on baseball. He asserts, "The game is square, absolutely square...there is no ambiguity."[34] For many athletes, this is the appeal of sport. Richard Raskind/Renée Richards describes the transformation: "Once again I would enter the clean, well-defined arena of tennis [where] there would be no complicated decisions to make. I would move from one tournament to the next."[35] Bill Bradley refers to the "platoon certainties" of the athletic life.[36] Oriard characterizes football as a realm where what is necessary for success is plainly understood, what is expected of the athlete clearly laid out. The football "player understands fully the skills demanded for his job.... He knows what he must do to maintain his ability to perform.... He has coaches who tell him what to do and when to do it, and who monitor his actions to see that he does." In a passage that echoes Koppett's distinctions between sport and life, the middle lineman describes the structure of football: "A football field is precisely 100 yards long and 53 1/3 yards wide. Everything the players can do on the field is governed by a set of rules that all understand and agree to. Violations are punished by any of six officials constantly watching for infractions. The object of the game is clear."[37]

Not surprisingly, athletes struggle to make the transition between the structured world of sport and that more ambiguous world outside. Aaron Pryor personifies this predicament. At one point, he is persuaded that the order of the gym had helped to improve his life. The young fighter comments, "I began to have a normal routine in my life which built discipline. I'd get up, go to school, get out of school at three, then go for a two-and-a-half mile run at four p.m. By five o'clock, I'd be in the gym working out."[38] All athletes seek order in their lives. Pryor's autobiography is framed in the context of a "born again" experience. His commingling of sport and evangelical religion isn't unique. The autobiographies of Steve Howe and Deion Sanders share this theme.[39] Religious conversions likely represent a parallel quest for order.

Writer and boxing fan Joyce Carol Oates saw the sport as obliquely akin to those severe religions in which the individual is both "free" and "determined," a unique, closed, self-referential world.[40] Cassius Clay found a sense of order in boxing, as he would find it later in the Nation of Islam as Muhammad Ali. He was lured by the asceticism and discipline of sport. "There was a side to Clay that relished leaving decisions to higher authorities who dictated what to eat, how to pray, what clothes to wear, and how to spend free time."[41] Boxing and Islam each supplied these needs in their own ways. The combination of Catholicism and football did much the same thing for Bill Romanowski. He describes the Jesuit priests at Boston College as "religious referees who became ideal support for an 18-year-old who had already set in motion his own Spartan regime for self-control."[42]

The ascetic dedication to sport can be compelling. Its practitioners thrive on denial and discomfort. Regarding his college football career, Romanowski comments, "Nothing—and I mean nothing—was going to stop me. There wasn't a party that was going to keep me from being the best I could be. There wasn't a class that was going to interfere. Not even a girlfriend.... If my teammates would head out for pizza and beer, I'd have pizza and milk. When they headed to parties after the game, I stayed behind to take care of my body and dream about the NFL."[43]

Lance Armstrong notes that cycling is so hard, the suffering is so intense, that it's absolutely cleansing. He elaborates:

> You can go out there with the weight of the world on your shoulders, and after a six-hour ride at a high pain threshold, you feel at peace. The pain is so deep and strong that a curtain descends over your brain. At least for a while you have a kind of hall pass, and don't have to brood on your problems; you can shut everything else out, because the effort and subsequent fatigue are absolute.[44]

Renée Richards who continued to play tennis through medical school, reflects: "All my life I had lived a life of intellectualization...I had always found my escape from this intensity in the straightforward physicality of tennis. It had offered me a chance to suspend the rational process and exercise my reflexes and my intuitions."[45]

Athletes may be drawn to sport by the physicality, the order and discipline, the simplicity, or for its insularity. But sport in the public arena proves to be an imperfect sanctuary. Athletes feel the need to seek out further asylum, an escape from the commotion of the crowd, the imposition of an adoring audience, and the intrusive prying of the media—for a place of personal time and space. The locker room has served this purpose well, until recently.

Sanctum Sanctorum

One can look at locker rooms simply as a place to change clothes and shower. From this perspective, we shouldn't make too much of what goes on there. But for the majority of athletes, the locker room is much more. Ken Dryden saw it not only as a place to change in and out of uniform and to wind up for and wind down from games. It was a refuge, a place to relax and get away from it all. The NHL goalie elucidates: "When restaurants, sidewalks, and theaters are taken away, when planes and buses, even our charters, are cluttered with press and ubiquitous 'friends of the team,' when autograph seekers, phone calls from a friend of a friend of a friend, petty crooks armed with out-of-town schedules intrude on our homes, the dressing room remains something that is *ours*."[46]

The locker room serves as anteroom, recovery room, and haven from the outside world. Dryden would linger in the locker room after practice to read his mail and the newspapers, to look at the plaques on the walls. For Bill Bradley, the locker room provided "a kind of home." The New York Knicks forward relates, "I often enter tense and uneasy, disturbed by some event of the day. Slowly my worries fade as I see their unimportance to my male peers. I relax; my concerns lost among the constants of an athlete's life."[47] Arthur Ashe encapsulates the feeling of sanctuary, "You walk into the locker room for the first time again, and you feel good and warm and comfortable. At times like these I actually stop and wonder why can't the whole bloody world be just like our locker room."[48]

Athletes assign the locker room a special place in their world. They arrive long before practice or a game and hang around afterward. Shep Messing was typical of those who liked to get to the locker room early and relax.[49] Athletes gravitate to locker rooms for a variety of personal reasons. For Pat Conroy it was a quiet place to meditate, to plan ahead. He writes, "I made my way to the locker room early that afternoon because I wanted some time to myself to shoot around and think about what I wanted to accomplish this season."[50] For others, the locker room simply offers a place to rest. One of Sands' college teammates felt so comfortable in the locker room that he took naps there before football practices.[51]

Joe DiMaggio enjoyed the before and after. He would arrive at the stadium by 11 a.m. for a three o'clock game. When the game was over, Joe would stay later than any of his teammates; maybe for two or three hours before he emerged from the locker room. It was like there was no place else he wanted to go. He would relax with a beer, a cup coffee, and a cigarette; often the last one to leave. After one night game, he stayed until 2:30 am.[52] Brian Piccolo's routine was much the same. Typically, he was the last one out of the Chicago Bears dressing room. When everyone else was leaving, he would be sitting in front of his locker, still in his jock and t-shirt, resting and thawing out.[53]

Locker rooms have their own distinct ambiance. Most of us remember them as being damp, dirty, and smelly. However, Pat Conroy celebrates the "olfactory essence" of his college's facility: "The room carried the acrid fragrance of the past three seasons for me, an elixir of pure maleness with the stale smell of sweat predominant yet blended with the sharp, stinging unguents we spread on sore knees and shoulders. Right Guard deodorant spray, vats of foot powder to ward off athlete's foot, and deodorant cakes in the urinals. It was the powerful eau de cologne of the locker room."[54]

The experience carries beyond the sensual; the shared space harbors communal dimensions. Oriard describes the Kansas City Chiefs locker room as the center of the players' world: the site of their meetings, of the pregame rituals and postgame celebrations or despairs, and less profoundly a place where for several hours each week players just lounged around. The sense of fraternity in the Chiefs locker room was reinforced by a plaque hanging on the wall, admonishing: "What you see here/What you hear here/What you say here/Let it stay here/When you leave here."[55]

Oriard observes that slogans on locker room walls reinforce the tradition of an inner sanctum where access is denied to all but the elect. Fans are prohibited from entering this domain. The minions of the news media are considered interlopers to be tolerated—but barely. Historically, even as reporters were allowed into locker rooms for postgame interviews, this facility remained a male enclave until the late 1970s when women journalists were first granted access. This too was accepted with varying degrees of resentment. Today's locker rooms are less a sanctuary than in the past. Even television cameras breach their sanctity to record victory celebrations.

Despite these assaults on the sanctuary of sport, athletes continue to see themselves as an exclusive fraternity. Their sense of shared identity may be centered in the locker room but it extends beyond it. Still, theirs is a limited world not without its drawbacks. Meggyesy characterizes his football career at Syracuse University as being part of a select group of athletes who were denied a normal college experience. They were expected to focus on football. Looking back at that period of his life, he now realizes he missed out on something.[56] Dave is the rare critic among athletes. Most of his peers seem willing to bask in the sense of comfort provided by their isolation from ordinary life experiences.

Meggyesy is not alone in questioning the narrowness of sport. Academics and sportswriters have joined in the criticism. A student journalist described intercollegiate sport as that separate realm "where grown adolescents participate in mythical battles in a struggle to forestall the aging process and avoid the realities of life."[57] Indeed, the athlete's narrow world can become a virtual Neverland where young men find escape from the wider world with its adult responsibilities.

PART II. SPORT AS NEVERLAND

From Peter Pan to Pete Rose

J.M. Barrie's character Peter Pan is the leader of a tribe of "lost boys" who inhabit the place called Neverland. In this magic world, no one has to grow up; the inhabitants remain boys forever. Popular psychology has appropriated the label Peter Pan Syndrome to describe grown men who avoid maturing. These real world Peter Pans tend to shun situations in which they are unable to cope; they shirk responsibilities or act irresponsibly. They often display other classic symptoms: fear of aging, obsessional behaviors, and narcissistic tendencies. In short, these are individuals characterized by their immaturity. In many ways, they continue to act like lost boys.

Play is preeminently a child's activity, and adults are made to feel self-conscious when engaging in play. To devote oneself to playing games on a regular basis would be considered juvenile behavior. Professional athletes are the exception. Tiger Woods *plays* golf for a living; the Green Bay Packers paid Brett Favre to *play* quarterback. What athletes do is generally regarded as distinct from the play of children. While play by definition is nonserious, voluntary, and casual, participation in games like golf and football is serious, work-like, even obligatory; and the results not insignificant. Coaches may diagram "plays" on chalkboards and athletes are expected to execute them, but there is little about organized sports that is playful. Notwithstanding, this imposed seriousness may prove fragile. Practice sessions and competition reveal occasional elements of playfulness despite the overriding atmosphere of earnestness. Indeed, coaches routinely admonish their charges to "stop playing around." It's fair to say that sport intermittently can be both work-like and playful.

Sports and games haven't always been adult occupations. We know that a few professional athletes were found in ancient Greece and Rome, but the idea of grown men (or women) making a career of playing games like golf or baseball is a fairly recent phenomenon. The noted American lawyer Clarence Darrow recalls a boyhood revelation regarding baseball in the 1870s. He remarks: "When we heard of the professional game in which men cared nothing whatsoever for [local] patriotism but only for money—games in which rival towns would hire the best players from a natural enemy—we could hardly believe the tale was true."[58] Of course, professional jockeys and boxers had been plying their trade for some time when Darrow made his observation about baseball, but most sports didn't offer steady financial remuneration until the 20th century. Tennis is typical. The professional circuit didn't exist until the mid-1920s. Before then, most players were collegians or recent graduates who played a few years during the summers and then went on to other gainful pursuits.[59] Professional football and basketball are even younger. Today, the American public supports over a dozen professional spectator sports. Moreover, many "amateur" sports have become full-time occupations. Olympic athletes now train year round.

The question to be explored is what effect does playing sports from child-hood through adulthood have on the emotional and social development of athletes. Is sport a kind of Neverland? The idea that participation in sport encourages arrested maturity has been around since Thorstein Veblen's *The Theory of the Leisure Class* (1899). The perception has endured among those who interact with and write about athletes, as well as athletes themselves. *Sports Illustrated* writer Frank Deford observes that the athlete begs a leading question of himself: "What will you do when you grow up?"[60] To critical observers like Deford, it's apparent that an athlete in many ways is always a kid. Indeed, there are athletes who have become notorious for their immature behavior.

Dennis Rodman has been described as "a man-child lost in suspended adolescence" and as "Peter Pan in basketball shorts." Rodman, who joined the NBA while in his mid-20s, cultivated his image as the League's "bad boy."[61] He was suspended for misbehavior at least nine times. Biographer Dan Bickley observed that in every Dennis Rodman story the same fundamental story arc is apparent, in which Rodman is good and loved but then gets bored, rebels, is punished, comes back and succeeds, and is forgiven. "Boys are always for-given," Bickley notes, and recognizes this as Rodman's "blessing and his curse." [62] Characteristically, Rodman always seemed to get along better with the chil-dren of his coaches than with his teammates.

Bill Tilden revealed similar traits. For much of his adult life, he lived with two maiden aunts. People who knew Tilden doubt whether he ever had a real friend his own age. He preferred the company of young boys. He was either mentoring them on the tennis courts or courting them. While the boys he taught and loved would grow up and put away childish things—which is what any game is—Tilden was the "child of his own dreams" until the day he died at age 60; his bags always packed for the next tournament. His pupil Sandy Wiener commented, Bill Tilden never grew up; champion of the world but always childish.[63]

Lance Armstrong did grow up, but it was a protracted process. During the final phase of the Tour de France, the 21-year-old cyclist called his mother back in Texas to ask her to come over and stay with him. She flew to France and shared his hotel room. Linda Armstrong did her son's laundry, prepared his meals, answered the phone, and made sure that he got enough rest. When Lance crossed the finish line, the first thing he did was look for his mother. He found her, and hugging her in rain exclaimed, "*We* did it! *We* did it!" [empha-sis added].[64]

George Herman Ruth could serve as the poster boy for immaturity. His moniker "Babe" was most fitting. Sportswriter Red Smith said of Ruth, "The man was a boy, simple, artless, genuine and unabashed." The young Ruth had been a "juvenile delinquent" (the term just gained currency). As an adult, he continued to give the impression of little or no impulse control. He had numer-ous run-ins with umpires, receiving five suspensions in one year because of misbehavior on the field. Off the field, he was equally uncontrolled. He indulged his appetites, engaged in crude and boorish conduct, and neglected his domestic responsibilities. Anecdotes of his immature behavior became legendary.[65] Ted Williams, Ruth's younger home-run hitting counterpart in Boston, also acquired an evocative nickname, "The Kid." It too suggested someone who never matured. Williams was notorious for his childish behavior at the ball park including spitting at the crowd and "flipping the bird" at fans, as well as for his petulance with the press.[66]

Pete Rose was born the year Ted Williams batted .400. An ability to hit baseballs wasn't the only thing the two held in common. Rose once candidly observed of himself, "I was raised but I never grew up."[67] His parents had made him "an icon in his own home just for being born a boy, and therefore a ballplayer. Nothing was ever expected of him except that he excel as an athlete.... He entered adulthood with one admirable value, his estimable work ethic toward his job: baseball." Unlike Williams, Rose limited his juvenile behavior to when he was out of uniform. He gambled compulsively, cavorted, philandered, and generally behaved like an adolescent. His escapades became notorious. Once at a strip club in Mexico City, Pete jumped up on the stage and became part of the show. While this incident was simply embarrassing, other behaviors led to more serious consequences. The player who held the record for lifetime hits found himself banned from the sport for betting on baseball games.[68]

Rose was a study in contrasts. He was all business on the baseball field, to the point of being off-putting to his more fun-loving teammates. They nicknamed him "Charlie Hustle." Indeed, Rose was exceptional for not engaging in adolescent pranks while in uniform. Most athletes enjoy a practical joke on occasion. Pitcher Steve Howe goes at some length describing stunts and hijinks among his Dodger teammates. He recounts, "Guys who left their pants out found the legs sewed, glued or taped together. Rick Sutcliffe was always in a hurry to get out of the locker room, so we cut the crotch out of his underwear"—and so on.[69] Brian Piccolo's teammates on the Chicago Bears were known as a rowdy bunch. The Bear's coaching staff actually hired a snoop to monitor them in training camp. In what became known as "The Great Stoning Incident," the Bears players climbed up on a dormitory roof one evening and pelted the spy with bags of nonlethal objects for entertainment.[70]

Usually, there is one player who acquires the reputation of "team clown." Steve Howe's teammate Jerry Reuss played this role on the 1980s-era Los Angeles Dodgers. To a Freudian, Reuss's pranks suggest a fixation with the phallic stage of development. On one occasion, a Dodger player threw a party to christen his new swimming pool. Howe recalls, "As everybody stood by the pool, beers in hand, Reuss intoned solemnly, 'God, it's a great pool.' Then urinated in it." Howe relates another incident when he and Reuss were in a public bar, and he [Howe] took a restroom break. "While I was gone, Jerry whipped out his schwantz and stirred my brew with it. After I had returned and taken a big swig, he told me about it."[71]

Sports biographies divulge what has become a well-accepted verity: that athletes in a group are known to engage in adolescent behavior. Indeed it begins when they are adolescents. Seventeen-year-old Mickey Mantle, playing in the minor league, naturally took to the locker room camaraderie. He would liken it to being back in high school. To keep from going stir crazy on the road, Mantle and his teammates would engage in regular diversions like water pistol duels and food fights.[72] Such camaraderie endured over the course of a career. Oriard describes playing Canadian football as, "A few weeks of feeling twenty-one again, getting drunk once a week with the boys." He recalls veteran football players yelling back and forth from dining room tables and sabotaging each others' trays of food.[73] The locker room banter, verbal jabs, practical jokes, and other "jock humor" may strike the reader as gratuitous. Veteran goalie Ken Dryden saw it as part of the ritual that accompanies men competing as a team. He argues that it keeps egos under control and relieves tensions.[74]

However, occupational tensions are not unique to sport. Many professions are competitive, create stress, and require ego control. The question remains: why do male athletes engage in immature behaviors to a degree that appears extreme? And why is such behavior excused. Too often when mature athletes act like juveniles, we tend to roll our eyes and comment, "Boys will be boys."

Living in Neverland

A young man's sense of identity as an athlete is often formed while he is still a child. NFL veteran Tim Green points out that in his case it was at age eight. He recalls that whenever people called out his name, the next words out of their mouths were "the football player." That's what he was in their minds. He elaborates: "There are pictures of you in your uniform, one in your mom's wallet, one on your dad's desk, on your girlfriend's dresser; your grandmother has one on her refrigerator. It seems inconceivable to you that you could be anything but the person portrayed in that picture." The attention and special treatment accorded young athletes continues into adolescence. Green recounts the favorable treatment accorded him and his young teammates; how the other kids gaze at them starry eyed and adults fawn over them simply because they are talented athletes. In high school, while their classmates struggle to impress admission officers and get into the schools of their choice, the star athletes are wined and dined by college scouts. They are even wooed by powerful alumni, university administrators, and faculty who implore them to come to their school.[75]

What's the effect of all this attention? Oriard cautions, "Football can become a seductive siren, whispering in players' ears... 'You're special... You're a hero; the world admires you and wants to take care of you. Don't worry about anything; sign autographs and let people buy you drinks. You can play forever.'"[76] Once this identity is established, life takes on a distinct pattern. Former New York Knick Bill Bradley expresses concern about the formative years of athletes. He writes, "Growing up, when most young people struggle to define their tastes and develop their own sense of right and wrong, the star athlete lies protected in his momentary nest of fame." He continues, "The adolescent who

receives such attention rarely develops personal doubts. There is a smug cocki-
ness.... Compared to the natural fears and insecurities of his classmates, he
has it easy. His self-assurance is constantly reinforced by public approval."[77]

Journalist David Halberstam comments on a crop of NBA recruits: "Most of
the new players had been coddled since the time they were in high school,
going to special camps, being stroked by sneaker companies, college recruiters,
and, in time, agents."[78] Typically, they had never held any job other than
basketball. They always held the leverage with their high school coaches, their
college coaches, and in time, their professional coaches. Pat Jordan, a high
school pitching ace, faults the stilted world that he inhabited as a young athlete:
"Our life was simple in a way that life outside baseball never was.... We delib-
erately thwarted growth because we feared it would lead to the realization not
that our little boys' dream was insignificant, but that it was not significant
enough to excuse our wasting all that time."[79]

Lance Armstrong describes the "hot-house" environment of sport and its
effects. The champion cyclist observes that athletes, "are too busy cultivating
the aura of invincibility to admit being fearful, weak, defenseless, vulnerable,
or fallible, and for that reason neither are they especially kind, considerate,
merciful, benign, lenient, or forgiving, to themselves or anyone around them."
Armstrong reflects on his youth and identifies overcompensation as a pattern
of behavior along with both repressed and expressed anger. By his own admission, he had carried a chip on his shoulder.[80]

The exceptional treatment accorded to athletes by coaches and other interested parties creates a double standard. Following an incident where Jackie
Robinson was charged with resisting arrest by the Pasadena police, the UCLA
athlete was allowed to enter a plea of guilty in absentia without penalty.
He was represented by a university attorney who arranged for the school to
pay his fine and reimburse his forfeited bail. An older and wiser Robinson
comments, "I got out of trouble because I was an athlete."[81] Fortunately, young
Jackie "straightened out" and became a responsible adult, but not all athletes
make this transition. Today's sports pages are replete with reports of athletes,
both adolescents and adults, running afoul of the law. Too many coaches act
as apologists for their misbehavior.

Mike Tyson was the textbook case of a young athlete whose inappropriate
behavior was repeatedly excused by his handlers. The previous chapter
described his youth on the streets of Brooklyn's tough Brownsville District,
running with gangs and getting into trouble with the law. By the time Mike
was rooming with boxing manager Cus D'Amato, he had developed into a
big, menacing kid. Despite his stint in reform school, by all accounts he was still
a juvenile delinquent. Whenever he got into trouble in school or in town, Cus
would bail him out and make excuses for him.[82] At Mike's high school, when
his classmates provoked him, his rage would reach a flash point. Another big
kid, nicknamed "God" because of his dominance over students, kept baiting
Tyson. One day he pushed too far, and Mike pounced. A frightened student

ran into the principal's office shouting incredulously, "There's a fight outside—Mike's beatin' up God." The humor in the remark was probably lost on school authorities. On another occasion when a hungry Mike entered the school cafeteria before lunchtime, he was told the cafeteria wasn't open yet. He impulsively grabbed several milk containers and splattered them against the walls. Mike was repeatedly suspended from school. After one suspension hearing, D'Amato was heard saying to Mike, "If they expel you, I'll get you a tutor."[83]

The overall impression was that D'Amato was more interested in exploiting the young boxer's talent than shaping his character. For Mike's part, he would continue to behave like a sociopath. His biographer compared the adult Tyson to a bad driver "who causes a twenty-car wreck behind him but emerges unscathed and keeps merrily rolling along, oblivious to the carnage he left in his wake." But Mike didn't remain unscathed. A rape conviction resulted in a prison sentence.[84]

Steve Howe, who grew up in a blue-collar suburb of Detroit, was known for his aggressive and cocky behavior. When not on the baseball diamond, he did drugs and got into street fights. The behavioral problems persisted into his adulthood. The underlying problem was transparent to Dr. George Mann, one of the physicians who treated Howe's drug addiction. He observed, "The thing that always came to the surface [over five years of treatment] that was outstanding was immature, immature, immature. Every test we gave, every psychological test, Steve came out very immature."[85]

Howe was forced to confront his emotional immaturity in mid-career; but other athletes often "get a pass" from the realities of life. It's difficult to imagine that anyone would reinforce emotional adolescence and deter the maturation process of a talented young man, but sports coaches—typically former athletes—have their own agenda.

Coaching as Paternalism

Robert Sands, playing junior college football in his late 30s, decries the, "mind-numbing obedience to autocratic authority" that is expected of athletes. Writing about his experience, he remarks, "We bowed to an autocratic regime, a dictatorship by a council of middle-aged men who determined players worth through their efforts of manipulating highly impressionable young minds." He notes that, "Drills were designed not only to condition and teach, but also implicitly reinforce the power of the coach."[86] Tim Green echoes these observations. He stresses that from the time they are children, football players have it ingrained in their minds that they must absorb every word from their coaches and "toe the line." In his words, "All football players are programmed to march to a certain beat."[87]

Authoritarianism leads to what Dave Meggyesy labels, "enforced infantilization." Coaches find it to their advantage to sustain the immaturity of athletes; it makes it easier to maintain control. They establish their authority over their athletes by treating them like boys. Meggyesy found this to be the norm in high school, college, and pro football. He remarks that the most significant thing about high school football was gaining the approval of the coach. "I would do anything on the football field that I thought would make him happy. . . . The more approval they [the coaches] gave me, the more fanatically I played. I wasn't playing football for any great love of the game but primarily to win approval."[88] Randy Matson describes his junior high school football coach as, "the only man I ever knew in my life who I respected and was scared to death of at the same time." Following an injury, Matson relates, "The hardest thing I had to do that summer was tell Coach Lyon that I wasn't going to play football. I would just about get up the nerve to tell him then I'd get cold feet and have to wait a few more days."[89]

Oriard attributes his decision to continue playing football in the NFL to a need to please Kansas City Chief's head coach Hank Stram, the latest in a long line of coach/father-figures for whom he had performed, and from whom he sought recognition since grade school. He recalls an incident that lies at the heart of the athlete's delayed maturation. While in his early 20s, he is cut from the team. He is called into the head coach's office, praised for his performance during training camp, and then asked to serve on the team's "taxi squad," which pays a minimal stipend for 14 weeks and means not suiting up for games. In effect, he must choose between continuing to live with his grandparents and work at a part-time job in a sporting goods store so that he can continue to play professional football, or join his fiancée and begin graduate school in preparation for a career outside sport. Oriard chose life on the taxi squad. This controlling relationship is particularly characteristic of football, but may be evident in any sport where an athlete competes under a coach or manager.[90]

Boxing managers, like football coaches, seem obsessed with control. Cus D'Amato boarded fighters under his roof with a strict set of house rules (although he indulged Mike Tyson). A similar case was promoter Al Weill who kept a stable of young boxers, including Rocky Marciano, during the post–World War II era. He would corral his fighters in a lodging house near Central Park in Manhattan and place them on a weekly meal allowance in the form of meal tickets redeemable at a local diner. Weill watched his charges like a mother hen.[91] For better than two years, he successfully blocked Marciano's marriage. Once at a reception, Weill admonished the fighter's fiancée in a toast not to stand in the way of her future husband's career. Unable to stop the marriage, he telephoned the new groom several times during his honeymoon and then summoned him back to New York three days early, preventing him from returning home with his bride. Marciano complained to his brother: "It's getting so this guy wants to do all my thinking for me. . . . I can't do anything on my own. He's got his nose stuck into my marriage, my personal friends, and everything else." But Rocky put up with it.[92]

The system of imposed control is quite evident during training camps and on road trips. Offensive guard Jerry Kramer groused about the rule-dominated Green Bay Packers camp of the 1960s. Coach Vince Lombardi was known to lecture his players sententiously. Kramer recounts, "Vince reviewed the training rules and the club rules and the league rules, all of which I think I've heard a million times."[93] Football coaches routinely subject their athletes to curfews and bed checks, and impose fines on those who break the rules. When Chuck Knox coached the Seattle Seahawks, he would require his players (many of them married) to check into a hotel by eight o'clock the night before a game, home and away. He scheduled team meetings and then a meal together before enforced bedtime at 11:00 p.m. Knox comments, "I run a standard curfew. The players rooms are checked by an assistant coach or trainer, along with a security man. It doesn't take long because we put all the players on the same hotel floor. Watching the floor is a Seattle police officer, standing guard for the entire night."[94]

Close monitoring of athletes by coaches and managers has a long history. When Babe Ruth played for the Boston Red Sox, manager Ed Barrow used to pay the night porter at the hotel to spy on his young slugger. Yankee manager Miller Huggins once slapped a $1,000 fine on the incorrigible Ruth for being out of the hotel all night. The Babe was indignant. When tempers cooled, Huggins rescinded the fine, but he had made his point.[95] Under Huggins' successor Joe McCarthy (manager from 1931 to 1946), the rules for Yankee players were unyielding. On the road, they were expected to show up for breakfast with a coat and tie at 8:30 a.m. in the hotel dining room. Unlike other managers, McCarthy didn't run curfew bed checks; he just checked the eyes of his players in the morning.[96]

Many athletes are first exposed to the institutional form of paternalism in college. When they arrive on campus, they discover that everything has been arranged for them. They have few financial or academic worries compared to other students. Tuition, room and board, and loans are taken care of. Summer jobs with minimal obligations are available. Meals are provided at training tables, and they may have their own special dormitories. Academic tutors are available free of charge and accommodating professors will arrange assignments and exams around travel schedules. Coaches will direct them to the easier classes so that they maintain their academic eligibility. All in all, there are few responsibilities outside their sport.[97] This arrangement may appear benign, but can clearly stifle athletes' self-sufficiency and initiative.

The segregating, controlling, and coddling of college athletes was well in place by the first decade of the 20th century. Glenn "Pop" Warner the coach at Carlisle College, a school for American Indians, didn't invent the practice but he added some bold strokes. The perquisites at Carlisle included special football quarters and a training table along with first-class travel, clothing allowances, and payments to players out of gate revenues. Warner also paid local police to keep a "gentle but close rein" on the players. The athletes had their own reading room, a special kitchen and dining room, and recreation amenities that included a music box and pool tables. On football trips, the team ate first class on the trains and hotel dining rooms. Warner paid a publicity agent to make sure his players got their pictures in the local newspapers. Most of the familiar amenities and conventions of contemporary big-time college football had been set in motion by Warner.[98]

The Carlisle coach openly flouted the spirit of amateurism. He would disburse payments of $10–15 a month to the players for expenses, some distributed in the form of loans which weren't expected to be repaid. There also were direct cash bonuses. Football and track star Jim Thorpe received $500 during the 1907 season, more than he would make playing minor league baseball the following year. As a product of Carlisle's system, Thorpe was an exemplar of its failings. He had come to Carlisle at age 21 with a reputation as an outstanding athlete. He stretched the patience of the school superintendent by his disregard for class attendance despite being excused from afternoon classes to attend football practice. Nor did Thorpe make much use of the paid tutors that were provided Carlisle athletes. As a member of the class of 1912, Thorpe would not qualify for a general or academic certificate.[99]

Later on, when amateur status and academic eligibility were more strictly enforced, college coaches made the necessary adjustments. Jesse Owens, who had attended public schools in rural Alabama and East Cleveland, was poorly prepared for the academic rigors of Ohio State University when he matriculated. The coaches made sure he signed up for easy courses, knowing that his secondary schooling hadn't been the best. Instead of an athletic scholarship they found Jesse a position running a freight elevator during the night shift so he would have time to study on the job. Like so many other college athletes, Owens was living in an academic Neverland. He left Ohio State without a degree. This deficiency didn't make life any easier in the postcollege world. However, his case was not that unusual. Most athletes of the era didn't have college degrees.[100]

The Wider World

It's not surprising that young men who spend most of their developing years in a paternalistic system cowered by authority and shielded from reality, should have difficulty functioning in the real world. Tim Green observes that some of his NFL teammates can't make airline reservations. They don't even know how to open a checking account, let alone do their taxes. Players have enough resources that they can hire people to do these things for them, and this becomes a pattern through their entire NFL careers.[101] Professional services aside, athletes seem to have particular difficulty handling money.

As a young ballplayer, Babe Ruth had no idea whatsoever of the value of money; his manager would dole out a little of his salary to him each day, and it didn't last long.[102] Likewise, St. Louis Cardinals owner Sam Breadon put 21-year-old Dizzy Dean (who joined the team in 1932) on a cash allowance of a dollar a day to be picked up each morning from the club secretary, because Dean was so irresponsible with money.[103] Pete Rose would joke that his lawyer

Ron Katz had him on an allowance. Katz was a sort of father figure who watched Pete's bank accounts for him, cosigned his checks, advised him on his investments, and told him how much he should spend each month.[104] Other athletes are provided with "total service management." An agent pays all the player's bills and sends him a monthly allowance. Everything is prepared for the athlete by the agent's office, from insurance to taxes, from budgets to marriage contracts.[105]

Aaron Pryor had no one to handle his financial affairs or put him on an allowance. He was known to go to the bank and withdraw $15,000 cash for "walking around money." Incredibly, Pryor went through five million dollars in boxing purses over the course of six years.[106] Boxers seem to have a special penchant for spending money. Early in his professional career in the 1930s, Joe Louis made some $750,000 in three years. He went through $200,000 entertaining his friends, according to wife Marva, who admitted to a $35,000 wardrobe. Joe, for his part, reputedly had a hundred suits in his closet. Failed business investments cost him another $100,000. Louis spoke openly of his inability to manage money when the federal government began filing tax liens against him a decade later.[107]

Mike Tyson may be the all-time champion when it comes to financial profligacy. He would routinely run up bar bills for his friends to the amount of $600 a night and spend thousands of dollars on rented limousines. Based on financial statements, his cash drawings averaged $6,400 a week during one stretch. Tyson reputedly grossed some $100 million during his professional boxing career (a record at the time), and spent most of it. By 1991, Tyson's fortune had dwindled to about $15 million. He took little personal interest in his financial affairs. During a deposition in 1991 regarding the international distribution of fees, Tyson commented, "I don't understand anything about the foreign affairs [sic]...I just go in and fight and hopefully get the fee." He once admitted that he had no idea where a $10 million check from a fight was deposited.[108]

Excessive generosity is a contributing factor to the financial problems of some athletes. Jack Johnson was known for his largess. Ed Smith, a sports critic and boxing referee, commented about the early 20th-century boxer:

> I know Jack to be possessed of one of the kindliest minds of any great athlete I ever came into contact with. Money never meant a great deal to this mighty man of brawn and ring brains. As far as the financial end of his dealings was concerned, Jack...wanted to do for others and always went the limit—sometimes, unfortunately for himself, beyond that.[109]

Johnson also was generous with himself. He was known to spend extravagantly on clothes, automobiles, entertainment, and other trappings of the high life.

Muhammad Ali revealed a similar tendency to randomly disburse large sums of money. He was estimated to have earned $50 million from boxing. By 1979 most of it was gone, in part due to his indiscriminate charity. Ali would ask his driver to stop the car so that he could hand out large bills to a needy person on the sidewalk. He also was overly indulgent to a large entourage of friends and hangers-on. However, Ali fared better than Joe Louis in his retirement. He survived his early excesses to enjoy a comfortable, if modest, life on his farm in Michigan.[110]

Michael Oriard offers a fitting coda to the above portrayals of the Neverland of sport. He writes: "Living in a largely physical, sensuous world; obeying strict rules handed down by a patriarchal coach; viewing conflicts as we and they, good and evil—this is more like a child's world than the adult reality we all must deal with."[111]

But a sense of reality does set in for some athletes. They grow up to become responsible and successful adults. In reading Don Schollander's autobiography, one finds no signs of repressed maturity; just the opposite. A teenaged Schollander had to grow up rapidly in the four years between the Tokyo and Mexico City Olympics. By age 18, he had won four Olympic gold medals and been voted best athlete in the world. The young swimmer had become a world traveler, yet found time to speak at dozens of banquets, assemblies, and press conferences; all the while completing a degree at Yale University. Following his retirement from competitive swimming at age 22, he served on the U.S. Olympic Committee.[112] Schollander's experience may be exceptional in that swimming is not a professional sport. In this sense, there was no prolonged adolescence. NFL veteran Dave Kopay observes that to the extent that sport is a rite of passage into manhood, many professional players act out the transition years after the event was expected to have occurred; more likely in their 30s or 40s than as a 20-year-old.[113]

Adversity has a way of accelerating the maturation process. Dave Dravecky became more reflective following the diagnosis of cancer in his pitching arm. He observed, "Baseball seems, like all boyhood games, as though it could last forever. It's the only life we know.... We can't imagine what's beyond. We just can't picture life without baseball."[114] Dave had to face what lay beyond when he lost his pitching career at age 33; two years later he lost his arm. Fighting testicular cancer helped Lance Armstrong mature. He comments, "This disease would force me to ask more of myself as a person than I ever had before, and to seek out a different ethic. I felt I had a new sense of purpose, and it had nothing to do with my recognition and exploits on a bike.... I was a cancer survivor first and an athlete second."[115]

Later, during a long day of training, Armstrong has an epiphany while climbing a hill. He writes, "As I rode upward, I reflected on my life, back to all points of my childhood, my early races, my illness, and how it changed me. Maybe it was the primitive act of climbing that made me confront the issues I'd been evading.... As I continued upward, I saw my life as a whole. I saw the patterns and the privilege of it, and the purpose of it, too. It was simply this: I was meant for a long, hard climb."[116] It is a metaphor that suggests growth.

For every Babe Ruth, Bill Tilden, Mike Tyson, or Dennis Rodman, one can find an athlete who did grow up. Some mature during their playing careers, others are forced to when they hang up their uniform for the last time. The more reflective athletes come to appreciate the transitory nature of sport. Bill Bradley was one of those who could temper his sentimentality about the game he loved with a dose of realism. Heading to the airport with his New York Knicks teammates, he contemplates grown men living and traveling together, giving each other identity through their association as athletes. A veteran Bill Bradley reflects, "We will miss this life of prolonged adolescence."[117]

3

Public Life, Private Space

Those who taste the joys and sorrows of fame when they have passed forty know how to look after themselves. But as for those who win fame when they are twenty, they know nothing, and are caught up in the whirlpool.

—Sarah Bernhardt, actress

Introduction

Athletes want the best of both worlds. They like to be noticed and appreciated, but they also value their privacy. Boxer Jack Johnson became cynical about all the public notoriety he received. He complained, "The more that is written and said concerning one who has held public interest, the less the public knows about that person."[1] All the same, Johnson cultivated a high profile. The fact is that athletes, like film actors and stage performers, require an audience. Dancer Rudolf Nureyev's biographer observes, "Whatever they may claim about a right to privacy, performers live to be looked at."[2] Most of them, however, prefer to be looked at when they're performing. Richard Ben Cramer writes of young Joe DiMaggio:

> Joe had a funny attitude about people watching him. He was sure they always did. That was fine on the ballfield, where he could be perfect, or pretty near. But any other time, anywhere he might show at a disadvantage—well, it made him edgy. From the start, he had to have it both ways: he wanted to be well known at what he was known for—and for the rest, he wouldn't be known at all.[3]

Those who write sport biographies are well aware of the point of contention between the right to privacy and the right to know, the art of balancing the athlete's dignity with the reader's curiosity. It's a fine line. The best writing abstains from voyeurism in its quest to provide meaningful insights into the life and character of the subject. Contemporary life stories of famous sports figures routinely reveal private behavior as well as public conduct. Athletes, for their part, must deal with public exposure on a daily basis in all kinds of venues. Having one's private life revealed between the covers of a book is a less immediate concern than the constant intrusion of cameras, journalists, and admirers. In this chapter, we'll examine how the athlete copes with fame and notoriety; how he establishes a sense of "self" distinct from his public image, and to what extent he can carve out a private space beyond the glare of media exposure.

COPING WITH CELEBRITY

The onset of celebrity can be sudden; the consequences dramatic. Charles Lindbergh was a classic case. The aviator's private life virtually ended when he arrived home following his solo flight across the Atlantic. Americans have a penchant for creating instant celebrities: aviators, astronauts, movie stars, and athletes. The world of sport has produced its share. A young Joe Louis journeying to New York City in 1935 and defeating the ex-heavyweight champ Primo Carnera provides a notable instance. Lance Armstrong winning his first Tour de France in 1999 is another.[4] Both of these young men arose from relative obscurity to world fame based on a single athletic event.

Fame carries its own baggage. The national infatuation with celebrity on this side of the Atlantic renders the notion of privacy practically obsolete. Americans tend to distinguish between public figures and private individuals as if the former had forfeited their right to avoid constant scrutiny. The adulation is fanned by a veritable industry of paparazzi and tabloid journalists who exploit the private lives of public personalities. Personal peccadilloes share the headlines with professional accomplishments, as Pete Rose and Dennis Rodman can attest.

One is reminded of Max Mercy, the snoopy reporter in Bernard Malamud's novel *The Natural,* who was more interested in the hero's shady past than his exploits on the ballfield. Max's legacy, the investigative reporter, has become a fixture in the press boxes and locker rooms.[5] Today's celebrity athlete—whether a self-promoting NBA "bad boy" or an introverted outfielder—can fully expect the details of private life to be revealed between the covers of a book or magazine, with or without his cooperation. However, the desire to engage in investigative reporting is tempered by the realities of sportswriting. As journalist Michael Sokolove notes, a writer's primary job is to write. He explains: "It's a big job that doesn't leave much time for idle investigating. If he doesn't keep his eye on the ball, he doesn't get the job done. If he prints stories about [private] matters that anger the players or the manager, he may lose access to his sources."[6]

Fortunately for Joe Louis, no skeletons were lurking in his youthful closet when he came into the limelight. The news media scrutinized his personal life, dissected his boxing style, analyzed his character, and manipulated his image. Louis was transformed into a national icon upon his signing for the match with

Primo Carnera. The fact that he was the first serious African American contender since Jack Johnson generated huge public interest. The 20-year-old from Detroit was deluged by New York City sportswriters and cameramen. The cascade of unending questions by reporters overwhelmed the unassuming young boxer. There would be no relief from the torrent of public attention. As he continued to win fights, the acclaim grew. The young heavyweight would become the most written about African American in popular journalism. The media, in effect, created the public persona that they wanted to believe in. Louis became a race hero to African Americans and a patriotic hero to all Americans in the pre–World War II era, following his victories in the ring over the Italian Carnera and the German Max Schmeling.[7]

It would seem that nothing in sports could top the media frenzy that surrounded Joe Louis, until 1941 when another Joe came out of a batting slump in rather dramatic fashion. During his 56-game hitting streak, Joe DiMaggio's name filled the air at every dinner table, barbershop, and construction site in the country. It was broadcast by radio stations and moved to the front page of newspapers. His life story and image were coveted by all the popular illustrated magazines—*Look, Collier's, Life,* the *Saturday Evening Post.* DiMaggio graced advertising billboards and lit up Hollywood with talk of a film, with him and his baseball-playing brothers portraying themselves. His fame triggered scores of requests for personal appearances, escalated the craze for his photograph and autograph, and even inspired a popular song, "Joltin' Joe DiMaggio." He routinely upstaged FDR and World War II in the news media.[8]

For better or worse, the reality of spectator sports is that athletes have to deal with public notoriety. A culture of fandom is created not only by live audiences but generated by the print and electronic media. This phenomenon predates the Louis/DiMaggio era. A 1926 boxing match between Jack Dempsey and Gene Tunney was witnessed by 130,000 spectators in a Philadelphia stadium while being broadcast to another 39 million radio listeners.[9] Today's television audiences easily surpass these numbers. The visibility of contemporary sports competition shapes the athlete's everyday existence. Olympic swimmer Mark Schollander characterized it as "life in a goldfish bowl."[10] Arthur Ashe observed, "It's almost like your life becomes a competition between members of the media."[11]

Athletes may find themselves in the public view at an early age. Adolescent celebrities have become common in sports like gymnastics and swimming. On the other hand, "precocious golfer" sounded like an oxymoron until the arrival of Eldrick "Tiger" Woods. Following three-year-old Tiger's appearance on national television, public attention remained focused on him throughout his youth. Shortly after turning pro at the tender age of 20, Tiger found himself stranded in Cleveland amidst a hailstorm. During this brief hiatus, his agents turned down interview requests from 17 television shows including *Oprah Winfrey, Jay Leno, David Lettermen,* and *Larry King.*[12]

More often, early celebrity is a local phenomenon. School sports create teen-age heroes in the hometown newspapers. At school pep rallies, young athletes are raised up on a stage with hundreds of schoolmates cheering them on. The frenzy follows athletes to college. Pat Conroy recalls being mobbed by fellow Citadel students in his dormitory after winning an important basketball game.[13] During his last year at Princeton University, Bill Bradley received some 50 letters a day because of the public acclaim surrounding his basketball success.[14] An added dimension of schoolboy celebrity is the attention bestowed by profes-sional teams. Pitcher Pat Jordan recounts, "In school, strange men in bright clothes wandered the corridors in search of my classroom, or waited for me in the school parking lot when I went outside to eat lunch. Those same men reap-peared later in the afternoon as I warmed up far down the left field foul line."[15] They were, of course, major league baseball scouts.

Horse racing is not a school sport, but talented jockeys attract the attention of racing stables during their adolescence. Tod Sloan initiated his professional career around age 14. Sloan already had earned something of a reputation by age 20. Following some impressive wins, the young jockey received an extraordinary amount of public acclaim. Newspapers chronicled his activities on a daily basis and created a following of rabid fans. George M. Cohan wrote a Broadway musi-cal "Yankee Doodle Dandy" loosely based on the colorful jockey before he turned 30. Sloan recounts, "After I made a few successes there was no end to the people who came up and claimed me."[16] The famous jockey's remark calls attention to an aspect of public recognition that would become more common as the century progressed: the intrusion of strangers into a celebrity's personal space.

Two-sport athlete Deion Sanders' public exposure in the 1990s could be just as taxing as that of Sloan. Deion complained, "People come after you. They start coming out of the woodwork. People start reaching at you . . . . Everybody wants a piece of you."[17] Athletes are talked about, pointed out, required to put up with untimely bothering for autographs and handshakes, and expected to endure these intrusions with a smile.[18] Writer Ring Lardner made his reputation, in part, by sneering at the public enthusiasm for sports heroes. He called the idola-try of worshipers at boxing matches a "national disease." Lardner described the crowds that would close in on Jack Dempsey at every public appearance as, "hoping a drop of divine perspiration might splash on their undeserving snout."[19] Sports teams that win big games on the road are often greeted by an ecstatic crowd at the airport when they return home. Former NFL coach Chuck Knox explains why the players try to avoid walking through such crowds: "We are whipped. It has been a long, long day and here we are, usually late at night, just wanting to get home. Our bodies and our minds can't withstand being beat on and touched and grabbed for five thousand autographs. It's suffocating. And often it's not secure."[20]

There can be a up side to the fan worship. Jackie Robinson was met with an intense blend of positive and negative encounters with the public during his first season with the Brooklyn Dodgers. The racial taunts and epithets from the crowds, along with the threatening letters, were an aberrant subtext in an overwhelming sea of adulation. Robinson's every action on the field was greeted with a reaction from the stands. Crowds followed him down the streets and mobbed him to the extent that areas outside stadiums had to be cordoned off and police officers assigned to protect him from adoring fans. His popularity crossed racial lines. One of his contemporaries quipped that it was the first time in American history that a white mob chased a black man down the street out of love. At home, Robinson's telephone rang constantly. Jackie became the most recognized figure in sports, the darling of the news media, and a riveting point of focus in the African American community.[21] It wouldn't be the last time a Black athlete was the object of ambivalent attention. Muhammad Ali would experience equal doses of public adulation and invective some two decades later.

Jesse Owens had experienced a mixed reaction to his feats in the arena a decade earlier. During the 1936 Olympic games in Berlin, Jesse became the darling of the German crowd, especially the youngsters, despite Adolf Hitler's personal slight of the African American track and field champion. Owens was constantly surrounded by autograph seekers and photographers. German children were fascinated by the unassuming American. He would wake up every morning in the Olympic village to curious faces pressed against his dormitory window. Owens handled the fishbowl existence with surprising good humor and equanimity.[22]

Olympic champions have celebrity status thrust upon them within the concentrated focus on the quadrennial games. By the 1960s, the media attention surrounding the event had turned into a feeding frenzy. Gold medal winner Don Schollander remembers climbing out of the swimming pool and being surrounded by a mob of people—reporters, photographers, friends—firing questions, popping flash bulbs, and not being able to get away from them for two hours! He recalls the media waking him up at 7:30 a.m. The young swimmer was inundated with gifts, bombarded with invitations to attend banquets, and received hundreds of letters to answer. He was invited to make speeches, to give interviews, to appear on television—and even received offers for a screen test. His life became a blur of ceaseless activity. Every day, dinner with different people in a different ballroom in a different city; people on the street pointing at you, coming up for autographs; people staring at you at parties. Just the fan letters and correspondence could be overwhelming; there is no way to respond to all of it without a secretary. Once in the hospital for several days recovering from mononucleosis, Don recalls, "I remember thinking...how good it felt just to lie in that bed and sleep and not have to catch any planes or answer any telephones or make any speeches or swim any races. Nobody was asking me to do anything."[23]

No recent athlete has received more attention from fans than Tiger Woods. Some 125,000 people passed through the gates of the Texas Open to see him play after he turned pro, a huge crowd for a golf tournament. Most of them wanted his autograph. Tiger was aware that his predecessors Jack Nicklaus and Arnold Palmer would stand and sign autographs for 90 minutes at a time.

But it would have taken Tiger four hours if he stopped to accommodate every-one. He had to pick his spots and keep moving.[24] Roberto Clemente was another athlete always willing to satisfy as many autograph seekers as humanly possible. He was one of those rare celebrities who could relate to fans as indi-viduals. One time in Houston, the Pirate announcer took Roberto over into the stands to meet a 14-year-old deaf child. "After he returned to the dugout, Roberto autographed one of his bats, went up into the stands, and walked some fifteen rows into the reserved seat section to personally deliver the souvenir to the boy."[25]

Clemente, who dabbled in ceramics, entered a store in Pittsburgh to buy some materials for his hobby. The store owner refused to take the ballplayer's money. He explained:

> You won't remember this, but when I was a kid—ten or eleven years old—I was sitting in the right-field stands at Forbes Field while you were out there. The batter hit a foul into the stands and when I went for it an older man grabbed the ball away from me. I sat there crying. The next inning you came over and said, "Here's a ball for the one they took away from you." That ball slept beneath my pillow every day of my life, until I married. Now I keep it in a place of honor in my home. That's why I can't charge you.[26]

Interacting with ordinary fans is one thing; dealing with other public figures is another matter. Prominent people vie to appear with the celebrity athlete of the moment. The practice has become institutionalized. Boxing's heavyweight title automatically grants celebrity status. Rocky Marciano recalls hobnobbing with movie and television stars as well as famous athletes in other sports. After winning the title, he appeared as a guest on several television shows, and was hustled around the country by his manager to make numerous personal appear-ances.[27] What is vulgarly referred to as "jock sniffing" transcends social and class distinctions. Shep Messing reports that Henry Kissinger, Robert Redford, and Mick Jagger all joined a locker room celebration of the New York Cosmos when he was a member of the team.[28] Even heads of state and royalty want to meet celebrity athletes. Following a string of victories that made Tod Sloan the most famous jockey in the United States and Britain, he was granted an introduction to Edward, Prince of Wales.[29] German Chancellor Adolf Hitler arranged a special reception for Max Schmeling after he defeated Joe Louis.[30] U.S. presidents routinely pose for pictures with winning athletes and teams. Photos of these occa-sions embellish sports auto/biographies.

Business and political interests maneuver to exploit the image of sports celebrities. Tour de France winner Lance Armstrong recalls that Nike when asked him to hold a press conference in New York, the mayor wanted to be there and so did Donald Trump. Meanwhile, the city of Austin wanted to have a parade. It goes without saying that local politicians would share the spotlight in parade vehicles. These invitations were followed by several offers to be on television talk shows. Armstrong was then invited to Wall Street to ring the opening bell at the New York Stock Exchange. Finally, the capstone of recognition: *Wheaties* put him on the cover of their cereal box.[31]

Athletes are routinely induced to lend their public persona to the marketing of commercial products. The practice carries as far back as 1905, when Honus Wagner, "The Flying Dutchman," signed a contract giving J.F. Hillerich & Son permission to use his autograph on Louisville Slugger bats. By the 1920s, Babe Ruth had to hire an agent to handle all his endorsement contracts. Jesse Owens' corporate clients included Ford Motor Company, Sears Roebuck, Atlantic-Richfield Oil Company, U.S. Rubber, and Schlitz beer. Pete Rose's 17 appearance on the cover of *Sports Illustrated* may account for his being sought out by so many commercial interests. He did endorsements for Aqua Velva, Grecian Formula, Swanson Pizza, Mountain Dew, and Zenith TV sets among others.[32]

However, Rose preferred rubbing elbows with the common people to the celebrity circuit. He would ride around Cincinnati in his car, honking his horn at pedestrians on the sidewalk and waving at them. Rose wasn't the country club type; he hung out at bowling alleys and Little League games, and he always signed autographs.[33] Chicago Bear running back Brian Piccolo also would lose himself in the common man, sitting in a bar, signing autographs. He rarely turned down an invitation to give a speech at a local event.[34] Carmen Salvino became a celebrity after his appearances on televised bowling shows. He seemed to enjoy the attention when people would stop him on the street or in restaurants for autographs. Carmen made a point to be nice to people who approached him.[35]

Muhammad Ali was a sports celebrity who also embraced the public and relished the attention. His reputation as "the peoples' champion" was well deserved. He loved crowds. He would have his driver stop the car so he could get out onto the street just to mingle with his fans. Ali's wife Belinda complained that all he did was sign autographs. Ali also liked to verbally spar with the media. Sports reporter Dick Schaap estimates that Ali held more interviews than any other athlete in history.[36] While Muhammad Ali and Pete Rose were exceptionally approachable, other athletes can be standoffish, even reclusive.

Mike Tyson never liked too many people around him and was noticeably ill at ease in public. While attending a fight at Madison Square Garden, fellow boxer Larry Holmes stood around joking with fans and admirers, signing autographs; Mike, in a ringside seat, began to look like a caged animal when people approached him to say hello or shake his hand. Finally, he retreated to the fenced-in area for the press, beyond the reach of the public.[37] During a press interview, the wary Tyson commented about the type of fan who wants to become the athlete's friend: "In my situation, it's very hard to find a real friend. The majority of people have their hands out.... I don't want new relationships. That's how these problems occur. Too many friends—excuse me—too many people who say they're your friends. I should have known from my background that people are basically not nice, the majority of them."[38]

Not all athletes are as paranoid as Tyson, but they may be ambivalent about the constant intrusion by the public. Michael Oriard notes, "When you're a star, businessmen want to buy you drinks, the parents of your children's friends want to meet you and talk about football, men and women of all ages find you fascinating." He recalls what it's like to be in a restaurant with teammates: "We talked and laughed, ate and drank, self-consciously oblivious to our surroundings but aware all the time that we had become the center of much attention."[39] When Roberto Clemente was eating breakfast in San Francisco with club photographer Les Banos, an elderly women in the restaurant kept looking at Clemente. Finally, she came over to their table and inquired, "Mr. Blue, can I have your autograph?" "I'm sorry," Clemente replied, "But I'm not Vida Blue." "Oh," the lady responded and walked away. Clemente looked at Banos, shrugged and said with a smile, "See? That's fame and fortune for you."[40]

All the inordinate attention can lead to feelings of dissociation, even alienation. Athletes find that they are living with an image of themselves that isn't quite real. They recognize that there is a conflict between the real self and the celebrity self.[41] High school phenom Pat Jordan writes of his "awareness that I could be superfluous to a discussion of myself. It was the talent they were interested in not the person."[42] Bill Bradley observes that the notoriety of being an athlete sets one apart from the rest of society, denies one the privilege of being an equal member.[43]

A worse fate may await athletes whose performance falters. Former heavyweight champion Floyd Patterson observes that the boxer, "is beaten under the bright lights in front of thousands of witnesses who curse him and spit at him, and he knows that he is being watched too, by many thousands more on television."[44] When an athlete's team is no longer winning, encounters with the public can become equally painful. Walking down the street as a winner invites hellos and congratulations. Walking that same street after losing produces criticism and derision, as Bill Bradley notes. The Knick forward often stayed in his room to avoid the latter type of attention.[45] Tim Green comments that being on a losing team is like carrying an infection that quickly spreads to every area of life. No one wants to associate with losers. He recounts one such occasion: "I slouched down the street so they might not see me, fearful of evoking pity or disdain, the two standard reactions people have to a loser. I preferred anonymity. The same went for dinner reservations. I would put them under my wife's maiden name...if they [the restaurant staff] knew I was a player, they'd make me wait for a hour, then seat us next to the kitchen."[46]

Negative public reaction can stem from events that occur in an athlete's private life. Richard Raskind played professional tennis as Renée Richards following a sex change. The surgery received a good deal of media exposure; then the six feet, one inch tall Raskind/Richards became the target of more public criticism for competing on the women's circuit.[47] Of equal notoriety was Arthur Ashe being "outed" as infected with HIV. This compounded his already ambivalent feelings of being the object of attention. As he put it, even more whispering and pointing than when he was an "ordinary" celebrity.[48] Personal problems and misbehavior of sports celebrities become grist for the media mill. Steve Howe made the sports page headlines as a result of his cocaine habit; Sonny Liston, upon his several arrests; Tod Sloan and Pete Rose because of their gambling problems; Jack Johnson for crossing the color line in his choice of women friends; Dennis Rodman for his unconventional body art and lifestyle. Stories covering such events would be buried inside the newspaper if the actors were everyday people, but these are celebrity athletes.

Veteran sports stars become increasingly wary of journalists. Joe DiMaggio, when returning to New York, would get off the train in Newark to avoid the bevy of reporters awaiting his arrival at the New York City station.[49] The only sportswriter he trusted was Jimmy Cannon. The two lived in the same Manhattan hotel and frequently dined together. Later, in the era of television, the journalist culture changed; such familiarity between reporters and players was frowned upon. Members of the two professions were less often friends than adversaries. The modified relationship with the press in the 1980s and '90s is chronicled in journalist David Halberstam's book on the Chicago Bulls.[50]

Traditionally, sportswriters had accompanied teams on road trips, which provided a lot of access. They flew on the same planes, stayed in the same hotels, and ate in the coffee shops together. The bus going from the airport to the hotel and the bus from the hotel to the arena carried both athletes and reporters. But gradually, these accommodations were phased out. Players took charter flights, and reporters no longer were invited on the bus going to and from the arena. In every way, access was becoming more and more limited; the coverage more cursory. Press sessions increasingly were dominated by quickie radio reporters.[51]

However, as travel arrangements became more segregated, the locker room was increasingly made accessible. The 1960s emerged as the "decade of the quote" in sports journalism. Following the end of a ball game, reporters would rush from the press box to the clubhouse for postgame interviews. This new style of sportswriting required writers to search out players who could fill up their notebooks with good quotes. Athletes began referring to writers as "flies"—in short, pests. The writers, for their part, were equally cynical about the task of interviewing athletes. Cincinnati sports reporter Earl Lawson remarked, "I saw a lot of players come and go, and damn few of them had anything interesting to say."[52] The more savvy athletes learned to cultivate a public persona that was blandly pleasing. While some athletes like Pete Rose were adept at handling journalists, others seemed overwhelmed and intimidated. A few could be outright hostile. Ted Williams and Mickey Mantle were notorious for their bad relations with the press. Mantle remained uncomfortable around reporters for most of his career, partly due to his innate shyness. Also, he wasn't particularly articulate. At times he would hide from the press or engage in boorish behavior around them. During interviews in the Yankee locker room, Mantle and teammate Yogi Berra occasionally "played catch" with the reporter in the middle to express their disdain.[53] Reporters aren't easily intimidated. Earl Lawson, who covered the Reds for the *Cincinnati Times-Star,* wrote tough stories and never backed down. On three occasions he exchanged punches with Reds players, twice with Vada Pinson.[54]

Physical intimidation and confrontations are the exception, but the interactions between reporters and athletes often become verbal fencing matches. Reporters try to lead players to statements which will confirm the reporters' own preconceptions, and players try to avoid saying anything that will make them look bad. The stilted dialogue deteriorates into a charade. Every event on the field of play must be followed with explanations of the self-evident. As many as two dozen reporters can descend on a locker room after a game. Accommodating players, often standing in little more than a towel, will talk to reporters for 20–30 minutes. In general, reporters are interested in the game more than the private lives of the athletes, unless the athlete has run afoul of the law or public morals. But either way, the athlete realizes that whatever words come out of his mouth may appear in the following day's newspaper.[55]

A young Roberto Clemente had two strikes against him in his early relationship with the press: the color of his skin and the language barrier. It didn't help that Clemente was opinionated and candid. Teammate Bill Mazeroski commented on how the press treated the outspoken Latino ballplayer: "They tried to make him look like an ass by getting him to say controversial things and then they wrote how the 'Puerto Rican hot dog' was popping off again. He was just learning to handle the language, and writers who couldn't speak three words of Spanish tried to make him look silly."[56] Mazeroski recalls that the writers would quote Roberto phonetically to make his English sound worse than it was.

Pete Rose was exceptional. Reporters genuinely liked him, and he treated the sports writers with respect. Moreover, Rose was good company. He had dozens of friends among sportswriters who helped him craft the "Pete Rose story." He and *Cincinnati Enquirer* writer Bob Hertzel coauthored two biographical books when he was playing for the Reds. Later with the Phillies, Rose struck up a close relationship with sports writer Hal Bodley. The two shared a beach-side condominium during spring training in Clearwater, Florida. While Pete was at the dog track, Bodley would play "Dutch uncle" to Pete junior.[57]

Following the gambling scandal, Rose actually hired a publicist to re-craft his public image. His objective was to gain sympathy with the American public and with the baseball writers who cast Hall of Fame ballots. The "repackaged Rose" was now a better husband, a more caring father, and charity-minded citizen. There were newspaper stories about Pete preparing breakfast for his five-year-old son Tyler before driving him to preschool. "A magazine photographer snapped a picture of him holding his new baby Carla, in his lap while also clutching one of her dolls, which she was still too young to take much of an interest in. He posed for a photo with a March of Dimes poster child."[58]

While the interview established the athlete's relationship with the media and the publicity campaign framed his image with the general public, autograph signing increasingly defined the athlete's relation with his fans. Celebrity autographs had been around since the time of Washington Irving (1783–1859), who referred to autograph collectors as the "mosquitoes of literature." The collecting of sports autographs appeared somewhat later in American history but quickly surpassed the demand for authorial signatures. "Autograph hounds" were still something of a rarity when Babe Ruth played in the 1920s and 1930s. Ruth, who was the original sports celebrity, always took time to sign autographs for kids.[59] Over the decades, autograph collecting became more common among adults as well. In the grand tradition of consumer capitalism, the practice would realize its full commercial potential. Organized autograph signings became an institutionalized ritual of fandom.

Shep Messing describes an autograph-signing event in 1977 that took place in Bloomingdale's Department Store in New York City. He stands in the Young Gentlemen's Department with a stack of 8 X 10 glossies on the table in front of him, ready to peel them off as fast as he can. He remembers a stout woman in a fur coat poking him in the ribs with a silver fountain pen and instructing "Right here, Mr. Messing, make it to Barry, the best center forward on the Gramercy Hornets. That's B-A-R-R-Y-E, please." Messing relates that he signed arm casts, T-shirts, shopping bags, knapsacks, comic books, visors, sneakers, and a lot of "grimy little hands." The laid-back soccer goalie depicts this event with a sense of detached amusement.[60] The collectors, of course, take these occasions quite seriously. Minor sport celebrities like Messing treated the practice of signing autographs simply as a nuisance. However, the more entrepreneurial have learned to exploit the craze for all its worth.

Few athletes have become more mercenary about trading on their signature and image than Pete Rose. He was a ubiquitous presence at autograph shows. With a short first and last name—compared to, say, the old Phillies manager Cornelius Alexander McGillicuddy who shortened his moniker to "Connie Mack"—Rose could scribble better than 600 autographs on various items within an hour, never pausing or looking up. It was possible to draw $20,000 from a promoter on such occasions. During the excitement of chasing Ty Cobb's all-time hit record, Rose exploited his notoriety by marketing posters, key chains, limited-edition silver and gold coins, and lithographs. He even sold the bat and ball involved in his record breaking hit for $129,000. He wore a different uniform in each inning of the record-breaking game and sold them all. Rose was undeterred by adversity in pursing his trade. On the night that he agreed to accept a lifetime banishment from baseball, he left his wife and day-old baby and flew to Minneapolis to appear on the Cable Value Network's "Sporting Collections Show." Sitting next to the host, he autographed balls for $39, bats for $229, and jerseys for $399.[61] The practice, of course, is not limited to baseball. Football, basketball, and hockey players will also sign jerseys and other paraphernalia.

The autograph shows constitute neutral ground. Everyone has agreed upon the protocol. But beyond these staged signing events, autograph seekers can be remarkably invasive. They routinely interrupt private conversations and intrude upon restaurant dinner parties. The usually accommodating Carmen Salvino reports being asked for autographs in public rest rooms.[62] No one was badgered more by autograph seekers than Joe DiMaggio; fans found him even when he was in a hospital bed. He countered by asking $150 and up for baseballs with his signature on them.[63]

Tim Green conveys the athlete's irritation with overzealous autograph seekers. He notes that most ballplayers don't appreciate having to stop and sign their name a hundred times after every ball game or while making the trek between the practice field and dining hall. Nor do they welcome the obligation to fake a smile and pose for a picture with some stranger's "Aunt Martha" from out of town. He remonstrates, "A fan is a nonparticipant, a watcher, a wannabe, a stiff in a shirt with an outdated tie, a goofy guy wearing a matching team hat and jacket with his arm outstretched, holding on to a crummy little piece of notebook paper and a pen. 'Gosh, shucks, golly-gee, can I have your autograph?'" Green relates that athletes go to great lengths to avoid fans, ducking out back doors, even wearing disguises. He claims he's known athletes to feign sight and hearing loss.[64]

The unappeasable demand for autographs can sour the athlete's general disposition toward fans. Mickey Mantle became notorious for his aversion to the public. The shy Oklahoman would sit in the clubhouse and drink beer with his buddies for hours after the game until the crowd cleared the streets. If he was confronted by lingering fans, his impulse was to bolt. Occasionally, he could be rude and mean spirited even to youngsters seeking autographs. Mantle's adverse reaction to intrusive fans increased during the media circus that accompanied he and Roger Maris' assault on Babe Ruth's home run record in 1961. As a retired player, he would attend autograph shows for a fee.[65]

A generation earlier, Babe Ruth suffered a similar level of visibility. He literally could not hide. Everyone recognized his cherubic face and ample frame. Wherever he went, he was on public display; few of his gargantuan appetites went unnoticed. He maintained a love-hate relationship with the public over the course of his playing career. Early on, he had toured vaudeville with a comic routine, and basked in the attention. Later, he began to regret his high profile. Ruth was so likely to get mobbed that he had to avoid hotel lobbies and would seclude himself in his room. A renowned gourmand, he seldom went to popular restaurants but frequented out-of-the-way places where he knew the owner.[66]

Joe Dimaggio went to great lengths to avoid unwanted contact with the public. Because of intrusive fans, he would rarely dine with his teammates in the hotel dining room. His buddy Lefty Gomez referred to him as "the King of Room Service." On the road, Joe and Lefty routinely had meals sent to their room. They would instruct the front desk: no calls—and don't give out the room number. But people (especially women) would find out where Joe was staying, and knock on the room door all hours of the night.[67] Joe's pal George Solotaire would run errands for him—to the cleaners, the drugstore—so that he wouldn't have to go out in public. DiMaggio never took the subway or the bus, couldn't eat in public places (excepting Toots Shor's restaurant where his privacy was protected), couldn't take a walk, go to a movie alone, or stop for a beer at a local tavern. He was constantly on his guard, as he became the target of cranks and schemers as well as admirers. At one point, he was stalked by a woman and required a temporary bodyguard. When he was in the hospital, reporters and photographers followed him (on crutches) up and down the halls. His marriage and subsequent divorce from movie star Marilyn Monroe brought public interest to heights as intense as any athlete has ever experienced. Increasingly, DiMaggio had to avoid public events. Ultimately, he became something of a recluse.[68]

In the age of mass media, basketball star Michael Jordan would experience an unparalleled level of public recognition. He topped Pete Rose with four dozen appearances on the cover of *SI.* But fame became a monster as the expectations escalated. There were endless demands to endorse products, to pose for pictures. Every other phone call was a request for something he did not particularly want to do. He became warier and more cynical, more brusque in dealing with the outside world. Like Ruth and DiMaggio, he often was a prisoner of his hotel room with the door protected by body guards. He couldn't go out in public without causing a mob scene, so his friends had to come to see him. Jordan was partly responsible for his high profile. No American athlete entered more homes via television to promote commercial products.[69]

On the global level, few athletes have been more popular or recognizable than the Brazilian soccer star Pelé. His method for gaining privacy in a public place was inimitable. As NASL teammate Shep Messing recalls, "He simply shuts his eyes to close off the rest of the world that wants to touch him, or cop an autograph on an airline napkin. . . . 'It is sometimes the only way to be alone,' he once told me. 'Very simple to close the eyes.'"[70] However, given the increasing intrusiveness of celebrity culture, most athletes find it difficult to simply tune out.

Coping strategies of former heavyweight champion Ezzard Charles illustrate the measures of deception that athletes have employed to avoid recognition. The night Charles won the title (1949), he stole off with a chum to celebrate. The two men ducked into a Chicago nightclub, with Charles sporting dark glasses and making every effort to conceal his identity. When people in the club asked him if he were the champ, he gave them an alias. But his cover was blown, and the two had to flee the club. Such extreme measures carried over to Charles' wedding ceremony. The event was held in the home of a friend where everyone was sworn to secrecy. The new groom continued to live with his grandmother while wife Gladys lived with her parents. The couple revealed their marriage only after the birth of their daughter. Charles explains, "I thought it was best to live apart, my being an athlete and everything, but when the baby came, my wife insisted that people should know we were married."[71]

    This clandestine marriage underscores the impact of celebrity status on the athlete's family. Jackie and Rachel Robinson provide a textbook case. No married couple in professional sports were closer. Rachel often traveled with Jackie on road trips and attended many of his ball games. She became caught up in the national frenzy when Jackie integrated professional baseball in the late 1940s. Jackie's wife shared the Jim Crow treatment encountered south of the Mason Dixon line and heard the racial epithets directed at him. Through all of this rancor, she had to field scores of questions from the pressing news media. Her education and poise—superior to Jackie's—served her well where most wives would have felt overwhelmed.[72] Indeed, most athletes' wives choose to remain in the background.

    If the athlete has children, they too are affected by the public notoriety and media attention. Carrying a famous father's name only compounds the difficulties. Joe DiMaggio Jr. lived with his mother, actress Dorothy Arnold, following his parents' divorce. He visited his father on rare occasions. When he did, he often was pawned off on one of Dad's cronies so Joe Sr. could avoid public scrutiny. As a schoolboy, Joe Jr. was expected to be an outstanding athlete like his father but could never live up to expectations. Later, he was exploited by the media, who used him to ferret out the details of his father's private life. This created friction between father and son, and the two men remained estranged throughout most of Joe Jr.'s adult life. His death postdated his father's by five months.[73]

    Jackie Robinson Jr. also lived in the shadow cast by a famous father. Because of his name there was no hiding place. To adoring fans, young Jackie Jr. was always more of a mascot than a child. Eventually, he became resentful of being Jackie Robinson's son. He often seemed befuddled about how to approach his father, and their relationship remained problematic. Jackie Jr. had chronic problems in the schools where his parents placed him. He gave up on both football and baseball. His adult life was marred by serious drug addiction. Jackie Jr. died in a tragic automobile accident before his 25th birthday.[74]

    Occasionally, a celebrity athlete's parent is thrust into the media spotlight. Shirley Rodman was left reeling from the "sudden whirlwind of attention" her son Dennis received. She still resided in her small apartment in Dallas when her previously uneventful life was interrupted. The now-famous mom with a listed phone number proved all too accessible. When her son's team the Chicago Bulls won the NBA championship, Shirley groused, "My life was hell. . . . All of a sudden, everyone wanted me on every [TV] show. I thought, 'what's going on?' It disrupted everything in my life." One night in Chicago, Shirley arrived at a restaurant for what she thought was a quiet dinner with her son, only to find a huge entourage there. She couldn't be seated immediately because there weren't any chairs left at the table. Her pride hurt, she walked out. Shirley merits an entire chapter in her son's biography, a testament to what its like to be the mother of a sports celebrity.[75]

    Of course, most athletes aren't celebrities. The majority are neither famous nor widely recognized. Pitcher Jim Brosnan, who described himself as an average ballplayer, introduces his diary *The Long Season* with the comment, "The daily life of the professional ballplayer is not really so exciting."[76] Journeyman athletes like Brosnan walk down the streets without attracting a crowd and dine at restaurants with little worry that their meal will be interrupted by autograph hounds. This was the fate of Pat Jordan, a hot prospect who drifted toward mediocrity and never made it out of the minor leagues. In the next chapter, the young pitcher describes his pedestrian existence playing ball in small towns and cities where the only people who recognized him were his teammates.[77] For these athletes, there are no award ceremonies, no autograph shows, no appearances on national television. No one holds a parade for them, and there are no photo ops with politicians and show business celebrities.

Fame is a mixed bag. While the everyday athlete dreams of being famous, the superstar longs for the refuge of temporary anonymity. Being a celebrity can distort one's perspective toward family, friends, and everyday life. If validation comes solely in the public recognition of behavior, what does it mean not to be a spectacle? Does anything in an athlete's life have meaning when it goes unacknowledged?[78] The late British novelist John Fowles once observed, "Audience corrupts. Even more than power." Indeed, fame is infectious: the praise, the adulation, the recognition of achievement, the reinforcement of self worth. How does one step away from all this?

The Roman historian Tacitus characterized the desire for fame as the "last infirmity to be cast off." Over time, the athlete's infatuation with fame is tempered by its unyielding demands. It is a rare individual like Muhammad Ali whose appetite for public exposure remains insatiable. His fellow athletes tire of the unrelenting attention and look for ways to escape the crowd. They seek a private space where they can live normal lives.

What do athletes do after the game, between games, on the road, and during the off-season? Who are their friends? What are their forms of entertainment; their uses of leisure time? In some cases, it's difficult to detect. DiMaggio was an intensely private individual who jealously guarded his personal life. Other sports celebrities have been more revealing. Confessional autobiographies like Renée Richard's *Second Serve* may tell us more than we want to know.[79] The majority of athletes fall between the poles of recluse and spectacle. They are revealing in some aspects of their personal lives, protective of others. The following chapter looks at the athlete's life outside the public arena, the often mundane reality of everyday existence.

4

In the Arena's Shadow

I wear no watch. On "practice days" it is "before practice," "practice," or "after practice"; on "game days," "before the team meal," or "after the meal." "Today is a 'practice day," as yesterday was; tomorrow and the next day are "game days." Today, we are "at home," tomorrow we'll be "on the road."

—Ken Dryden

Gladiator's Holiday

Janus the Roman god of gates symbolizes change and transition. This two-faced deity provides a fitting icon to represent athletes, as these modern-day gladiators struggle to reconcile the demands of their sport with life outside the arena. They describe an existence that feels compartmentalized and disjointed. Football players seem particularly conflicted. Michael Oriard, recalling his experiences in high school and college, observes: "I led two lives: my life on the football field and my social and educational life away from it. The two halves of my existence were mutually influential but still distinct and separate."[1] Dave Meggyesy resorts to clinical terminology in describing his bifurcated existence. He compares being a football player to enforced schizophrenia. He writes, "I was a football star half the year and another person for the rest, and I could not give myself completely to either identity."[2] Linebacker Bill Romanowski refers to his alter ego "Romo," the obsessively driven, wild man who takes over his identity when he enters a football stadium. He recounts the draining transformation "going from the monster on the field back to being Bill."[3]

Like all maturing humans, athletes must undergo the process of individuation, the struggle to form a clear boundary between self and world. Part of this process involves separating who they are as a person from their role in sport. At the same time, the athlete must maintain a sense of integration between

these two identities.[4] Each individual copes with separation and integration in
his own way; some do it better than others. Arthur Ashe commented that when
he thought of tennis, he thought of a whole existence: "playing and traveling
and meeting people and being with the guys."[5] Ashe seems to be saying that
his identity as a tennis player extends into peripheral areas of his life in a positive way. In contrast, when Dennis Rodman began receiving the attention he
was desperate for by playing basketball, he realized the benefits in being eccentric. The quirks of Dennis Rodman the individual carried over onto the court to
define Dennis Rodman the athlete.[6] A continuing struggle with personal identity shaped his public persona and perturbed his private life.

An athlete's ability to establish an identity outside the arena is exacerbated by
feelings of temporariness and isolation. Team sport athletes seem particularly
vulnerable. Much of their time is spent traveling, they can be traded abruptly,
and their team may even relocate in another city. Younger athletes tend to
inhabit rented apartments or live in hotels, delaying the decision to establish a
permanent residence. This sense of transience carries across sports. Ashe was
constantly on the road. He kept an apartment on the East Side of New York City
that he referred to sardonically as his "clearing house." Like most Manhattan
dwellers, he didn't own a car.[7] Bill Bradley was someone who often felt isolated
from his immediate surroundings. He wrote about the eccentric routine of sport
that creates a sense of unawareness of the larger world beyond. To him every
day was a struggle to stay in touch with life's realities.[8]

This quotidian predicament could be offset by the satisfaction that an athlete
receives from his sport: looking forward to participating in it, carrying positive
feelings away from it. And, indeed, athletes describe such sentiments. But many
veterans portray their life in the arena as little more than a job. For them, sport
has lost the excitement and passion that characterized its earlier days. Oriard
laments, "My most difficult adjustment to professional football came from the
recognition that the game was no longer a quest for self-discovery or an
emotional crusade shared with a group of teammates. It was my employment."[9]
Time spent on the bench can be especially tedious and unfulfilling. Pitchers Pat
Jordan, Jim Bouton, and Jim Brosnan all write about their acquired lack of
attention to the ongoing ball game while sitting in bull pens. Jordan recounts,
"We watched the games with but faint interest. They were being played by
someone else and influenced their careers, not ours."[10]

In the midst of competition, athletes can become as task oriented as
assembly line workers. Lance Armstrong describes the feeling of being "on
the job" racing six or seven hours a day. He recalls that his mental state was
totally focused on cycling. "My mind didn't wander. I didn't daydream.
I thought about the techniques of the various stages.... I worried about my
lead. I kept a close watch on my competitors, in case one of them tried a break-
away.... I stayed alert to what was around me, wary of a crash." This narrow
focus blots out the *gestalt* of road racing. Armstrong acknowledges, "You don't
really see the mountains as you ride through them. There is no time to dwell on

the view, on the majestic cliffs and precipices and shelves that rise on either side of you, looming rock with glaciers and peaks, falling away into green pastures. All you really notice is the road in front of you, and the riders in back of you."[11]

The "work environment" of sport can contribute to a sense of burnout. Shep Messing complains that playing minor league soccer often includes second-rate facilities, running on aging Astroturf, and dealing with menacing fans. Yet, athletes who make it to the top of their profession enjoy superior accommodations and amenities.[12] From the fan's perspective, these professionals have enviable jobs. Even if the grass is not always greener on the playing fields, what athletes describe is no different than what the typical worker expresses about lack of job fulfillment. Most professions become routine at a certain point. People compensate by finding relief and relaxation off the job. Even with heavy travel obligations, sports schedules offer ample opportunities for rejuvenation.

Athletes identify with their sport and their lives are defined by their sport, despite the fact that much of their time is spent away from the arena. How they fill this time is instructive. The way that some of them employ leisure brings to mind the relentless tedium of Sisyphus. Ben Hogan would spend most of his free time on the fairway hitting golf balls, hour after hour. On the road, Ted Williams could be found in his hotel room compulsively swinging his bat until four o'clock in the morning. Not all athletes take a "busman's holiday" when they are given a day off, but the examples of Hogan and Williams illustrate an important fact of life in sport. Whether one makes his living playing golf or playing left field, the honing of skills and the obligation to stay in shape impinge upon an athlete's free time and his ability to relax.[13]

PRACTICE TIME

When athletes aren't competing in the arena, their main preoccupation is training and practicing their skills. Whether a scheduled practice called by coaches, a regimen exacted by a personal trainer, or the self-imposed agenda to stay in shape, the obligation is always there. The typical sports fan rarely sees an athlete at practice and cannot appreciate the time and effort devoted to it. Without question, preparation takes up a greater proportion of an athlete's life than competing. Boxers train several months for a fight that may end after a couple of rounds. Mike Tyson's cumulative time in the ring in his first 19 fights totaled less than an hour and a half, but he had spent hundreds of hours training to get to that point. Likewise, gymnasts may prepare their entire young lives to execute a key routine that lasts a minute or two. Sprinter Jesse Owens commented on the oddity of training so many years for an event (the dash) that would be over in mere seconds.

For team sport athletes, training and practice are what they do during their typical "workdays" over the course of a season. It dominates their daily schedule. Brian Piccolo complained about, "so damn much practice." He described his everyday existence as living "from week to week—getting ready, always getting ready."[14] Ken Dryden describes what it's like to play professional hockey: "Practice is the routine, unseen link in a season. One practice a day every day with few exceptions from season-opening to season-end: an hour the day before the game, and hour and fifteen minutes or more on other days, twenty minutes the day of the game." He adds, "Sometimes it is drudgery, sometimes pure remembered fun, usually it is just fast-paced emotionless routine."[15]

Don Schollander would swim laps daily for more than three hours: an hour and a half before school commencing at 6:30 a.m. and then two hours after school. During the summers he often swam eight miles a day. The workouts were long, monotonous, incredibly boring, and left him absolutely exhausted. He recalls that these practice sessions consumed so much time and energy that, in the few hours left, all he would do is rest or watch television. He describes a life so dull, mechanical, and impoverished emotionally and intellectually that, in his words, "swimmers begin to feel like robots." Clearly, Don didn't enjoy the regimented existence, but he accepted it as the price one pays to be a champion.[16]

Schollander's experience underscores that point that this obligatory regimen can shape the athlete's use of time when he is not training. Soccer's Paul Merson relates, "Each day I would go to training, come home, sit myself down in the front room and watch television until it was time to go training the next day. I was becoming a groundhog."[17] Practice schedules keep athletes from doing other things they would like to do. At one point, Ken Dryden's hockey coach actually changed practice time from 10 a.m. to noon to discourage outside activities. On the other hand, practice fills empty time. Dryden notes that early morning practice, "is something to get out of bed for, to get to, to get undressed and dressed for, to do, to get undressed and dressed again, to get back from—to get one through two hours of an otherwise uneventful day."[18]

Training camps can be particularly intense. Athletes are billeted away from home and placed on a 24-hour-a-day schedule. Dave Meggyesy describes a 1960s-era NFL camp. Days started at seven in the morning, and players had to be dressed and on the field at 8:45 for nine o'clock practice. Morning practice lasted about an hour and a half. Players could relax until afternoon practice at 3:30. Team meetings were held at 8:00–9:30 p.m., then players were free until enforced bedtime. (Coaches conducted bed checks.) This routine would go on day in and day out for 7–8 weeks before the season began. Of course, football squads continue to put in their hours on the practice field during the playing season.[19]

Jerry Kramer's diary of his 1967 season with the Green Bay Packers devotes a good 80 pages to what its like in training camp. Kramer opens his account of the second day at camp with, "I went to jail today. I started an eight-week sentence in Sensenbrenner Hall [a dorm at Norbert College, the Packer's training site].... The whole thing is a pain in the ass. The worst part is that you're completely a captive of [Coach Vince] Lombardi." Kramer describes a daily routine similar to much of what Meggyesy experienced, beginning with breakfast at 7 a.m. and ending with curfew. He writes, "For obvious reasons we try not to spend too much time in the rooms, except for playing cribbage and sleeping." Players bring their TV sets, sound systems, and recorded music to pass the time. But mostly, they convalesce from the day's grueling regimen.[20]

Boxing, like most competitive sports, underwent an increasingly protracted training regimen over the course of the 20th century. Early on, boxers would wait until a couple of weeks before the fight to begin training. The day before Jim Corbett fought Bob Fitzsimmons in 1896, he ran eight miles in the morning, four in the afternoon, shadow boxed for an hour, played two games of hand ball, and took an hour's gymnasium workout.[21] Three decades later, heavyweight champion Gene Tunney (who held the title from 1926 to 1928) would go up to Maine or to New Jersey a few days before the battle to put in his hours of work so that he was "in trim." Tunney's training regimen: a little road running of about 10 miles a few times a week, plenty of walking and exercise followed by the usual gymnasium workout.[22] Recent fighters have taken a less occasional approach. They train for months to prepare for a fight.

No boxer was more motivated than Rocky Marciano. He and buddy Allie Colombo devised their own training program early in their careers. They would run through the streets of Boston every morning, varying the routes and tossing a football back and forth to break the monotony. In the afternoon, the two would continue the workout at the local YMCA. Marciano would hit the heavy bag for a couple of hours, topping it off by throwing uppercuts underwater in the swimming pool.[23] Unlike many athletes, Marciano seemed to have a knack for incorporating an element of enjoyment into his training. Muhammad Ali also was dedicated to training. His regimen would begin with a predawn run of three to five miles. He would drink some tea or juice and then sleep until late morning, when he'd get up for his daily ring work. Ali started with stretching, followed by a two-hour workout which included rope jumping, speed bag, heavy bag, sparring, and exercises. Abdominal and neck exercises capped his long day.[24]

Historically, golf was known for its leisurely lifestyle of a few rounds in the morning before retiring to the bar. At a time when no one on the professional tour practiced rigorously, Ben Hogan would hit balls for hours on end. Hogan's typical day, when he wasn't playing in a tournament, consisted of driving 150 balls then playing six holes, then another couple of hours on the practice range. He persisted in this rigorous routine throughout most of his career while other golfers were having drinks or playing cards at the clubhouse. The results spoke for themselves.[25] Contemporary golfers are more inclined to emulate Hogan than his cronies on the bar stools.

For sports that require strength training (a growing list), the weight room supplements formal practice sessions. Michael Oriard's routine at Notre Dame was typical for college football players: an hour and a half a day in the weight room during the winter season.[26] Basketball's Dennis Rodman routinely followed his mornings at team practice with a long afternoon in the weight room, prior to playing an evening game.[27] Weight training can be pure drudgery. Randy Matson's biographer poses the question, "Why would a man now shouldering the same responsibilities you and I endure—mortgage, family welfare, a career—relinquish his afternoons to perspire in the stifling confines of a dingy health studio, lift weights [that] dock workers wouldn't...while his neighbors were in their backyards barbecuing [or] playing golf[?]"[28] The answer is that an athlete has to remain strong to compete and stay ahead of the young guys coming up who attempt to break his records and take his job.

Training is a given; all athletes must endure it. Pitchers run the outfield, cyclists pedal down country roads, golfers hit drives, gymnasts stretch, boxers spar, swimmers flail, and bowlers genuflect. And they do it for hours on end, day in and day out. If training takes up most of an athlete's time outside the arena, traveling must come in a close second. One might expect it to be a bit more enjoyable.

ON THE ROAD

"I like the road," goalie Ken Dryden declares; "I like the feeling of moving, of being in a hurry, of doing something even when sometimes I'm not. Of being in one place, and a few hours later being some place else. I like the energy I get from airports and planes, from hotels and tall buildings, from downtown sounds.... I like traveling a continent to walk on its streets, to see its people.... I like finding places I'm supposed to find."[29] That's the upside. But traveling with the Montreal Canadiens during the 1970s came at a price.

Dryden reckons the toll of life on the road: 80 games over a 26-week season, the shuttling from plane to bus to hotel to bus to arena to bus to plane; four games in five nights in four different cities, a game at night carrying into the early morning hours, waking up you-don't-know-where, needing an afternoon nap but not being able to sleep, "going from nap to nap and from game to game." The veteran goalie portrays life on the road as a revolving door: home, away, home again.[30]

The travel experiences for athletes have changed over the decades, and they vary from sport to sport. Golfers on the professional tours in the late 1920s formed convoys of cars, often with three or four passengers per vehicle. They would assemble after a tournament and proceed to the next event, from Miami to North Carolina; from the Phoenix Open to the Texas Open. There were no car radios, so they talked to each other. Married golfers and their wives lived on the road, driving as far as 1,500 miles to a tournament. Ben Hogan figured that he and wife Valerie were on the road for at least half the year.[31] Early on, professional bowlers also traveled by auto, often sleeping in their cars. They hopped from town to town across the Midwest for three- or six-game tournaments vying for prize money in the hundreds of dollars.[32]

Throughout most of history, sports teams traveled by rail. Sportswriter Fred Russell traveled cross-country to the Rose Bowl with the University of Alabama football team in 1937. He notes, "Back then it was four and a half days on the train going, four and a half days coming back."[33] Players ate and slept on trains. It was a makeshift existence. Ty Cobb recalls traveling in the World War I era when players washed their uniforms "in sinks on trains and hung them out windows, where the uniforms were peppered with flying cinders. Bathing facilities at ballparks and at second-rate hotels were few and primitive; men often dried in their own sweat upon leaving a city." Most of the team slept sitting up on the trains, and the dining wasn't much better than the sleeping arrangements. Cobb recalls, "Road meals came cold and unappetizing."[34]

Travel arrangements broke down on occasion. Lou Gehrig recalls one trip the Yankees made in 1927. They left Boston for Detroit shortly after their game with the Red Sox. The train's departure was delayed, necessitating an all-night train trip with no meals, arriving in Detroit at game time the next day. Players grabbed hot dogs and soda pop on the way to the dugout.[35] The cycles of travel for a baseball season (including spring training) lasted from the second week of February through early October. The 154-game regular season included a cycle of 11 games at home and 11 away against each of the seven other clubs. A particular road trip was repeated three times a year. Today, air travel, league expansion, and realignment of divisions and playoff structure have changed much of the old routine for major league ballplayers.[36]

Minor league baseball, however, has continued to offer exhausting automobile and bus trips. Steve Howe recalls that playing ball for San Antonio included a 16-hour bus trip to Jackson, Mississippi, for a road game.[37] Pat Jordan, who played minor league ball in the 1960s, describes 13-day road trips with 12-hour drives in station wagons. Even short trips were taxing on players. Jordan notes that in Nebraska D Class ball, many away games were overnight stands with three-hour road trips, arriving home at 4 a.m.[38] When Pete Rose played with the minor-league Macon Peaches in 1962, the team would endure all-night road trips in jam-packed station wagons. Once, to break the monotony, Rose climbed out the back window of the vehicle, slithered down the roof, and plastered his face on the windshield, nearly causing the driver Tommy Helms to veer off the road.[39]

Spring training in the Negro Leagues was equally grueling. For Josh Gibson's Homestead Grays, it often meant playing two and three games a day, traveling from Hot Springs to New Orleans, back north through Kentucky, then over to St. Louis, and finally back home in Pennsylvania. In the early 1930s, the Grays traveled in two large Buicks, each with nine men inside, racks on the sides to hold clothes and a box on back with the equipment. Travel could be hazardous. Once on the way to Shreveport, Louisiana, a blown tire on a dirt road flipped one of the cars and threw most of the occupants through the canvas top. Fortunately, everyone survived. In 1932, when Gibson was with the Pittsburgh Crawfords, the team played 94 games in 109 days (plus 13 rainouts) from the last of March through the middle of July. This left two open dates. The team had logged 17,000 miles. On the upside, the new Mack bus that Gus Greenlee provided for the Crawford players was a lot more comfortable than packing into a Buick. Long road trips on the bus were filled with marathon pinochle games and the ubiquitous pranks. When they weren't traveling, the team would hang around the hotel or motor lodge, playing cards or talking baseball. If they weren't playing cards, they might go into town to drink a couple of beers. Few of the players had much money to spend. Occasionally, the local town folks would put on dances.[40]

Pat Jordan spent much of his minor league career on the road in strange towns. He observes, "There was nothing in Kokomo to differentiate it from Waterloo or Decatur. . . . [The] games were our only reality. Our lives were lived within their nine innings. . . . The rest was nothing but dead time somehow to be filled."[41] Jordan describes his daily routine as reading the newspaper and occupying the rest of the morning wandering around town, looking in store windows, occasionally going inside a store, wandering up and down its aisles. He recalls spending a lot of time drinking coffee in drugstores and shooting pool in the afternoons.[42]

Sports vary in their road schedules. Professional football teams make trips on the average of two a month over a 16-game season. Basketball and hockey have comparatively long seasons which can turn into an endless procession of one-night stands. An NBA player may spend 100 days a year on the road. Bill Bradley remembers five games over seven days in four different cities. He would attempt to combat the loneliness on the road by making chitchat in hotel lobbies or passing time with strangers in bars. Occasionally, he would venture out into the city to take in an art exhibit or visit an interesting section of town; but often there was too little time for these excursions. Then he would sit in his hotel room reading books or listening to the radio.[43] Few athletes prove to be adventurous travelers. They rarely seek out new restaurants or visit cultural or historical sights while on the road. Instead, they tend to frequent the same spots year after year, the same steak house, movie theater, or the nearest bar.[44]

When DiMaggio was playing in the California minor leagues of the 1930s, the players went to a lot of movies. Once they'd been around the league a few times, they would have friends in town and might be invited to dinner. Some of the veterans arranged liaisons with women. Curfew was usually midnight or two hours after a night game. How athletes spent their time had a lot to do with personality. DiMaggio's roommate Steve Barath would hang out at the dime-a-dance emporiums, while young Joe, the introvert, would sit in the hotel reading the *Sporting News*.[45]

For athletes in individual sports, the schedule can be just as fatiguing. Bowlers typically play one tournament on their "home court." By the mid-1980s, the Professional Bowlers Association was sponsoring 130 national and regional events.[46] Although no individual bowler would attempt to compete in all these, it still meant a lot of time on the road. Golf imposes a similar schedule. Two generations after Ben Hogan, the means of travel had improved but the professional tournament schedule was just as daunting. During one short stretch, Tiger Woods traveled from Oregon to Wisconsin and then to Canada for the Canadian Open. The following week it was on to the Quad City tournament in Iowa, the B.C. Open in upstate New York, the Southern Open in Las Vegas, then to Texas. At that point, his immediate plans included playing the Disney Classic (Florida) and then the Tour Championship in Tulsa, Oklahoma.[47]

Yacht racing entails thousands of miles of international travel. Ted Turner recalls going to Oslo, Norway, on July 13 for the Skaw race; then on July 26, to Isle of Wight for the Admiral's Cup; August 25 to Sardinia for the World One-Ton championship; and then September 28 to Malta for the Middle Sea Race during one season in the 1970s.[48] Tennis players also traverse the globe. Arthur Ashe notes that in the year from June 1973 through June 1974, he made 129 plane trips and slept in 71 different beds while playing in 25 tournaments. He once flew 6,000 miles in four days, and on another occasion made 12 flights in 11 days. Ashe's reaction: "I don't feel I'm traveling, I feel like I've been shipped somewhere."[49]

Ashe's lifestyle on the road stood in stark contrast to that of the old timers like Cobb and Hogan. The tennis star ate in the best restaurants, stayed in the best hotels, socialized with celebrities, and could fly from city to city on a whim. In his autobiography, he comments on where to shop internationally for the best bargains, where the finest caviar can be found, and on the superior hotels and restaurants. World-class tennis players and yachtsmen are the "jet setters" among athletes.[50]

The days of long auto and train trips are disappearing. Most professional athletes now travel by air. However, as leagues expand geographically and tournaments proliferate, even this means of transportation can become time consuming and tiring. By the time you get to the airport, check your baggage, go through airport security, wait in line for takeoff, and then upon arrival go through baggage and catch your ground connections, it can make for a long day. The veteran Pelé ragged his young teammate Shep Messing, "I bet you I spend more time in airplanes than you spend on the field your whole time in soccer."[51] Roberto Clemente notes that years ago when teams traveled by train, at least they had time to adjust to the time change. With air travel, he observes, "After a night game, you go to bed at 1 o'clock there, but it is really 4 o'clock in your head because we come from the East.... Even when you think you're resting, you're really not."[52]

One might assume that athletes might avoid traveling when they are not required to by the schedule of competition. However, the obligations of public life encourage more of the same. Rocky Marciano was constantly being hustled around the country by his manager to make personal appearances. For a good four years, he was on the road more than he was at home with his family.[53] Jesse Owens' wife Ruth pleaded with her husband to slow down and enjoy life. The "retired" track star chronicles a typical week on the road: "I attended a track meet in Boston, flew from there to Bowling Green for the National Jaycees, then to Rochester for the blind, Buffalo for another track meet, New York to shoot a film called, 'The Black Athlete,' Miami for Ford Motor Company, back up to New York for 45 minutes to deliver a speech, then into L.A. for another the same night."[54]

Arthur Ashe, once he became a celebrity, found himself involved in a constant stream of promotional events, business deals, and charity appearances. Ashe's diary chronicles his typical nontournament schedule during one year. It records appearances at resorts and store openings, parties with tournament backers, coaching stints at tennis camps, conducting clinics, representing commercial interests on tour, various promotional appearances in conjunction with product endorsements, appearances at conventions, doing media commercials, lunches with corporate board chairmen, appearances at charitable events, as well as promoting the Arthur Ashe line of clothes—on and on. Although Ashe groused about the hectic tennis circuit, he obviously enjoyed the stimulation of traveling places and meeting people.[55]

One way or another, travel makes up a major part of athletes' lives. It's not all negative. Sport can transport young men like Jim Thorpe or Randy Matson out of rural, small-town America and show them the world. Pitcher Jim Brosnan reflects on his professional career: "In my twelve years in organized baseball I've played professionally in forty-one of the fifty states, several Caribbean islands, and some Far Eastern countries, including Japan. Had I joined the Navy in 1947 instead of the Chicago Cubs organization I doubt if I would have seen much more of the world."[56]

An athlete may tour the minor league cities of mid-America or travel the international circuit; but whether in Omaha or the Olympic village, one constant is lodging. While the range in accommodations is wide, a sense of sameness permeates the experience.

Hotel Living

Throughout modern history, athletes have sampled a wide range of lodgings. Rookie Ty Cobb found a room in an $8 weekly "bed and board" near the Tigers' Bennett Park when he arrived in Detroit in 1905.[57] Jockey Tod Sloan had a predilection for hotel suites that ran a 100 (turn-of-the-century) dollars a night when he was "in the chips."[58] In the pre–World War II era, many of the bachelors on the New York Yankees would reside in modest hotels in the Bronx, while the married players had houses in New Jersey. The well-paid DiMaggio boarded at some of New York City's finest midtown suites.[59] These practices haven't changed much over the decades, and the accommodations continue to vary from penthouses to boarding houses. The majority of athletes, however, limit their hotel living to road trips.

World-class tennis players like Arthur Ashe can choose between luxurious hotels or the private homes of star-struck admirers. But the typical athlete on the road stays in accommodations rated fewer than five stars. Whether at the Waldorf or the Red Roof Inn, hotel rooms become as much a part of the athletic experience as locker rooms. Travel accommodations traditionally have been rather austere. Early on, lodging lacked air-conditioning or laundries. Ben Hogan recalls that he would sit in the lobbies under the ceiling fans and then retire to his room to do his laundry in the bathtub.[60] Lance Armstrong complains that the discomfort of road cycling (much of it abroad) extends to tiny, unclean rooms and terrible hotel food.[61] Even the jet-setting Ashe complains of washing his laundry and going stir crazy in his hotel room. He remarks on the monotony of road trips: "The courts, hotels, and restaurants are different, but the experience will be the same."[62]

For lack of alternatives or a dearth of imagination, athletes on the road spend an inordinate amount of time sequestered in hotels. New York sportswriter Dan Daniel, who accompanied the Yankee teams on the road in the 1920s and '30s, recalls, "After the game you came back to the hotel, had your dinner, went up to your room...then you went down to the lobby, and who was in the lobby? The manager, the coaches, and a few players."[63] Pat Jordan recounts that he and his teammates generally stayed close to the hotel. "We did nothing for hours on end. We waited impatiently for each meal. We made dozens of trips to hotel coffee shops, and spent hours slumped in the lobby's easy chairs. Day after day, the same."[64]

A few athletes don't even venture as far as the lobby. Paul Merson recalls holing up in his room more than 12 hours a day.[65] Ken Dryden would alternate between the bathtub and the bed. Otherwise, he would be on the phone. He preferred to be alone but is required to room with a teammate. He worries about disturbing him. Roommates are part of life on the road for most athletes. Occasionally, the situation can get testy.[66] Bill Bradley remembers arguing with roommates over trivial things like whether the TV should be on or not.[67]

Hotel rooms provide refuge. Carmen Salvino would go out and bowl, and then retreat to his hotel room to contemplate in private. During a time he was struggling with his game, Salvino locked himself in his hotel room for five days, phoning only his wife.[68] Once air-conditioning became standard, hotel rooms offered a welcome level of comfort. Athletes in outdoor sports would retreat to their rooms to recover from the heat and humidity after a game or practice. After training long hours in a humid swimming pool, Don Schollander would retreat to an air-conditioned motel room and rest.[69] During the Tour de France following the day's racing, an exhausted Armstrong and the other riders would have their legs massaged each evening, eat dinner, and then watch French television sequestered in their rooms before retiring.[70]

Time endured in hotel rooms leads to compensatory behaviors. Ashe recalls sitting in a room and endlessly changing TV channels. Pat Jordan recalls, "I passed the time standing for hours in front of the mirror on the wall. I practiced my motion in pantomime. I threw a thousand pitches a day in front of that mirror."[71] At night, Ben Hogan would take his putter, a wedge and some balls, and practice putts and chip shots.[72] These are the introverts. Others are more sociable. A laid-back Shep Messing relaxed by playing Frisbee in the hotel hallways.[73] Sonny Liston shared accommodations with his traveling buddy Foneda Cox. The two men would party in their room.[74] Because Michael Jordan couldn't go out without causing a mob scene, his hotel room became the center of the action, filled with his friends and the ever-present body guards.[75] Muhammad Ali routinely "held court" in his hotel room, accompanied by the hangers-on in his traveling entourage.[76]

When it came to having fun in hotels, no group was more creative than Jim Bouton's Yankee teammates: climbing around on hotel roofs or setting up telescopes in hotel windows to gawk at women.[77] This is not to imply that athletes limited their escapades to the hotel environs. Babe Ruth set the standard for gregariousness. He seldom remained in his room for long unless he was ducking intrusive hotel guests. Normally, he was out on the town partying. Ruth would come in on the train and go directly to the commercial district. He might show up later at the hotel for a change of clothes. When teammate Ping Bodie was asked what it was like to room with Ruth, he replied, "I don't room with him, I room with his suitcase."[78]

Hotels are a constant; the personalities of their occupants are the variable. Hotel living may present a skewed image of the ways that athletes occupy their leisure while on the road, but it offers a preview to how athletes generally cope with time outside the arena.

TIME IN; TIME OUT

Based on the actual time spent competing in the arena, athletes should enjoy quite a bit of leisure when not on the road. What Joe DiMaggio and Mickey Mantle did as baseball players, they did for three hours a day during spring and summer afternoons or evenings. Alter the time of day or the season, and most team sports feature similar schedules. Individual sports competition isn't much different in its demands. Arthur Ashe played in maybe two dozen tournaments a year during his peak. Most tennis tournaments last less than a week, and only winners keep playing. Boxing is not a seasonal sport, yet professional boxers compete less often than ballplayers. Once they win the title, they may fight only a couple times a year—encounters that last about an hour. Veteran welterweight Aaron Pryor fought twice in 1983, and once each during the following five years. Of these seven fights, three ended within three rounds.[79] Whatever the sport, the same point can be made: performing takes up a relatively brief part of an athlete's life.

But competition and its corollaries—training and practice—have a way of impinging on free time as noted above. Pitcher Dave Dravecky observes, "You're on the road fifty percent of the time, and even when you're home most of the games are at night. I generally leave for the ballpark at two in the afternoon and arrive home after midnight."[80] The experience for basketball players is analogous. Bill Bradley notes that even though an NBA workday was only about four hours it seemed to structure the remainder of his day. The same was true for weekends. He comments, "Saturday doesn't begin for me until 1 p.m. whenever we return from a late road trip; the next day is always a jumble."[81] Ken Dryden points out that in professional hockey you normally play only three games a week, but it is routine that can fool you. It should allow time for other things, but it doesn't. It takes away your weekends and occupies your nighttime. He observes, "it can't be a full-time job. But it is." He declares, "I have become a full-time hockey player and a part-time everything else."[82]

Schedules shape the athlete's orientation to time. Oriard describes teammates for whom life was just "marking time" between football games. Being an athlete, he remarks, is being aware of the insistence of time. "Not only the brevity of careers, but a concentrated focus on the *now*. . . .the past is meaningless and the future irrelevant except for the game just ahead."[83] Don Schollander experienced time as waiting: "waiting for the morning workout, waiting to go to sleep, waiting for the evening workout. Finish the workout and wait for the next. Wait for Saturday. Wait for Sunday. Wait for the next meet."[84]

Sports seasons play out in rhythmic patterns. The daily and weekly cycles with their imposed schedules can feel unnatural. Dryden describes the routines within an eight-month hockey season: "Our time is fragmented and turned upside-down. Awake half the night, asleep half the morning, with three hours until practice, then three hours until dinner, nighttime no different from daytime, weekends from weekdays. At home, in the rhythm of the road, on the road, needing to go home. Then home again, and wives, children, friends, lawyers, agents, eating, drinking, sleeping. . .and we're on the road again." Traveling to or from the West Coast, Dryden's team occasionally has a day with no game or practice, a travel day. Less often, perhaps once a month, an off-day. After eight years of doing this, he confesses that he still is not very good at off-days.[85]

Historically, no sport had a more grueling schedule than horse racing. Todd Sloan recalls that the turn-of-the-century turf season in the East consisted of a continuous 176-day meeting with races on Christmas and New Year's Day. Some of the California tracks raced on 200 plus days a year. Only when Sloan became successful, did he ride when it suited him.[86] During the course of the 20th century, sports seasons generally got longer. Baseball went from 154 to 162 games with the World Series in late October. The NFL season, including playoffs, now runs into February. What were originally seasonal sports have expanded to nearly yearlong endeavors. Soccer preseason in Britain begins in July, and the formal season runs from August through May with World Cup games the following summer. Paul Merson notes that while competing in the World Cup, he was away from home for six weeks. During one year he had only four weeks off.[87] Dennis Rodman recalls that his basketball team reported back to camp just 14 weeks after winning the NBA playoffs.[88] At the same time, sports seasons are becoming more congested. Bradley noted that during the NBA season there is usually no longer than one day at a time without a basketball game; no long weekends or national holidays. Players may have a game on Christmas night or New Year's Eve.[89]

Even amateur sports are increasingly demanding of an athlete's time. Gymnast Bart Conner remembers being home only two days for an entire three months in 1984. As a student athlete, Conner was forced to workout between 7 and 10:00 p.m. because of scheduling conflicts with classes. He would then go home, eat dinner and go to bed. Conner's autobiography depicts little of life outside the gym.[90] Schollander observes of his life as a student athlete, "You cut down on studying, you give up dates, you rest in the afternoon. You read, you watch television, you eat and sleep. You indulge in no outlet for your tension. I'd go to bed the same time every night, to get up at the same time every morning."[91]

There are athletes who willingly immerse themselves in their sport so that it becomes virtually their entire life. Young Carmen Salvino would bowl three to four hours every weekday while going to high school, and up to 12 hours on Saturdays and Sundays. After graduating, he took a day job and continued to bowl evenings and weekends. Sometimes he would bowl through most of the night, rolling as many as 50 games.[92] For Bill Tilden it was five sets of tennis a day. Even when he was 60 years old, Tilden would spend the entire day on the court.[93] Cycling became Lance Armstrong's whole life. He recalls, "I was too busy being a pro athlete...to do the things most people in their 20s do, to have fun.... I'd completely skipped that phase of my life." He describes his routine during training and competition as eating, sleeping, and riding his bike.[94]

Later, a married Armstrong endured a hectic morning and afternoon schedule, culminating in exhaustion: out the door at 8 a.m. after a brief breakfast for a training ride; riding straight through lunch until about 3 p.m.; returning home to shower and lie down until dinnertime, dinner with his wife "Kik," and then early to bed. This routine might continue for months.[95] Athletes literally can be "married" to their sport. Mark Wetmore, a distance runner at Rutgers University, and later the cross-country coach at the University of Colorado, describes himself thus: "I don't play golf. I don't have any hobbies. I don't have a wife." Simply put, cross-country is Mark's life.[96]

In addition to competing in their sport, some athletes have jobs. When Michael Oriard was playing Canadian football in the 1970s, he noted that many of the players held down second jobs both during the season and between seasons.[97] Virtually all minor league soccer players worked at second jobs according to Messing, during the early years of the NASL.[98] Likewise, the early bowling tour supported very few top professionals. Bowlers played the tour for a few months and then went home to earn a living.[99] It's not uncommon for athletes to hold jobs during the off-season. Brian Piccolo worked in real estate between seasons while playing in the NFL.[100] Pete Rose's teammate Jim O'Toole sold insurance during the winters, while Jim Maloney sold used cars.[101]

Yet, there remains "downtime," gaps between games, practice schedules, and part-time jobs. Some athletes do better than others in filling this time.

Positive pastimes include reading, recreation, or just relaxing. Less desirable options for use of leisure involve habits such as compulsive gambling or taking drugs. But a lot of athletes simply pass the time doing little of significance.

FILLING LEISURE TIME

Paul Merson, a recovering drug addict, spends more time at home than most athletes. On match days, he lays around on the bed watching TV until it's time to leave for the soccer stadium. He recalls playing computer games for an entire morning. On a typical nongame day, he is up at 8 a.m. for a morning training session, then back home by 1 p.m., watching soccer on television all afternoon. On Sunday at home, he watches television for six hours. Occasionally, he pops sleeping pills and then sleeps for 12 hours straight. Clearly, Merson is strug-gling to cope. He professes, "As I have discovered in trying to recover one day at a time from an addictive illness, there is life outside the game." At one point he asserts, rather unconvincingly, that he is not one to sit around a swim-ming pool all day. Occasionally he does break out of the lethargy. "I escaped into physical activity, running three miles a day and playing a lot of tennis," he reports. Such bursts of activity are episodic.[102]

Athletes who do find meaningful ways to occupy their free time often are drawn to physical recreation. It seems a natural fit. Cobb played polo with the same reckless abandon he ran the bases, according to his teammates. Todd Sloan shot skeet. Many athletes hunt or fish in the off-season. Deion Sanders was an avid fisherman who liked to take along teammates. Steve Howe fished and hunted, and did some snowmobiling in the winters. Gene Tunney vaca-tioned in the Maine woods where he spent the summer fishing and reading. DiMaggio and a buddy would take a couple of weeks for golf and deep sea fish-ing, or head to South Dakota for some hunting and freshwater fishing. Gehrig enjoyed deep sea fishing. Ted Williams was a passionate angler who devoted an inordinate amount of time to the sport. Tiger Woods was a convert. On a rare break from tournament play, he allowed fellow golfer Mark O'Meara take him fishing on one of Florida's lakes. But he couldn't resist a round of golf the following day.[103]

Golf is by far the most popular recreational sport among athletes who don't play professionally. Babe Ruth, Gene Tunney, Joe Louis, Joe DiMaggio, Mickey Mantle, Arthur Ashe, and Lance Armstrong all played golf. Michael Jordan became engrossed with the game. For him, it was both enjoyment and escape. When he was on the course no one could bother him. But it soon became an obsession. Jordan was known to play from seven in the morning until the sun went down. After the 1991 championship season, Jordan and his friends played an ongoing five-day marathon.[104]

High-profile athletes like Joe DiMaggio and Michael Jordan have to find ways to enjoy their free time without drawing a crowd. While Jordan was inclined to seclude himself on private golf courses, DiMaggio proved more eclectic in his diversions. He became a regular at the upscale New York City bars and restaurants. He also liked to attend boxing matches. When he could maintain his anonymity, he would frequent the dog racing tracks in Florida. Joe occasionally went to movies and attended Broadway plays.[105] DiMaggio was typical of athletes who enjoy indoor as well as outdoor activities. These are the guys who can be found regularly at the local watering holes and clubs. Dennis Rodman spent many evenings in an all-night bar with friends and liked to gamble at the casinos. Brian Piccolo was always ready for a night of social drinking after a day at the stadium. He would routinely stay out with friends until 3 a.m. Pete Rose also liked to drop by the neighborhood bar and socialize with friends over a few beers.

Physical and social activities trump the more cerebral forms of recreation. Given the option of spending their day off at the local bar, the golf course, or the library, few athletes choose the latter. Lance Armstrong reflected on his youth by noting that he had a short attention span and couldn't sit still for long. He didn't care much for books.[106] Pete Rose boasted that the only book he had ever read was *Pete Rose: My Story*.[107] Rogers Hornsby, who played major league baseball from 1915 to 1937, made a point not to read during the season on the theory that his batting eye would be adversely affected—but he excepted racing forms from this rule.[108] Babe Ruth read menus not books.

When journalist Jeanne Parr interviewed athletes' wives for her book *The Superwives*, she noted very few volumes on the shelves in their homes.[109] But contrary to the jock stereotype, one does find athletes who read in their leisure. Jerry Kramer comments that every time a reporter came to his home and saw books, he seemed surprised: "The Beast reads!"[110] In fact, athletes read on airplanes, in hotel lobbies, even in locker rooms. Ashe always traveled with books; he either read or worked crossword puzzles to kill time. Among those who do read, the material covers quite a range. Joe Louis liked to read the comics in the newspapers; among his favorites was fictional pugilist Joe Palooka. DiMaggio read Westerns and comic books, but was so self-conscious about his image that he would inveigle friends to purchase these items for him. Paul Merson preferred self-help books. Jockey Red Pollard grew up reading the classics, Shakespeare, Omar Khayyám, Emerson, and he never lost interest in them.[111] Ty Cobb, the son of a school superintendent, read history and biography. Roberto Clemente read in two languages. When he traveled to New York or California he could find books in Spanish. He also read Westerns and adventure stories in English.[112]

Reading serves as recreation and a way to fill time. Tim Green was probably more literate than most of his NFL teammates. He went from playing football to writing about it, and then wrote some fiction. During his professional career, he would read Dickens and Tolstoy. Green notes that there was always a book in his locker. He describes himself as an inveterate reader, picking up a volume during any break between meetings or before practice, waiting for the horn to sound to go out on the field. He recalls that he even read during lunch and sitting on the training table getting his ankles taped. His reading would draw looks of suspicion, and even disgust, from some of the other players and coaches.[113]

Another future author Pat Conroy received similar reactions from his college basketball buddies: "My teammates thought my reading habits both odd and off-putting, another way of not inhabiting the world around me."[114] Jim Bouton wrote at length about the anti-intellectual atmosphere in the baseball clubhouse, and his teammates' general discomfort around anyone who would attempt to share thoughts formed from reading.[115] Like most professions, one can find serious readers, light readers, and nonreaders among the ranks. While reading is a selective activity among athletes, card playing is ubiquitous and often involves wagering.

Playing Cards and Gambling

Playing cards certainly is more sociable than reading. It provides a way for athletes to interact while killing time. Whatever the sport, one can find athletes engaged in some type of card games. Poker was the typical game at football training camps. NFL rookie Michael Oriard discovered that both high- and low-stakes games of stud were a feature of the Kansas City Chiefs camp in the 1970s.[116] Ballplayers also alleviate the boredom of long trips by playing cards. Clemente's teammate Steve Blass recounts the monotonous flights from Pittsburgh to Los Angeles: "On airplane trips, we'd play cards a lot. The six or seven of us that played would confiscate a few rows of seats and get out the blankets, and everybody had to bring change. The guys who played that afternoon would get the most comfortable seats, facing ahead, and us pitchers who hadn't worked had to lean over the other seats, facing down."[117] He remembers Roberto would occupy a corner seat and try to eat dinner while playing seven-card stud.

Messing writes about teammate Hubert Eusebio who was obsessed with poker. Eusebio would play anytime, anywhere, on buses, planes, in locker rooms, hotel rooms, coffee shops, and bars. The games often would last all night.[118] Michael Jordan and his buddies on the Chicago Bulls engaged in marathon card games that lasted through the night and into the early morning.[119] Bill Tilden was an inveterate card player. Although he detested poker, he could be enticed into games of pinochle, hearts, or gin rummy. But bridge was his passion, and he was an expert player. Tilden not only indulged in long games at the local tennis club, but when on the road he sought out the best players in whatever town he was in for a serious game.[120] Ashe played casual poker with other players on the tennis tour. Joe Louis had a reputation for winning at the poker table. DiMaggio played poker with teammates and *Briscola,* an Italian game, with friends. Salvino would play poker and gin rummy to relax after an evening of bowling. Pat Jordan reports that the older minor leaguers played a lot of bridge.

Pete Rose loved to play cards but with no money involved. One of his favorite pastimes was to play hearts and gin rummy while sipping Miller from a can at the local bar.[121] It's paradoxical that an athlete who played cards without wagering would become the symbol of professional baseball's gambling problems. Gambling at cards has a long history in sports. Ben Hogan notes that early on in professional golf there was much drinking and betting on cards after a daily round or two on the course.[122] Sometimes, high-stake card games among athletes would lead to hard feelings. New York Giants manager (from 1902 to 1932) John McGraw refused to permit his teams to play cards as the stakes got so high the losers were brooding, and it was affecting their play.[123] Messing recounts that high-stake poker games in the NASL would cause such hard feelings that one player refused to pass to another during the game, informing him, "You take my money in poker, I never give you the ball."[124]

Card games weren't the only venue for gambling. Indeed, some sports seem inextricably linked to betting. Bowling is a prime case. Salvino would wage bets much like a pool hustler does. He notes that most games during the post–World War II era had a wager on them. Bowling pools were common with contributions by frame, for example, 20 cents for each open frame.[125] Horse racing probably wouldn't exist without betting, but the wagering is supposed to be limited to the spectators. Sloan was an inveterate gambler who occasionally bet on the races he rode in. He even roomed with a professional gambler at a time when horse racing was the greatest gambling enterprise in the country. It's estimated that his gambling debts and high living depleted his earnings by some $300,000. Sloan's betting on races eventually cost him his career.[126]

Gambling on baseball was not uncommon in the early 20th century. At one point, Brooklyn and Philadelphia actually allowed open betting pools in their baseball parks. Betting by fans became part of the scene, and poorly paid players had opportunities to make money with gamblers who could always be found in hotel lobbies. The most notorious incident involving players was the "Black Sox" scandal which revolved around a group of Chicago White Sox players meeting with gamblers who offered them bribes to throw the 1919 World Series. Commissioner Kenesaw Mountain Landis dealt lifetime bans to eight of the players accused of fixing the Series, even though they were acquitted in criminal trials. Seven years later, Ty Cobb and Tris Speaker were implicated in a scheme to fix a game, but were exonerated by Landis.[127]

Rumors spread that professional football players were engaged in some high-stakes betting on games during the 1920s when Jim Thorpe was playing for the Canton (Ohio) Bulldogs. Thorpe was reported to have written a $2,500 check to cover a bet, but his manager Jack Cusack vehemently denied it. Earlier, during a congressional investigation of corruption at Carlisle College, there was testimony that Thorpe's old coach Pop Warner had bet heavily on the 1913 Dartmouth game, and told his team at half time that if they won he would cut them in.[128] The gambling problem persisted in sports. The 1960s-era Detroit Lions were known as a bunch of rounders and hell raisers. Six players were fined heavily by the NFL commissioner, and defensive tackle Alex Karras was suspended, for gambling on a league football game.[129] During the course of the 20th century, commissioners in various professional leagues did all they could to eliminate gambling by players in order to protect the integrity of their sport.

Gambling infiltrates all levels of sport from the World Series to the local country club. Tiger Woods was hustling on the golf course when he was still in elementary school. He'd come home every day from the course with his pockets full of quarters, from the "skins" won on the putting greens.[130] But he was an amateur at the time. There's no indication that he gambled on the game once he turned pro. The more prudent professional athletes limited their wagers to sports and games that they weren't directly involved in. DiMaggio hung out at dog tracks during spring training, but was discreet enough to have friends place bets for him. Babe Ruth reserved his gambling for the horse tracks and the casinos. Dennis Rodman was a heavy casino gambler. It's estimated that he squandered most of the $2.5 million he earned with the Spurs due to gambling and high living. Dennis would spend consecutive evenings at the Las Vegas casinos, once burrowing himself in a hotel there for a month with a loss of some $35,000.[131]

Few athletes have gambled more compulsively than Michael Jordan. The habit began in college at 25 cents a free throw, with bets on games of "Horse" and the outcome of video games. Later, Michael would bet heavily on golf. At first he was wagering $100 a hole or $100 a putt. Eventually, the bets reached $1,000 a hole. He soon became a mark for golf hustlers, the type of characters who carry $30,000 cash in their pockets. Once, after a five-day spree Jordan owed $150,000 to two of his golfing partners. The NBA investigated Jordan's gambling after reports of a $300,000 settlement with a self-proclaimed gambling addict named Richard Equinas. Significantly, none of Jordan's gambling was on the sports he played professionally.[132]

For Pete Rose, gambling was a career-long habit. He began wagering bets during his rookie season in 1963. There were periods when he spent nearly every day at River Downs, the local thoroughbred track in Cincinnati. This was perfectly legal and within baseball rules. But Rose would place bets through bookmakers which was a violation of rules, and he also bet on pro sports. Mike Bertolini, who often joined Rose at the track, recalls that Pete would throw $1,000–$1,500 a race. According to Ron Peters, an Ohio bookmaker, Rose was betting as much as $30,000 a day on various sports in the summer of 1987. Dennis Schrader, a greyhound owner and bettor, recalls that one night Pete handed him and his wife a stack of losing tickets worth 10,000 dollars as he left the track. "He loved the action," commented Schrader. Between 1984 and 1987, Rose made nearly five million dollars in baseball, of which more than two million dollars went to taxes. It is estimated that he lost hundreds of thousands of dollars to bookies. Peters testified that he took in one million dollars in wagers from Rose on baseball and other sports.[133]

The Rose gambling scandal broke publicly in 1989. The official report coming out of the Baseball Commissioner's Office offered testimony and documentary evidence that Rose had bet on baseball and particularly on the Cincinnati Reds during three seasons when he was manager of the team. His compulsive gambling and wholesale exploitation of sports memorabilia led to other serious problems. Rose pleaded guilty to two felony charges of concealing income on federal tax returns and served five months in federal prison. He was banned from baseball and excluded from consideration for the Baseball Hall of Fame.[134]

Tim Green has given the matter some thought; he sees sport as a spawning ground for gambling. He recalls watching teammates lose 5,000 dollars in a poker game on a coast-to-coast flight, and then win back twice that much rolling dice on the way home. Why are athletes particularly prone to this behavior? Green believes that it is because they are programmed to be competitive, to win. He describes it as a "buzz in the brain that can't be turned off. The better the athlete, the bigger the buzz."[135] Thus, in his view, the very nature of competitive sport fosters and supports a gambler's mentality.

While some athletes are compulsive gamblers, others become habituated to alcohol and drugs. Paul Merson had a problem with all the above. He reminds himself following a relapse, "I am a gambling addict, an alcoholic and a drug addict."[136] He's not the only athlete who's struggled with the latter two afflictions.

RECREATIONAL DRUGS

When it comes to drugs, athletes run the gamut from abstinence to abuse. It's fair to assume that most drink alcohol; fewer use other recreational drugs. Steve Howe estimates that probably half of his former teammates on the Dodgers "were into substances other than liquor, [but] alcohol was still the team's universally accepted tribal method of blowing off steam."[137] Social drinking has been the norm among athletes. Brian Piccolo would spend evenings with friends drinking and socializing; Pete Rose liked to drop by the neighborhood bar for a few beers. Joe DiMaggio would have a beer in the clubhouse after games, and frequent New York City's upscale watering holes on a regular basis. While DiMaggio would be described as a heavy drinker in today's terms, Babe Ruth imbibed hard liquor and beer in prodigious quantities. *New York Times* reporter John Drebinger recalls, "I saw Babe Ruth take down a Coca Cola bottle full of whiskey one time. Gurgled it right down."[138] Sport has had its share of alcoholics.

Josh Gibson's drinking escalated over the course of his baseball career. Early on, he would drink beer with his teammates over card games or in taverns on the road. Seldom did alcohol go any farther than that, as drunkenness wasn't tolerated among the players in the Negro League ball parks. Winter League play in Latin America was another matter. The schedules included a lot of leisure time, and many of the teams were owned by liquor magnates. It wasn't unusual for a team owner to award good performance with a case of beer. Josh began his heavy drinking with buddy Sammy Bankhead; the two would vie on how many Mexican beers they could "down." Soon they were drinking between games of doubleheaders. Later, Gibson suffered spells of dizziness and disorientation, and his performance on the field began to deteriorate. He was occasionally benched. Field manager Vic Harris once caught him sitting in the team's bull pen drinking beer, a gross violation of the rules. But he did most of his imbibing outside the ballpark. One night in Chicago in 1945, teammate Jimmy Crutchfield found Josh drinking straight whiskey—shot after shot without a chaser. By then Gibson was making little effort to stay in shape. Things continued to go downhill until he succumbed to a stroke at the age of 35.[139]

Mickey Mantle acquired a reputation for hard liquor and late hours. He often showed up for games hung over. Yankee management became so concerned that they once had Mantle and his drinking buddies shadowed by private detectives. Mantle drank throughout his playing career (1951–1968) and into retirement. The habit eventually destroyed his liver.[140] Alcohol abuse has remained a problem in professional sports up to the present. Baseball players coming into the major leagues receive mixed messages about what constitutes appropriate drinking. Some of the role models are less than exemplary.

St. Louis Cardinals president Mark Lamping was formerly an executive at Anheuser-Busch brewery. The Cardinals play in Busch Stadium named after the family who owned the brewery. Until quite recently, team management allowed drinking in the clubhouse and on charter flights returning from road games. During spring training in Florida in 2007, Manager Tony LaRussa was arrested by Palm Beach police when they found him slumped behind the wheel of his vehicle and registering a blood alcohol level of .09. The team manager's imprudent conduct coupled with a club environment conducive to imbibing alcohol were prelude to a tragedy. The following April, 29-year-old Cardinal pitcher Josh Hancock was killed in an early morning automobile accident after crashing into a tow truck on a Missouri highway. He had pitched three innings that afternoon and then spent some three hours drinking at a local steak house. The restaurant manager reports that the pitcher declined an offer of a taxi ride. The offer was prescient, as the autopsy revealed that Hancock's blood alcohol level at almost twice the legal limit. Police also found 8.5 grams of marijuana in his car.[141]

Clearly, alcohol hasn't been the only recreational drug used by athletes. Steve Howe's drug of choice was cocaine. For a period of time, his life consisted entirely of playing baseball and snorting the white powder. In 1981, during spring training he blew $3,000 on cocaine over a period of less than four months. Steve notes that he spent so much on drugs he had to declare bankruptcy. When a baseball strike left him with endless time to kill, he partied continuously, staying out all night at least one night a week. One binge lasted for five straight days. He admits to inhaling nearly $1,500 worth of coke a week at one point. By spring training in 1983, Howe was staying out six nights a week doing drugs. Eventually, his problem became public, and he was suspended from baseball. After a long struggle involving several suspensions Howe eventually beat his addiction, but it had destroyed his career.[142]

Aaron Pryor devotes two chapters of his autobiography to his cocaine addiction. At one point, he was staying high for two weeks at a time. He and wife Theresa went through $200–300 of crack a day. His life got totally out of control. On one occasion he got into a gun battle with drug dealers; on another, he jumped from a three-storey window when police raided a crack house. His habit eventually led to an arrest for drug possession. Things continued to deteriorate to the point that he no longer cared about his boxing career. He commented, "The crack had such a grip on me, I didn't want to live anymore." He actually went into his bedroom and placed a loaded 9mm pistol against his temple. Later, he was shot by an intruder. Eventually, Pryor finds religion and gives up cocaine. His story is that of a talented athlete who self-destructs and is then redeemed.[143]

Paul Merson's chemical dependencies alternated from alcohol to sleeping pills to cocaine. Somehow he was able to maintain his position as a successful soccer player in the throes of all these mind-altering chemicals. He kept a diary of his struggle with addiction and writes at length about his experience in his memoir. At the time the book was published he had been three years without a drink, a drug, or a bet (he was also a compulsive gambler). He chronicles how a recovering addict lives one day at a time, observing that the disease is called alcohol*ism* not alcohol*wasm*.[144] The soccer star's account of addiction, recovery, and relapse is honest and sobering. Many of his experiences echo those of Steve Howe.

Athletes are probably no different than most professional performers. The great majority can control their use of recreational drugs while a few allow drugs to destroy their careers and occasionally, their lives. They do differ from most people in one regard; they have plenty of money to spend on expensive consumer items and entertainments. Most athletes enjoy a taste of the "high life" at some point in their careers.

LIFESTYLES OF THE *NOUVEAU RICHE* AND FAMOUS

The lifestyles of athletes run the gamut from Spartan to extravagant, but the general inclination has been toward the latter. Tod Sloan was the quintessential dandy who wore the best clothes, smoked the best cigars, drank the best liquors, and dined on the best cuisine. Before he ran out of money, he kept a valet, a chauffeur, and servants.[145] Sloan's contemporary Jack Johnson also had a knack for high living. The flamboyant boxer bought fine clothes, indulged in fast cars, wined and dined women, toured the capitals of Europe in style, purchased his own nightclub, and generally enjoyed wealth and fame while the opportunity lasted.[146]

The 1920s-era Yankees' habits were on a scale approaching decadence. Bootleggers and bookmakers followed them around like servants. Their champion debaucher was Babe Ruth. The highly paid slugger would spend money lavishly on food and entertainment. When the Yankees were on the road, Ruth often reserved his own suite in a separate hotel from the team. He could be found lounging around in red slippers and a red robe, cigar in mouth, cleanly shaved by his private barber. Over his career, he bought a series of splendid automobiles, demonstrating a preference for convertibles and sports cars.[147] Across town, heavyweight boxing champion Jack Dempsey was carrying on the tradition of Jack Johnson. The Dempsey formula for enjoying life incorporated wine, women, and song. The champ lived it up on Broadway, making the rounds of New York nightclubs and speakeasies, buying drinks for the house, and tipping liberally.[148]

Examples of high living were still evident two generations later, as the salaries of professional athletes soared into the seven-figure range. Deion Sanders became the highest-paid player in the history of the NFL. His sobriquet "Prime Time" and the title of his autobiography, *Power, Money and Sex,* bear testimony to his lifestyle. In the tradition of Sloan and Johnson, Sanders' quickly became known for flashy clothes and glitzy jewelry, heavy-duty partying, and womanizing—although he abstained from drugs and alcohol.[149] Professional athletes with million-dollar contracts are among the most visible *nouveau riche* in American celebrity culture.

Pete Rose came from a working-class background. Once in the money, he accumulated Corvettes, Porsches, Rolex watches, and yards of gold chains and bracelets. He boasts of a nine-room home, with four and a half baths, eight telephones, and five color television sets. "That's living," Rose offers.[150] When Tiger Woods arrived in Las Vegas for his first pro tournament, he rode in a stretch limo to the MGM Hotel and took a private elevator up to the penthouse. Dinner was in a private reserved dining room where he was toasted with Don Perignon. The kid who was now known as the richest college dropout in America had had to borrow $20 from his mother earlier that same week so he could go to MacDonald's.[151]

Lance Armstrong became wealthy through his success in professional cycling. At age 25, Armstrong signed a two-year contract with a prestigious French racing team Cofidis for $2.5 million. He bought a mansion on a riverbank, purchased a Porche, and put a fortune in the bank.[152] Gymnastics may be an amateur sport, but the endorsement contracts can be lucrative. Olympic gold medal winner Bart Conner either drove a Porsche or rode around in furnished limousines. In his autobiography, he describes himself floating on a raft in the middle of his swimming pool with an iced tea in one hand and a portable phone in the other. Out of the pool, he rubbed elbows with movie stars.[153] Money can provide a taste of leisure and luxury in stark contrast to the ascetic, regimented existence of an aspiring athlete in training.

Country club sports have always represented the lush life. Traditionally, golfers spent as much time at the club bar as on the links. Hogan was the exception. Tennis clubs have provided a similar atmosphere with lush locker rooms, inviting bars, and bridge tables. One could usually find Bill Tilden in this setting when he wasn't on the courts. The yacht club stands at the apex of the social hierarchy. America's Cup competition has featured summer parties, pickup soccer games on the club lawn, and gourmet food. Those who crew on yachts somehow are able to combine this lavish lifestyle with rigorous training. Ted Turner was adept at making the transition from a padded bar stool to the helm of a racing yacht.[154]

While Ted Turner and Bill Tilden were born into wealth, boxers tend to come from the lower classes. Like professional ballplayers, they can become wealthy almost overnight. Heavyweight champion Mike Tyson entered the ranks of millionaires at age 21. He quickly acquired all the trappings of success, including an apartment in an exclusive building on Manhattan's chic East Side and a bachelor pad in upstate Albany. Following his marriage to actress Robin Givens, Tyson and his new bride purchased a Victorian Castle replete with marble floors and gold leaf on the ceilings. Mike showered his new bride with expensive gifts. He also treated himself to luxury items that included gold and diamond jewelry, a $150,000 Piaget wristwatch, a fleet of automobiles including a Ferrari Testarossa ($205,000), a Rolls-Royce Silver Spur ($120,000), a Jaguar, a Corvette, and a Mercedes-Benz, along with an expensive collection of motorcycles.[155]

Such lavish lifestyles aren't typical of all sports figures. When Parr interviewed athletes' wives, she reported that most of the sessions took place in modest homes in the suburbs. A typical residence was that of Olympic track star Jim Ryun. Milers don't earn big bucks! The former world record holder and his wife Anne resided in a middle-income tract in the Santa Barbara foothills. The view from the window of their southern California home revealed rows and rows of houses just like theirs. Parr characterizes their residence as the type advertised in the newspaper as "Get back to the basics and buy a commonsense home!" There were no crystal chandeliers, no marble floors, no luxury automobiles in the driveway.[156]

A few athletes don't even make it to the middle class. Although Josh Gibson was inducted into the Baseball Hall of Fame, his family didn't benefit economically from his professional baseball career. Following Gibson's death, reporters sought out the home of the famous Negro League catcher. What they discovered shocked them. The Gibson family lived in an area of Pittsburgh misnamed Pleasant Valley. It was actually a run-down ghetto that the town's cabbies advised tourists to stay away from. There was no illusion of prosperity in this residential neighborhood with painted-on house numbers and old people sitting on the sidewalks in ragged overstuffed chairs. The predominant commercial establishments were taverns. When visitors arrived at the Gibson's home, they found the living room windows covered with plastic.[157]

The great majority of athletes grow up in modest circumstances. For those who come into huge amounts of wealth in midlife, it can be an overwhelming experience. They don't always make wise decisions about how to budget their money. Many of them overcompensate; they purchase more luxury items than any one individual could possibly consume. Profligate sports stars have been known to go through huge quantities of money in a brief time. The sports world has its share of "rags to riches" stories, and there are more than a few accounts of "rags to riches to rags." Todd Sloan's early extravagances reduced him to hustling in pool rooms for spending money.

TEAMMATES AND BUDDIES

Athletes routinely eat, train, shower, and travel together. They may or may not socialize, however. Bill Bradley comments that outsiders envision ballplayers as having intense personal relationships with each other. The perception is that they share their innermost thoughts, fears, and hopes. In his experience on the NBA Knicks such intimacy rarely occurred. Players seldom saw each other off the court in New York City. Contact was limited to buses and hotels.[158] On the other hand, Coach George Halas's 1960s-era Bears were exceptionally close as a team. The players did a lot of partying in homes and elsewhere even when they were struggling through a losing season. There was always lots of joking, ribbing, and pranks.[159] In truth, team relations can range from chummy restrained to antagonistic. Messing portrays the NASL New York Cosmos as burdened with inflated egos, ethnic jealousies, language barriers, and management-employee tensions. The upshot was bickering, occasional fights, benchings, fines, and firings.[160]

Discord among players can adversely affect performance. Even in sports like cycling, elements of cooperation are required. Lance Armstrong points out that cyclists don't win a road race on their own. They depend on their teammates. Each rider has a job, and is responsible for a particular part of the race. The slower riders, called *domestiques,* do the "pulling," blocking the wind for the other riders and protecting the team leader. Cyclists have to work together and be willing to make personal sacrifices. It helps if they get along with each other between races. He observes that cycling is not a sport for *prima donnas.* However, Armstrong himself always seemed something of a loner.[161]

Housing arrangements play a pivotal role in framing the social life of athletes. Two athletes rooming together can develop a strong bond. The most famous roommates in sport in the late 1960s were Chicago Bears running backs Brian Piccolo and Gale Sayers. The Bear's management had paired them off as an experiment in race relations. Despite their rivalry for a position in the backfield and their cultural differences, the two men became fast friends. At first, Sayers hung out with his African American buddies and Piccolo with a white crowd, but the two came to prefer each other's company. They ate out together, joked causally about their ethnicity, and exchanged mementos of their friendship. It was an unusually close relationship tragically cut short by Piccolo's death from cancer.[162]

Lodging arrangements vary for athletes. Bart Conner recalls six to seven sharing a two-bedroom apartment in the Olympic Villages.[163] Robert Sands describes the living arrangements in junior college as five football players jammed into a room big enough to hold two or three. If that wasn't crowded enough, the room also accommodated two televisions, two VCRs, a huge bank of stereo equipment, and collection of video games. But the roommates seemed to enjoy each other's company. He recalls, "We would watch football games on ESPN after practice, drink beer, shoot the shit about the team." And there was always pizza. Sands recalls that on one occasion the apartment ordered 24 pizzas in 30 days.[164]

The rigorous regimen of professional football imposes a level of intimacy on players. Football players live together virtually 24 hours a day for the six weeks of training camp. When camp is over, teammates may spend six hours a day together on weekdays and longer on weekends during the three-and-a-half-month regular season.[165] Jerry Kramer's NFL training camp diary describes life in a college dorm with two players squeezed into a room. Coach Lombardi's regulations and bed checks seemed more appropriate for student athletes than grown men. The fun-loving Packers responded predictably, by breaking curfew to sneak out for pizza in the middle of the night.[166]

This camaraderie masks an underlying tension that is part of the internal dynamics on a football team. An unwritten law in training camp is that veterans do not associate with rookies—at least until they make the team. Rookies receive constant abuse from the established players, designed to intimidate them and break their confidence. Other factors play a role in distancing players from each other. Despite the fact that athletes are on the same team, they still battle each other for starting positions or for a place on the roster. Careers and livelihoods are on the line. Verbal threats and eruptions of fisticuffs between offensive and defensive football players are not uncommon. Players remove their helmets and swing them at each other like battle-axes.[167] Oriard gets right to the nub. He explains, "When competing for a starting position, one's teammates become the opposition."[168]

Player contracts with performance clauses can create divisiveness. These clauses create a situation where the amount of money an athlete receives depends on how well he plays or how badly his position teammates play. Green expresses his ambivalence about teammates in these circumstances: "You secretly prayed for one of the two veterans who play your position to get hurt. You didn't want them to get hurt too badly, not paralyzed, just a knee or hamstring or something. Something that would put them out for the season. Something to give you a chance."[169] In addition to the internal competition, the frequent trading of players inhibits the forming of close friendships. All of this on-the-job conflict influences relationships off the field.

Team members generally have ways of segregating themselves by identity, habits, and interests: black and white, drinkers and nondrinkers, card players and noncard players, carousers and noncarousers. Religion also can create divisions among athletes. Dave Dravecky describes a group of players on his minor league team forming what they labeled "The God Squad." He reflects, "I will always remember the closeness we had with a bunch of players and their wives there," Davecky reminisces. "We were all new Christians, very excited about learning together." The members of the clique tended to socialize exclusively with each other in their homes. He makes it clear that other players on the team weren't welcome unless they adopted the same religious interests.[170]

Dave Meggyesy recalls how his radical political activity in the 1960s affected his status with the St. Louis Cardinal's players and coaches. It was a mutual standoff. The other players kept Meggyesy at arms length, while the hirsute linebacker would never "let his hair down." Dave simply couldn't "get into" the boozing, bar fights, and card playing. He recalls little contact with his teammates off the field. Characteristically, he chose nonathletes who were politically active as his close friends.[171] Meggyesy recollects the racial partition among Cardinal players of the era. Room assignments were racially segregated; players seemed to self-segregate in the dining hall; and they went their separate ways in socializing. He remembers the wives of white players hosting segregated parties.[172]

Despite the above instances of tension among players, the norm seems to be for athletes to maintain a modicum of camaraderie on the playing field and in the locker room. But many go their own way once they leave the sports scene. Dryden observes that off the ice, members of his hockey team each went pretty much in separate directions.[173] Dravecky comments that when players are constantly on the move, they don't often become close. "Typically, you say good-bye at the ballpark."[174] Pat Jordan recalls that when he was playing minor league ball, he saw teammates only during the games and occasionally downtown, by accident.[175] Several athletes across sports recounted that they rarely hung out with teammates beyond the stadium; they found their friends elsewhere. Some athletes tend to be natural loners. Don Schollander admits that he tended to stay in his room. He notes that he had virtually no friends or the time to make any friends.[176]

Ty Cobb provides the textbook case of an athlete who couldn't get along with teammates. Rarely has such a confirmed misanthrope graced the fields of play. In truth, the "Georgia Peach" was more of a prickly pear. He was bigoted, humorless, foulmouthed, and prone to violent outbursts. Scarred by a recent family tragedy (his mother had shot his father), the young ballplayer broke into the major league with a weight on his shoulders. He continued to carry a "chip" on one. Cobb didn't cotton to the teasing and pranks that rookies are meant to endure from veteran teammates; he took offense at most remarks directed his way; and he generally pursued a policy of hostility toward those in his vicinity. Much of his free time was spent in his hotel room immersed in his own thoughts. His combativeness and gratuitous violence on the field endeared him even less with opposing players. He once went into the crowd to attack a heckling fan. Yet he endured for over 3,000 games as a player and nearly a thousand more as a manager.[177]

Professional jealousy, envy, and unequal status may be factored into social relations between individual athletes. Among jockeys, a fierce competitiveness impinges on close friendships. Tod Sloan had no pals who were jockeys, never took meals with them nor spent time with them away from the track. Fellow jockeys respected Sloan but didn't particularly like him.[178] Some ballplayers are respected more than liked. As Michael Jordan's career advanced he increasingly limited his contact with teammates, in part due to his phenomenal success and relentless public exposure. Joe DiMaggio's celebrity impeded his relations with his teammates. He came across as rather imperious. Joe would select one or two close friends (usually not athletes) to hang out with. He would let the others know with a word or a glare that they were not welcome. Tommy Heinrich, who played next to him in the outfield for 11 years, recalls that the two of them never even went out to dinner together.[179]

Joe DiMaggio and Pete Rose both seemed less interested in friends on an equal level than surrounding themselves with gofers, personal servants, and court jesters. Rose cultivated a bevy of errand boys, small-time hoods, and drug pushers who washed his cars, placed his bets, visited his home, and "kicked up their feet" on his manager's desk at Riverfront Stadium. Rose always had his retinue. A local restaurant owner once commented, "When he closed the door on one friend, there was always twelve sycophants standing in line waiting to be his friend."[180] Given all the high-fives and fanny pats that Pete exchanged with teammates on the field, he remained very much an outsider. When it came to team camaraderie, he never fit in—never really wanted to fit in. Like DiMaggio, he had few close friends in baseball.[181]

Other athletes relish the company of teammates. Mickey Mantle hung out with his fellow Yankees both on and off the field; he enjoyed the needling, the pranks, and the rowdiness. Mick and his teammates would sit in the clubhouse and drink beer after the game until the crowd cleared the streets. Out of the clubhouse, they were known to "paint the town." Mantle also would vacation with fellow players like Billy Martin.[182] Brian Piccolo preferred a big night out with his buddies on the team after a game to being home with his family. Paul Merson, once free from his drug-related depression, spent a good deal of time socializing with his teammates off the field: shooting pool, playing golf or table tennis, going to movies, watching sports on TV. He also went to bars with his teammates—a dangerous setting for a recovering alcoholic.[183]

Athletes may find friends among competitors. Professional tennis players, like jockeys, not only share a locker room with their opponents but often socialize with each other. Arthur Ashe counted among his closest friends his opponents on the court.[184] Red Pollard and George Woolf were probably exceptional among jockeys. Despite a fierce rivalry on the racetrack—and opposite personalities—they remained lifelong friends.[185] But intimacy carries only so far among competitors. As for "sleeping with the enemy," Don Schollander advises, "You never room with anyone you will be competing against, no matter how close a friend."[186]

DiMaggio and Rose weren't the only athletes to cultivate a coterie. Boxer Aaron Pryor labeled it the "retinue phenomenon." Celebrities tend to attract a following, and they can accumulate a throng of hangers-on. Deion Sanders observed that rap music artist M.C. Hammer employed all his friends on a payroll. He recounts, "I used to go to his house in San Francisco and I'd see all these people around him, most of them doing nothing…they were just living off his success." Deion remained leery of would-be friends who wanted to cash in on his success, but a lot of athletes prove unable to avoid this syndrome.[187] For some reason, boxers seem particularly inclined to cultivate an entourage of courtiers. Pryor relates:

> Slowly but surely, I began to gather what the press and my closest friends called an "entourage." At the time, I desperately wanted some sort of family. Because of my own family's inability to love me for who I was, I replaced them with a group of people who I *thought* loved me. Boy, was I ever wrong. They loved being around the champ. They loved the perks of fame. The loved my wallet and once all of my money was gone, so were they.[188]

The entourage got so out of hand that Pryor recalls checking into a hotel on one occasion with 34 bags.[189]

When Mike Tyson went out on the town he arrived at a club in his Rolls Royce with his personal entourage. He would pay the admission charge for all his friends, order some Dom Perignon, and rack up a bar bill of several hundred dollars for the night. He once "dropped" $200,000 on clothing for the group at Versace's in Las Vegas.[190] Muhammad Ali acquired an impressive retinue of characters who went along for the ride. Traveling companion Herbert Muhammad once referred to the burgeoning group as "a little town." Besides Ali's trainer Angelo Dundee, as many as 10 hangers-on could be found in the champ's company—including the importunate Drew "Bundini" Brown who played the role of cheerleader and court jester while he was in favor. The overly generous Ali was known to pick up the tab for the entire group.[191] Michael Jordan acquired an entourage of media types. "What had been a handful of familiar reporters whom he knew personally…had morphed into a giant mob of strangers who cared nothing about basketball." His father even joined the group at one point. Over time, he would become increasingly wary of hangers-on.[192]

Successful athletes have to figure out who their real friends are and separate them from the sycophants and parasites whose only intentions are to bask in the reflected glow of celebrity or join in for a taste of the high life. Where athletes go, what they do, and who they do it with cannot be casual decisions. Cultivating a meaningful life outside the arena remains problematic. Athletes must find ways to shed the role of public performer and escape the intrusive obligations of their profession. The athlete's life can indeed resemble a Janus-like existence.

REVEALING THE INNER MAN

Samuel Johnson was convinced that the examination of a subject's personal life reveals character. If the great British author is correct, then we should have learned something meaningful about athletes by scrutinizing their behavior and activities outside the arena. But too often the peeling back of one layer only exposes another. Life is lived on two levels. At the surface level, the individual is what he does in everyday doings, routines, and daily tasks. At the deeper level, the person constitutes an inner self. This deep, inner identity is infrequently shown to others. The question remains as to whether the inner man is revealed by examining the athlete out of uniform.

Observers of sport suggest that athletes, as a type, are not known for their interior lives; that they are neither contemplative nor reflective, let alone "deep." A reviewer of Tod Sloan's biography comments that the subject comes across as all outside and no inside. This characterization might be applied to other athletes, but not all of them. Paul Merson allows us a glimpse of the inner man when writing about his struggles with drug addiction. The cerebral Bill Bradley's memoir has been faulted by some for revealing too much "inside" and not enough "outside." Tim Green, Dave Meggyesy, and Michael Oriard all wrote revealing memoirs about their inner lives as professional athletes.

On the surface, athletes' day-to-day lives outside the arena fall into distinct patterns. Merson is characteristic of those whose problem is filling time. Dryden experiences free time as severely bracketed by his obligations to his career. He is among those athletes who express time as recovering from, waiting, or getting ready for. Ashe, on the other hand, filled time more easily. He was the quintessential extrovert whose personal calendar became as crowded as his tournament schedule. The Epicureans like Babe Ruth pursue lives filled with sensual pleasures. Mike Tyson purchases expensive toys as compensation. Others turn to drugs to drown out reality; Josh Gibson did it with a bottle, Steve Howe with white powder. Finally, there are those whose single-mindedness in the arena carries over into leisure-time compulsions: Michael Jordan playing golf from dawn to dusk and then playing cards all night; Ted Williams releasing the grip on his bat only to grasp a fishing pole and disappear for days on end into the woods.

Paul Weiss wrote about sport from a philosophical viewpoint. He perceived the athlete as a kind of a fanatic, a far cry from men dedicated to the attainment of balanced, fulfilled lives.[193] NFL offensive lineman Jerry Kramer takes exception to this observation. He demurs, "I'm simply not a one-dimensional figure. I'm a business man much of the time. I'm host of a syndicated TV show . . . and I'm involved in a half dozen advertising ventures. I follow the stock market."[194] He reminds us that he also reads literature. Arthur Ashe seems just as able to balance the demands of the tennis tour with a wide range of intellectually and emotionally fulfilling activities: charity events, political causes, commercial ventures. From all appearances, these two athletes led fulfilled lives.

However, the general perception persists that athletes are one dimensional and unreflective. If so, it well could be the result of the insistent demands placed upon them. This highly physical life can stifle the inner realm of consciousness. At training camps, athletes exist at a minimal level, their lives centered on the simple physical needs for food, drink, and rest.[195] Don Schollander speculates on the effect of increasingly intense training for competitive swimming. He comments, "They'll have to figure out how to train swimmers more effectively in fewer hours, or else they will have only swimmers with low intellect. An intelligent guy could live like that and work like that for a while, but he couldn't sustain himself over a long period of time."[196] Lance Armstrong makes a convincing case that competition itself can be just as mind numbing. Athletes must find ways to balance their lives inside and outside the arena or they will become the automatons that Schollander predicts.

One facet of life outside the arena where balance seems most problematic for athletes is their relationships with women: wives or ex-wives, the mothers of their children, fiancées, romantic partners, admirers, and casual acquaintances. The following chapter explores the exaggerated masculine culture of sport and how it shapes attitudes toward the opposite sex.

5

SEX AND SEXUALITY

Girls in general played no role in our football world, except as cheerleaders at games. Men performed; women watched. Female beauty was an ornament on male prowess.

—Michael Oriard

From its beginnings, American sport established boundaries between men and women. The rise of sport was concurrent with the closing of the American frontier, and urban civilization carried connotations of feminization. Men searched for a separate sphere of life where true manliness could be appreciated. Sports provided a gender-segregated enclave for the demonstration of male prowess. Historian Roderick Nash observed, "Whether clearing the forests or clearing the bases...[t]he sports arena like the frontier was pregnant with opportunity for the individual. The start was equal and the best man won."[1]

At the same time, there was a strong prejudice among Victorian men against athletic sports for women. James E. Sullivan, founder and secretary of the Amateur Athletic Union opposed the hiring of teachers of athletics for girls, training programs for girls, and interschool competition for girls.[2] The idea that sports were for men and boys carried into the 20th century. The PSAL (Public Schools Athletic League) was formed in 1903 to provide *boys* in crowded tenements with opportunities for vigorous exercise and wholesome play. In a congratulatory letter sent to the League's founder, President Theodore Roosevelt proclaimed, "It is a great disadvantage to a boy to be unable to play games; and every boy who knows how to play baseball or football, to box or wrestle, has by just so much fitted himself to be a better citizen."[3] The president didn't seem concerned about young women. A girl's branch of the PSAL did form in 1905, but at first refused to sponsor school sports. If men in the Progressive Era had their way, women's sports would remain limited and segregated.

Early spectator sports provided a refuge from the feminizing elements in American culture. These public events offered a self-consciously masculine milieu. For the most part, ladies did not attend public sporting events—except horse racing in the South. Through the World War I era, ballparks, like boxing arenas, had the reputation of a stag environment with smoking, drinking, gambling, and rough language.[4] The literature of sport also reflected a male bias. Sports "pulps" remained popular into the 1920s and 1930s. These cheap magazines were remarkable for the absence of women characters, suggesting that their readers were looking to escape the complications of relationships with the opposite sex.[5] But while men's magazines were presenting a world without women, revolutionary changes were taking place in American society.

The strict distinctions between masculine and feminine culture eroded in the 1920s as young women began working outside the home—at least until they married. These women had money, independence, and leisure time. They took up sports like tennis, golf, and cycling, and began attending men's sporting events. Sports managers responded by modifying the environment of stadiums so that they were more amenable to a mixed crowd. For working women, the ballparks were an inexpensive form of entertainment where casual dress was allowed. They could go with girlfriends or on a date. Male athletes acquired female fans.[6]

Despite a growing presence of women fans in the stadium bleachers, most sports still remained male bastions. Ballplayers could always retreat to the locker rooms and clubhouses. Things didn't change much in men's sports over the next four decades. Michael Oriard commented that women's exclusion from the NFL locker rooms represented a larger exclusion from "the sacred mysteries of our football world."[7] However, a second revolution in women's equality was brewing in the post–Word War II era, and it would have direct consequences for the all-male world of sport. In 1972, Congress acted to provide girls and women with equal access to school sports. For the first time, students of both sexes competed with and against each other on organized teams. Then in 1978, a judge ruled that women journalists had the right to enter professional athletes' locker rooms. Suddenly, female reporters were interviewing male athletes draped in towels, while their sister sportscasters integrated the broadcast booths.

The question looms: how have these inroads changed the climate of men's sport and the attitudes of male athletes toward women? This chapter explores the cult of masculinity and the relationship between male athletes and the women in their lives. The accounts range from the post-Victorian perceptions of boxer Jack Johnson to the contemporary viewpoint of Tour de France winner Lance Armstrong. While sensitive to the broad historical narrative, most of what follows is drawn from the recent past.

Male Enclave

From the American perspective, masculinity not only refers to what one *is* but what one *does*. Real men work hard and play hard. Consequently, sport ranks prominently in the hierarchy of masculinity. This ethos defines what a "real man" is in terms of who is the strongest and who can withstand the most physical and emotional pain. The sport of boxing symbolizes the male quest for toughness and vitality. Heavyweight champion John L. Sullivan routinely boasted, "I can lick any man in the place." He was a symbol of invincibility, and the idol of young men across the country. Huge crowds followed his career in the ring.[8]

Sport in general reinforces the highly regarded male attributes of control, discipline, force, and dominance of others. Routinized aggression and violence are rewarded within a male culture in which femininity and weakness are despised. Sporting prowess is understood as symbolic proof of men's "natural" superiority over women. Thus, sport continues to provide a separate, male-defined world where boys and men can distance themselves from aspects of femininity. It long remained a domain in which women were marginalized or excluded outright.[9]

Until quite recently, young men who became athletes performed in an all-male environment. The primary vehicle for their individual success depended upon the personal and professional relationships they formed with other men. The intimate social networks that develop under these circumstances are significant. Athletes often live together and spend much of their time more or less undressed in locker rooms and clubhouses with their attention focused on bodies—their own and other men's. The emotional bonding is carried on far from the presence of women, yet they are expected to develop as normal heterosexuals within this milieu of hypermasculinity. Morris observes that the fully successful hero in baseball novels is the man who can: (a) begat a child in wedlock, (b) form an unsuspicious yet intimate personal bond with a male teammate, and (c) lead his team to victory in the Big Game.[10] Baseball biographies also touch on themes of gender role.

For many young men, sport has provided the primary means through which they establish a sense of manhood. Michael Oriard attended an all-male Catholic high school and later predominantly male Notre Dame. He notes that as early as 12 years old he had absorbed the notion that football was a man's world in which he had to prove himself worthy, and "whose sacred mysteries were incomprehensible to females." He recalls an incident where he was taken to the hospital following a football injury accompanied by his mother, and resenting her intrusion into this world.[11] Dave Kopay enrolled in a Catholic seminary to get away from a troubled home where his mother and father quarreled. He described the seminary as a well-ordered, all-male paradise where football players like himself reigned supreme.[12]

Psychologists suggest that any intense friendship among men that excludes and demeans women cannot be without a homosexual element. A thin boundary exists between the homosocial bonding of athletes, considered the highest form of male friendship, and their view of homosexual intercourse as the lowest form of perversion. Enforced heterosexism coexists with homophobia.[13] It doesn't take a Ph.D. in clinical psychology to recognize the coexistence of homosocial behavior and homophobia among athletes. Fans watching a San Francisco 49ers game in January 2003, observed teammates Terrell Owens and Garrison Hearst hugging each other, doing their helmet-touch thing, and patting fannies following an Owens' touchdown. This was the same Garrison Hearst who proclaimed earlier in the season, "I don't want any faggots on my team," and "I don't want any faggots in this locker room."[14]

Former NFL running back Dave Kopay's autobiography is exceptional among books by athletes for its depiction of football as a sport in which the culture of hypermasculinity coexists with a homosexual taboo.[15] Most sports biographies don't address the issue. The myth of exclusive heterosexuality among athletes has been perpetuated in both fiction and nonfiction. Morris observes, "There are no really gay men in baseball novels."[16] But it turns out that there are gay men in the real world of sports, and Kopay wasn't the first.

Bill Tilden is one of the great ironic figures in sport. In the 1920s when tennis suffered a "fairy" reputation, Tilden presented a swashbuckling, athletic image although he was privately a homosexual—the only great male athlete in that era we know to have been such. Tilden's proclivity was for young boys. It's quite likely that in his whole life, he never spent a night alone with an adult, man or woman. He spent his days hanging out at tennis clubs teaching and socializing with young men. Tilden was arrested for a homosexual offense late in his life and served time. The case received a good deal of publicity. Ultimately, he was dismissed by the public as the exception to the rule for male athletes.[17]

The myth of requisite heterosexuality in men's sports persisted into the late 1970s when Dave Kopay publicly acknowledged his homosexuality three years after retiring from the NFL. He was the first professional team-sport athlete in the United States to "come out." His openness sent shockwaves through the athletic world, although Kopay, unlike Tilden, limited his relationships to consenting adults.[18] Subsequent to Kopay's coming out, very few well-known athletes have openly acknowledged their homosexuality. Seven years after he retired, Olympic diver and gold medal winner Greg Louganis announced that he was gay. He revealed in his autobiography *Breaking the Surface* (1995) that he was HIV-positive.[19] In late 1991, Earvin "Magic" Johnson had announced that he was HIV positive. But the married Lakers point guard maintained that he had contracted the infection through promiscuous heterosexual liaisons. He continued to play in the NBA off and on through 1996.

British-born center John Amaechi became the first NBA player to announce he was gay in February of 2007. Like Dave Kopay, he waited until he was retired (although his sexuality had been a topic of speculation for some time). Amaechi's coming out was tied to the promotion of his autobiography, *Man in the Middle*.[20] The announcement met with a mixed reaction among his fellow athletes. One of the more rabid responses came from former Miami Heat guard Tim Hardaway. When asked about Amaechi on a Miami radio show, Hardaway responded starkly, "You know, I hate gay people." The public reaction to his remark was even more negative; his planned appearance at a promotional event for the NBA was quickly cancelled. The NBA veteran realized he had gone too far, enrolled himself in sensitivity training, and backed off from his comment. Hardaway claims that these actions were an indication of sincere regret, that he wasn't doing it just to resurrect his image.[21] Regardless of his motives, this episode provides a marker for the continuing ambivalence within the sports fraternity toward openly gay athletes.

Revelations of sexual nonconformity may have had some effect on the culture of men's sports. The distinct barrier between masculinity and femininity began to fade, at least in regard to athletes' personal presentation. In the early 1990s, Dennis Rodman challenged the enforced masculinity of sport through cross-dressing, wearing makeup, and dropping comments about a desire to be bisexual. Most of his friends saw this behavior as little more than a promotional stunt by someone who was clearly heterosexual.[22] Nevertheless, Rodman's high profile made it easier for other male athletes to express both their individuality and their feminine side through grooming and body art.

Hair style had been a point of contention between American coaches and male athletes since the first training camp sought to imitate military boot camp. The long hair trend started in the mid-1960s with the popularity of the British rock group, The Beatles. Jim Bouton recalls an incident when he was with the Seattle Pilots in 1969. Manager Joe Schulz began harassing Bouton's teammate Steve Hovley on his first day with the club: "Where's your barber? Don't you need a haircut? You're getting awfully mangy looking. Are you sure you don't need a trim, Steve?"[23] Joe Pepitone, who joined the Yankees in 1962, was one of the first major league ballplayers to wear his hair below his ears. When he stepped up to the plate at an Oakland A's game, the eccentric team owner Charles Finley instructed the announcer in the broadcast booth to introduce him as "Josephine Pepitone." The announcer refused, and then resigned before his imperious boss could fire him.[24]

By the laid-back 1970s, coaches and managers were finding it increasingly difficult to dictate traditional images of masculinity like military haircuts and restrictions on facial hair. Following Rodman's appearance in NBA in 1986, athletes not only let their hair down, they began to wear earrings, sported tattoos, and dressed unconventionally. The world of men's sport began to reflect the androgynous grooming and clothing styles of popular culture. However, while coaches and athletes adjusted to less masculine images displayed by liberated team members, their actual relations with women would change more slowly.

CHEERLEADERS, TEMPTRESSES, AND CENTERFOLDS:
MARGINALIZING WOMEN

Despite gay athletes coming out and the blending of masculine and feminine lifestyles, most athletes have remained "straight men in the process of reinforcing their straightness," to borrow Morris's phrase.[25] Homophobia may have waned ever slightly, but misogyny continued to ferment within the enclave of male sport. Sociologists tell as that one inevitable effect of "men's clubs" is that women are demeaned. This occurs on several levels. Much of the banter between athletes in the locker room or on the bus includes insults directed at players' wives, sisters, mothers, or girlfriends. Kidding aside, the restricted male environment can hinder an athlete's ability to establish and maintain intimate relationships with women. For some young men, sport serves as a surrogate for heterosexual relations. Morris refers to the ballplayer who would rather fondle his glove than a dame, a world of preadolescent sexuality directed toward cowhide rather than human flesh.[26] Reading Don Schollander's autobiography, one is struck by the absence of romantic or sexual interests, notwithstanding a brief mention of casual women friends. The impression is given that competitive swimming preempts normal relations with the opposite sex.[27] Lou Gehrig's biographer Frank Graham comments on the "Iron Horse's" retarded interest in the opposite sex. He notes that until the adult Gehrig fell in love for the first time, girls had played no part in his life. Girls didn't interest Lou when he was a boy. "Later, when he was going to high school and college, he had no time for them. There was too much else to crowd his hours—his home life, his sports, and the work that had to be done." Commerce High School was a boys' school, so Lou was not thrown into the company of girls during his school hours. Most of the other boys had girl friends and went to dances and parties, but such affairs had no appeal for Lou. There were girls on the Columbia University campus, of course. But Lou was more interested in home runs, three-base hits, forward passes, and rolling blocks. Now and then he would be seen with a girl, but not often and never twice with the same girl.[28]

If a young athlete did show an interest in the opposite sex, his coaches were less than encouraging. Pat Conroy recalls an apprehensive moment while playing basketball at The Citadel, a military college in South Carolina: "I had to summon up the courage to ask Mel [his coach] if he would allow me to have a date after the game. I would rather have asked Mel if I could moon the entire Corps of Cadets when they passed in review the following Friday." (Note the homosexual allusion.) Conroy continues, "Not once in my cadet career did Mel ask me if I had a girlfriend or if I was interested in meeting one." He concludes: "Now I believe that Mel was the enemy of all passion and all sense of engagement where one of his players might drift into realms Mel couldn't control, and I include the carnal arena in this appraisal."[29]

Dave Meggyesy recounts an incident from high school that illustrates the hostility toward heterosexual relationships. His football coach called him out of study hall and lectured him: "There are three things a person can do when he is in high school," the coach began. "He can play football, he can study to keep his average up, or he can go out with girls. And you can't do more than two of these things well." His coach went on to inform him that "there was a 'certain girl' in the school who had 'destroyed' one of our top players the year before."[30]

Coaches compete with girlfriends and wives for control of athletes. They discourage intimate attachments with women but may tolerate, or even encourage, casual contact. Meggyesy who went on to play football in the NFL, reflects on the general attitude of his school coaches toward male-female relationships: "The prevailing opinion was that it was somehow healthy and manly to go out and get drunk, pick up some girl, lay her and maybe even rough her up a bit. To the coaches, this was 'normal' behavior, but they got upset if you began to develop a genuine relationship with a woman."[31]

A theme runs through sports narratives: that ballplayers become real men, and real athletes, by treating women as objects. Jim Bouton's *Ball Four* gained notoriety for chronicling such practices as "beaver shooting" by his teammates. This euphemism for voyeurism—along with the above comment by Meggyesy —illustrates the conflation of sex and aggression that attends the objectifying of women. The association is conspicuous in the rhetoric of athletics. Kopay observes that much of the language of football is involved in aggressive sexual expressions. He recounts, "We were told to go out and 'fuck those guys'; to take that ball and 'stick it up their asses' or 'down their throats.' The coaches would yell, 'knock their dicks off, or more often...'knock their jocks off.'" Kopay continues, "I've seen many a coach get emotionally aroused while he was diagramming a play...on the blackboard. His face red, his voice rising, he would show the ball carrier how he wanted him to 'stick it in the hole.'"[32]

A revealing use of sexual imagery is recalled by Robert Sands: "I dropped the next pass, and [Coach] Garrett told me to frame my hands in the shape of a pussy."[33] This remark, while perhaps instructive, contains an implicit "put down." Coaches routinely employ sexual references to emasculate athletes. After he made an inept tackle, Dave Meggyesy's coach told him "that he almost looked feminine." Meggyesy considers this technique to be the coach's "doomsday weapon." It almost always works, he notes. "The players have wrapped up their identity in their masculinity, which is eternally precarious for it...is something that can be given or withdrawn by a coach at his pleasure."[34]

Detroit Lions guard Bob Kowalkowski recalls an incident in training camp with his new offensive line coach Chuck Knox:

> I miss an incidental block in an incidental drill, and then I hear this foghorn, "Know something, Kowal?" he [Knox] asks in a voice that could shut down an assembly line, "You're a sissy." I look up. I stare. This was my second year, and nobody had ever talked to me like that. I want to fight the son of a gun. I get ready to charge—hell, he's not much older than we are—but a teammate grabs me.[35]

Kowalkowski turns his anger on a rookie during a one-on-one drill; blocks become punches, and they end up rolling in the dirt until the rookie's face mask comes off his helmet. The offensive lineman looks up at Knox. This time his coach is smiling.

Pat Conroy recalls a graphic illustration of emasculation. It came not from his coach but from his overzealous military father, a former semipro basketball player. Driving home after one of Pat's basketball games, Col. Don Conroy berates his son: "You don't get it, do you, mama's boy? This is a kick-ass world that doesn't have time to wait around for pussies like you to wake up and read the fucking headlines.... They're eating your jock. Because you've got a pussy between your legs instead of a dick."[36]

Most of these anecdotes come from young men still in high school and college, or just breaking into professional sport. In spite of these uncertain beginnings in forming relationships with women, the great majority of athletes eventually marry. The nature of their relationships with wives, and other women in their adult lives, is to a great extent a product of the masculine culture into which they were initiated at a young age. How these men view women in their maturity and how they relate to them is equally revealing.

The emphasis on differences between women and men within the culture of male sport obscures distinctions among women. This mind-set makes it difficult for athletes to judge women as individuals and leads to stereotyping. Examples are not difficult to come by. Tim Green writes that in the world of football there are two categories of women, "groupies" and "nongroupies," the former term referring to women who make themselves available to athletes.[37] Dave Meggyesy comments on teammates who view their wives as virginal creatures kept at home with the kids, while other women are "meat on the rack."[38]

In her book *Superwives,* Parr points out that athletes' wives tend toward a *type*: the petite woman with a sensational body.[39] Not all sports auto/biographies describe the physical appearance of wives, but the ones that do tend to corroborate Parr's observation. The 6′2″ Carmen Salvino writes that he fell in love with a "slim girl with a blond streak in her hair,"[40] who comes up to his chin in photos. Pitcher Steve Howe describes his wife Cindy as "petite, blond and innocent."[41] Babe Ruth towers over his 17-year-old bride Helen.[42] But, of course, the Babe dwarfed most people. Running back Brian Piccolo married a petite brunette. A publicity photo for an Armed Forces game shows him with a diminutive WAC perched on his shoulder. The message is clear: big athlete, small woman.[43] An even more striking image was the huge, hulking Mike Tyson with his small and delicate actress wife Robin Givens.[44]

A number of the wives interviewed by Parr had been cheerleaders who met their husbands in high school or college. Why do athletes tend to marry cheerleaders? Carmen Salvino suggests that the male athlete, accustomed to being cheered in public, expects his wife to continue the cheering when he comes home. The champion bowler elucidates: "To reach the top of a big-time pro sport, you have to have a big ego and tunnel vision, and be able to administer the *coup de grace* to a wobbly opponent. None of those characteristics go over big around the house"—unless the wife can adjust to a submissive role.[45] Lance Armstrong observes that most athletes, "are too busy cultivating the aura of invincibility to admit being fearful, weak, defenseless, vulnerable, or fallible, and for that reason neither are they especially kind, considerate, merciful, benign, lenient, or forgiving" to anyone around them.[46] This include wives. An unmarried Arthur Ashe observed that being married to a tennis player can be very demeaning, and there's little his wife can do about it.[47]

Parr noted that a third of the wives she interviewed found it difficult to deal with their athlete husband's fame.[48] This never seemed a problem for Rachel Robinson, however. Jackie's wife made it her business to go out to the ballpark and watch her husband during spring training and into the regular season. Each morning they would "set out for work together." For 12 years, until Jackie retired from baseball, Rachel would attend virtually every one of his home games. "How could I miss them," she remarked. "That's where the action was, that's where the drama was."[49] The moral of the story is that when an athlete's wife is involved in her husband's career, she is relegated to the role of cheerleader or spectator. Ted Turner's biographer describes yachtsmen's spouses as "those friendly, loyal souls who had spent hour after hour aboard tenders and other observation boats watching their men…all summer, who had dutifully toed the line…in their roles as second-class citizens; who had endlessly babysat the children and had been models of decorum."[50] The glaring exception is the wife who draws attention to herself. Joe DiMaggio never could accommodate the public notice that wife Marilyn Monroe received. He may have been the star in Yankee Stadium, but she was the main attraction outside the arena.[51]

Wives differ in their ability to adjust to these traditional roles. Arthur Ashe's diary includes a chapter entitled, "Wives and Strange Bedfellows," in which the young author comments on the relationships of married couples on the tennis tour. He concludes that "marriage seems to work best only at the extremes." Ashe describes the successful types: "There is, for example, Sally Riessen, who is a designer in Chicago. She is extremely independent and rarely travels with [husband] Marty; they have no children, just their two disparate careers." But this relationship seems exceptional. Ashe then describes the opposite type: "Others of the most successful marriages on tour are made up of women who have pretty much submerged themselves to their men. Annemarie Okker is content to stay in Tom's shadow, although she will pick her spots and speak up on occasion." He continues, "On the other hand, Nikki Pilic had made it plain to [wife] Mia where she stands. Before they were married he told the other players, 'She must gif up everythink for me. Everythink! [sic]'"[52] Jim Bouton's marriage leans toward the second type. Parr writes of his wife Bobbie, "Women's lib may not approve of her housewife role, her submissiveness, her obvious adoration of her husband at the cost of her own identity, and her lack of concerns over her own accomplishments, but no one can fail to see that in spite of all this, Bobby [sic] Bouton is happy."[53]

Pete Rose's first wife Karolyn could play the role of classic baseball wife. Rose's biographer writes, "She cooked at any hour of the day or night to accommodate Pete's irregular hours. She sat behind home plate with the other wives and cheered her husband's every hit. Each February, she dutifully packed up the family for their annual trek to spring training." Karolyn became unusually popular in baseball circles, although experiencing some initial resentment from other baseball wives. "This is a marvelous woman," Cincinnati manager Sparky Anderson gushed. "I loved her. My wife loved her. I think everyone who ever came into contact with her loved her." Karolyn also learned to accommodate the more difficult aspect of being married to Pete Rose, the fact that he played around. She stayed with Pete for 15 years even after he had taken up with blue-eyed, blond former high school twirler Carol Woliung (who became the second Mrs. Rose). Finally, Karolyn got fed up and filed for divorce in 1979.[54]

While some wives remain content in their supporting roles, others come to resent their athlete/husbands' professional careers. Joe Louis's wife Marva complains, "I wish Joe would quit fighting. You know, we've been together only two weeks since he won the championship." Marva feels she is speaking for both of them when she laments, "We want to be together. We want to raise a family—live a normal life. But we can't do that while he's fighting." The Louis's marriage went well for a short time but soon ran into difficulties that led to divorce.[55]

The fact is that the wife and family often take a back seat to the athlete's sporting interests, professional and recreational. There's a classic golf joke about two buddies on the fairway near a main thoroughfare. As the first tees up, a hearse comes into view on the road. The golfer interrupts his swing, removes his cap, places it over his heart, and waits until the funeral procession passes. His partner is somewhat taken aback by this gesture and comments that he has rarely witnessed that kind of respect for the deceased. "Yeh," the first golfer replies, "She's been a good wife." The punchline plays on the perception that avid sportsmen have been known to miss important family events—or reschedule them.

Joe Louis scheduled his wedding for 7:45 on the same night he was to fight Max Baer at 10:00 p.m. It's obvious what *he* considered to be the main event.[56] Apparently, not much changes after the wedding for many sports couples. Ted Williams spent most of his free time during his three marriages on fishing trips. That's where he was when one of his children was born.[57] Chuck Knox's wife Shirley recalls that when she went into labor with daughter Colleen, Chuck was on the practice field. She comments, "Back then [1960s], we just didn't bother the husband with things like that. I know it sounds funny today, but that's the way it was."[58] When Mickey Mantle's third son was born, he was off hunting with Billy Martin. His wife Merlyn once commented about her husband, "He was married but in a very small geographic area of his mind."[59] Unlike his own father, Mickey spent very little time with his sons. He was more like a visiting uncle than a father. In 1957 Mantle's marriage ended, a casualty of his frequent absences, his drinking, and womanizing.[60]

Karolyn Rose once observed that she ranked fifth in her husband's life, behind baseball, their two children, and his Rolls-Royce. Bill Plumber played with the Cincinnati Reds as a backup catcher in the 1970s. The Plumbers and the Roses would spend quite a bit of time together during spring training, but often without Pete. Bill recalls, "More often than not, it was me and the two wives and the kids...and we would just ride around Tampa, go to a K-Mart or something. Pete wouldn't be with us. He was at the track." Things didn't change much with Rose's second marriage. Wife Carol groused about her often distracted husband: "When Pete comes home he turns on the TV and watches sports. Sometimes it's like he is in a trance." And, Pete still had a roving eye.[61]

Male bonding competes with womanizing as a preoccupation of married athletes. Joe DiMaggio spent little time at home after his son was born. Joe Jr. may have been a "feather in his cap," but he was first wife Dorothy's responsibility. When the baby was fussy, Joe would be out the door headed to Toots Shor's restaurant for an evening with the guys.[62] Brian Piccolo also preferred drinking with his buddies to dinner with his wife and daughters. Some nights he would show up at home at 3:00 a.m. His family saw little of him. Steve Howe would stay out at all hours, night after night, even when his wife was pregnant. The two lived parallel lives. She went to school and had her own set of friends. Steve, played ball and hung out with his male buddies.[63]

Michael Messner, who studies gender roles of athletes, offers an observation on such behavior. He notes that the more success oriented a man is, the greater the psychological and emotional distance between himself and his family. The work success of male athletes is an expression of male privilege and ego satisfaction, and comes at the expense of wife and children.[64] Parr translates this into the vernacular. For the married athletes, their sport comes first; the wife comes second.[65] The athlete never learns how to leave the game, and the wife may never learn how to live independently of her athlete/husband. At least, this seems true for many relationships.

Athletes' families are forced to lead nomadic lives, and this puts added pressure on relationships. In addition to the normal travel schedule, team sport athletes are subject to being traded repeatedly and on short notice. Hockey player Gary Smith and his wife had to relocate every two or three years during his 17-year career. Gary began playing professionally with the Toronto Maple Leafs in 1964. Following his season with the Maple Leafs, he played for the Oakland Seals, Chicago Blackhawks, Vancouver Canucks, Minnesota North Stars, Washington Capitals, Indianapolis Racers, and Winnipeg Jets. In addition, he had intermittent stints on several minor league teams in just about every league that existed. His peripatetic career earned him the nickname "Suitcase." Gary's retirement was no less settled. He went from job to job before his marriage ended in divorce.[66]

Baseball is similar to hockey in this regard. Bouton points out that players are, in effect, "owned" by the teams and can be traded indiscriminately, short of a preemptive clause in their contract. He cites the case of infielder Eddie

Brinkman who was traded five times in one year. His wife spent most of her time packing and unpacking.[67] A lot of minor league couples don't even bother to unpack. The wife may read about the trade in the newspapers, if her husband is on the road. Soccer's Shep Messing relates how his wife Arden reacted to his being traded on short notice to the New York Cosmos: She tells him that she doesn't care about the money, but remonstrates that she will miss her friends, lose her job as a rental agent, and have to abandon the home they established—all the things a transient athlete's wife has to endure. "I don't mind living out of suitcases," she grouses, "but there is no such things as drip-dry friends. We're so happy here. Why does it have to end?"[68] Messing is rare among athletes for acknowledging his wife's point of view in his autobiography.

Lance Armstrong's cowritten autobiography includes considerable material on his wife Kristin ("Kik"). The book even discusses her experiences with IVF, labor, and delivery. We read of Kik's feelings, her perspective, and her reactions to his career. Yet, it's quite clear that Lance's career takes precedence over his marital relationship. He admits that during training, the couple didn't do anything or go anywhere. They simply ate and then went to bed, so he could get up the next morning and train. That would be their life for several months on end. The wife's role was to maintain the household and run errands.[69] This marriage didn't last either.

There are more successful relationships on varying terms. Jim Bouton conveys a close connection with accommodating wife Bobbie in his diary *Ball Four*. He routinely talks to her on the phone while on the road.[70] Ben Hogan preferred his wife Valerie's company to that of his golfing buddies. He is that rare athlete who seems closer to his mate than his teammates. Hogan never embraced the social life of the clubhouse when he was playing. In an era before air travel, he trekked cross-country to tournaments on long car trips accompanied by Valerie. They shared hotel rooms and all the other life experiences of a struggling young couple. When he was recovering from a serious auto accident, Valerie literally moved in the hospital to be with him. Later in his career, she would join the tournament gallery to watch him play. Most golfers' wives of that era rarely went to the golf course to watch the competition. Instead they would spend a lot of time in each other's company, playing cards or doing needlework.[71]

It's noteworthy that athletes who have personal problems or are experiencing difficulties with their careers seem more revealing about relationships with their wives. Jim Piersall credits his wife Mary with helping him recover from a series of mental breakdowns.[72] Arthur Ashe's wife Jeanne is acknowledged in his memoir about retirement from tennis and his struggle with AIDS. A reflective Ashe writes, "In the long shadow of the announcement [that I had AIDS], family is more important to me than ever. They have rallied beautifully to my side.... Jeanne shares this sense of family with me; it helps bind us." On Mother's Day, the couple travels to Chicago to have brunch with her mother.[73] In his younger days, Ashe most likely would have been on the road on a promotional venture.

Dave Dravecky, who endured recurring bouts with cancer, sentimentalizes, "One valuable lesson I've learned in the past few years is how important it is to keep a balanced perspective on life. In the long run, family has to be the top priority." Dravecky writes at length about his relationship with wife Janice and family. The impression presented is that Dave doesn't go out on the town with his male teammates but stays at home. Any socializing with other players—primarily born-again Christians—includes their wives. There are accounts of the couples reading the Bible and praying together. Dave recalls an occasion with friends when, "We stayed up until 5:00 a.m. We discussed our marriages and the importance of putting our wives first in our schedules."[74]

Dravecky presents himself as an athlete whose family comes first. In point of fact, when he was healthy his baseball career took priority over his family. He admits that wife Janice "has never been fond of the way baseball affects our family life." At one juncture, she angrily lets out all her resentment: "There is a point where you have to put other things ahead of baseball.... Would you put your children through another year like this one? It's been hard on [children] Tiffany and Jonathan. If you don't need to put them through it, why would you? What would be your motives for that? Is baseball that important to you?" Dravecky concedes, "Janice wondered whether she was really ahead of baseball in my love."[75]

Paul Merson, recovering from drug addiction, writes at length about family, the relationship with his wife Lorraine and their three sons, his parents, brother, and in-laws. Merson complains repeatedly of feeling homesick, missing his wife and children while on the road. He and Lorraine regularly talk to each other on the telephone while he is away on tour, including several heated arguments. Merson describes playing with his sons, picking them up from school, taking them on vacations, bringing them gifts, letting his wife sleep in, and preparing breakfast. He makes it a point to be with his family to celebrate birthdays and holidays. All this despite the fact that his marriage was coming apart. Against Merson's claims about being a good family man, Lorraine complains about his being a part-time husband and father. In her words he is, "the hero who came round and did all the nice things with them," while she had to cope with the children's home work and their moods. These scenes are preview to their impending divorce.[76]

HOME AND AWAY

Sports wives routinely complain about "part-time" husbands. Indeed, athletes who play team sports probably see more of their fellow players than their wives during the season. Bill Bradley observes that in professional basketball your roommate is someone you're with 100 nights a year on the road, and someone you see virtually every day for practice and games.[77] The sports wife's role may be marginal in comparison, leading to expressions like "football widow." The frequent absences due to the schedule of competition can create emotional distance between the athlete and his wife. When the season is over, athletes come home to a family who has learned to cope without them.

Intimate relations between athletes and their wives are curtailed by the various rituals of sport that include separation during training camp as well as frequent road trips. Add to these intrusions, the self-imposed or coerced sexual abstinence prior to a competitive event. Rocky Marciano would abstain leading up to his fights, as he had heard that intercourse took something away from a fighter.[78] During the 1960s, St. Louis Cardinal football coaches kept players from going home to their wives the night before home games. Apparently, they had bought into the belief that sex would sap the players' energy and keep them from playing well.[79] Bill Romanowski recounts that during Thursday team meetings before a game, San Francisco 49er Coach Bill Walsh would turn to Assistant Coach Tommy Hart and inquire, "Green light or red light." Green light meant that players could have sex during the days before the game; red that they could not.[80] The myth about sex and physical performance has been deeply engrained in the psyches of athletes, married and single. Minor league pitcher Pat Jordan recalls a resolution he made during one road trip: "I had sworn off romantic entanglements. . . . I was sure that God had punished me for my indiscretion with Sally [a girlfriend] by damming my pitching. My celibacy at Davenport would be rewarded with a string of gems (no hitters, shutouts, etc.) that would lift me out of the Midwest League and deposit me in the majors."[81]

In spite of the myth about sexual intercourse adversely affecting performance, the behavior of athletes on the road could be described as less than abstinent. When DiMaggio played in the minor league in the 1930s, curfew was usually midnight or two hours after a night game. More than a few of the veteran players, married and single, had "special friends" around the circuit, women whom they'd visited over the years. This was strictly a "winking matter," seldom talked about and never flaunted. The players seemed less worried about their wives back home or the morality of their behavior than getting caught breaking curfew.[82]

Ashe shares an anecdote about the colorful tennis player Richard "Pancho" Gonzales, who was married six times. In Brazil in 1966 for the Davis Cup, Pancho ran into an old friend Ingrid in the lobby of the hotel and invited her up to his suite. Ashe relates the incident:

> Brazil is very proper about this sort of thing, and a house dick tailed Gonzales and confronted him just as he and Ingrid were about to go into the room. The detective said that since Richard was not married to this woman, he could not permit them to enter a room together. The way Richard responded to this was to reach back all of a sudden and slug the guy square on the chin. Absolutely cold-cocked him. Then he put the key in the door, Ingrid and he stepped around the fallen form and went into the suite.[83]

A standing joke circulated among players in the NBA is that the hardest thing about going on the road is wiping the smile off your face before you kiss your wife goodbye. This is not to say that athletes' wives and girlfriends are totally naive about what goes on when their husbands are away. Anicka Bakes, a 23-year-old model from California, lived with NBA star Dennis Rodman for two years. Although not married at the time, she assumed the couple had a monogamous relationship. In a 1988 interview, a pregnant Bakes told *People* magazine, "I would find as many as fifty women's names and telephone numbers written on scraps of paper in Dennis's clothes... *in a month*."[84]

The sport of boxing has had its share of philanderers, and the wives aren't completely naive about what is going on. Once when Aaron Pryor was heading for training camp at Lake Tahoe, he told his wife Theresa that he wanted her and the children to accompany him. Pryor then changed his mind and waited to inform his wife in the lobby of the hotel. She responded, "I ain't going home, Aaron Pryor! You just wanna go out with them bitches!" Six weeks later, Theresa served her husband with divorce papers.[85] Some wives put up with the infidelities longer than others.

A photograph in Robert Cassidy's biography of Muhammad Ali shows the champion boxer standing with Joe DiMaggio on the occasion of their receiving awards from the Ellis Island Foundation. In the background, one can make out the fog-shrouded image of the Statue of Liberty.[86] The representation is deficient in one respect; the two athletes in the photo had more than one woman in their background. Indeed, both were legendary womanizers. As a young man, Ali hadn't been around girls that much, and most of the interaction with them never went beyond flirting. However, following his divorce from first wife Sonji, his behavior changed. A mature Ali admits, "I used to chase women all the time." He rationalizes, "I was young, handsome, and heavyweight champion of the world. Women were always offering themselves to me." He acknowledges fathering two children with women to whom he wasn't married. Ali's second wife Belinda put up with the indignities, including his highly publicized affair with Veronica Porsche, for nine years before divorcing him.[87]

Joe DiMaggio also was rather shy as a young ballplayer. Later, he would acquire quite a reputation as a Ladies Man. Following his brief marriage to actress Marilyn Monroe, he dated a string of showgirls and Miss Americas. Joe routinely found his name in the gossip columns of the New York newspapers. There also were private stories circulated among male friends of his sexual prowess, rumors of countless one-night stands in hotel rooms, and visits to Polly Adler's fashionable New York City whorehouse, where he famously complained about the sheets. Joe, like many celebrity athletes, was approached constantly by women in restaurants and public places. Clearly, the attraction—at least among the amateurs—was mutual.[88]

Pete Rose had a girlfriend in every National League city. Rose "went beyond what was acceptable adulterous behavior even within baseball's mores, by having outrageously flagrant affairs." Philadelphia Phillies' club president

William Giles once called Rose (then his playing manager) on the carpet for allowing his extramarital activity to become too public. Giles recalls, "I said to Pete, 'You got a nice wife. If you chase women, why do you flaunt it so much?'" Rose countered: "Let's look at the four sins of the world, Bill. There's drinking, there's gambling, there's smoking, and there's woman-chasing, right? Now let's look at you. You drink, I don't drink. You smoke, I don't smoke. And you gamble, and I gamble. We're both gamblers. I don't think you chase women. So I got two vices and you got three."[89]

Babe Ruth cultivated most of the world's vices. Sportswriter Lee Allen remembers him as "a large man in a camel's hair coat and a camel's hair cap, standing in front of a hotel, his broad nostrils sniffing at the promise of the night."[90] Ruth was notorious for his sexual appetite at home and on the road. His young bride Helen was unable to cope with his exuberant ways. She routinely was left on the farm while Babe was out on the town. Babe and Helen separated in 1926 while he was having a publicized affair with Claire Hodgson and avidly chasing other women all the while. On road trips, Ruth would go directly into town looking for women and check into his hotel later, if at all. He was known occasionally to spend an entire night in a bordello.[91]

While athletes like Ruth and Rose aggressively pursued women, there have always been women who are equally aggressive in seeking out liaisons with athletes. This practice culminated in the phenomenon of "groupies." These women are savvy as to where athletes hang out and readily make themselves available. Bouton refers to the "Baseball Annies" who line up to provide sexual services to ballplayers in every major league city. Generally, they frequent the local bars, but the more aggressive women even show up at the hotels where athletes are staying. Bouton recounts an occasion when he returned to his hotel room to find a naked women lying in his bed with a rose in her teeth. He kicked her out, but she continued to stalk him for weeks.[92] He describes another occasion where, "Police arrested a twenty-two year-old-blonde who had climbed a tree outside our clubhouse and was peeping in at us in the shower. A female beaver-shooter."[93]

The women's motives occasionally include more than sex. Paul Merson recalls an incident that occurred in London:

> Me and Bozzy [roommate Mark Bosnich] went into the Met Bar off Park Lane . . . One girl came up and announced herself as an Arsenal [Merson's team] ticket holder. She just wanted to talk about football. Then her mate came up to say that she had overheard a couple of girls saying that if they could get Paul Merson into bed tonight they could make a packet [of money] from the newspapers. That was it for me. I didn't want to be there any more. I went home pretty soon afterwards.[94]

A circumspect Bill Bradley hints at the sexual freedom of a basketball player's life on the road. He comments on the phenomenon of women who regard athletes as show business figures with a particular brand of masculinity:

"An athlete can recognize the absence of interest in him as a person. He more than most males understands the unnaturalness of being a sex object."[95] Bradley's following observation brings to mind the turbulent relationship between Joe DiMaggio and actress Marilyn Monroe. He writes: "A strong and inseparable bond exists between the innocent, beautiful girl and the pampered athlete. Both are objects in the eyes of most people. Both are given credit only for their physical attributes, and receive inordinate prizes for them: Miss America and the All-American."[96] DiMaggio actually dated two Miss Americas.

The idea that male sports celebrities can become sex objects presents a certain irony. Athletes may find themselves on the receiving end of sexual advances; however, most of the time they prefer to be the aggressors. Indeed, several of them pursue sexual conquests with the same mind-set that characterize feats performed in the athletic arena.

SEXUAL ATHLETES

Norman Mailer maintains that sexual prowess is the second-most admired athletic ability after "a good straight right."[97] "America 'adores and worships its paid athletes as supersexual gods,'" Dave Kopay proclaims; "that is, when we're not dismissing them as 'simpleminded robots.'"[98] Kopay is attuned to a phenomenon beneath the radar of many heterosexual athletes: that sport and sex comprise a relationship marked by contradictions. If society is conflicted about the sexual role of male athletes, so are athletes confused about the purpose and meaning of sex. Dave Meggyesy observes of teammates: "The way they talk, players seem to see sex as something close to athletics. That is, they worry a lot about 'staying power' and 'performance.'" [99]

Sex as performance often shades over into sex as aggression and dominance. Meggyesy recalls a Cardinal teammate, who would talk eagerly about returning to see his wife and "punishing" her when the team had been away for a while.[100] Foneda Cox describes the sexual practices of boxer Sonny Liston, with whom he traveled and shared women. He relates that Sonny really "let loose" on prostitutes. This may be so much braggadocio, but the fact is Liston was implicated in several sexual assaults.[101]

Mike Tyson exhibited similar proclivities. José Torres, a friend of Tyson's, commented that Mike, "had a problem with women. He told me he likes to hurt them when he makes love to them."[102] Early in his life, girls rejected Tyson and made fun of him. In reaction, he became a sexual predator beginning in his adolescence. Cus D'Amato, his mentor and guardian, smoothed over more than one situation where the young boxer had sexually harassed or impregnated a woman. Throughout his professional career, Mike's approach toward women consisted of crude innuendos and uninvited fondling. A romantic relationship with the young actress Robin Givens was marred by verbal and physical abuse. Tyson's pattern of sexual aggression culminated in his conviction for the rape of an 18-year-old Miss Black America pageant contestant in 1992.[103]

In no way should Liston's and Tyson's behavior be represented as typical of all boxers, or of athletes in general. But the question remains: are male athletes incapable of regarding sex as something other than performance? Can they not engage in sex as a shared emotional experience? Transgendered tennis player Renée Richards remarks, "Most jocks save their emotionalism for the heat of the game. Off the field they may be rather controlled and often unable to express their feelings."[104] Athletes live in a physical world taking care of their bodies for their sport, but they are not sensual, observes Parr.[105] When athlete's win, they don't need sex. Winning is a form of sex. They are more needful when they are not winning. This mind-set may explain some athletes' inclination to engage in sex as a group activity. Richards recalls her early experiences as a male tennis player (before sex-change surgery): "Our sexual moments were primarily ones that could be shared by all, like trips to burlesque shows.... Had we known how to go about it we would have gone to whorehouses."[106]

Jockeys knew where the bordellos were in the towns on the racing circuit. One of the most prominent venues in the 1920s and early 1930s was Tijuana, Mexico, where many of the apprentice jockeys like Red Pollard received their sexual initiation. Up the hill from town was the notorious Molino Rojas, reputed to be the largest house of prostitution in the Western world. It was a great occasion in the young men's lives. They came back down the hill from the establishment a "half dollar poorer, twenty minutes older," and with a decided swagger in their walk. Then it was on to the Turf Club Saloon and wild exploits at the motel, chasing girls buck naked down the corridors. The element of public performance was a frequent feature in these escapades.[107]

In the absence of commercial establishments, athletes regularly bring women to their hotel suites, motel rooms, or apartments. Not infrequently, one finds collaboration and sharing of women among athletes and their buddies during these encounters. The handsome and charming Foneda Cox was not only Liston's side kick but his procurer. When they couldn't get free women, they went with the "store bought," in Cox's words. Sonny would give Foneda money to purchase the services of the women. Cox remarks about Sonny, "When he wasn't training, his big sport was women." He describes their modus operandi: "We would go into a new town, and we would have girls in there. When Sonny would have sex with women, I would have sex with them too." He continues, "We'd pick up a girl and keep her all night, and then, the next morning that's when they [*sic*] would leave. So, then we'd have more the next night." Cox relates that sometimes they shared one women and sometimes they shared several. Elements of voyeurism run through Cox's descriptions. He comments with relish on the size of Liston's organ.[108]

From a somewhat different perspective, Meggyesy describes a group of his teammates on the St. Louis football Cardinals' who got together for what they called "sets," a mass sex scene at one of the player's apartments with several prostitutes, beginning immediately after practice and extending well into the night. One player would hire prostitutes and invite Cardinal teammates to "work out" in front of certain of his business associates who were excited by the spectacle.[109] Kopay recalls a similar voyeuristic practice among some of his teammates on the Detroit Lions in the late 1960s: "Three or four times, Alex [Karras] asked me to go along when he and a friend had 'a scene going' with prostitutes in a motel room. . . . I always passed on these scenes. Similar ones I've been in seemed to me examples of men relating to one another and using women as an excuse."[110]

Kopay considers these occasions when male athletes get together to mutually share a woman as "bisexual" experiences. Clearly, the encounters had overt homosexual implications for him—if latent ones for his buddies. He recounts one occasion when he was on active Army reserve duty in Texas: "[A] college friend and I would share a room—and a prostitute—when we had leave time off the base. What I enjoyed was making it with her after she had been with him. If we hadn't shared her, we wouldn't have had relations with her at all."[111] Kopay describes another incident that occurred while at a golf tournament in Palm Springs. An All Pro NBA player, who had been married since college, told Kopay that he and a buddy had sex with a prostitute, and commenced to describe some of the details. The basketball player concluded with, "It was really hot." Kopay inquired, "Don't you think that's at least a kind of bisexual experience?" His masculinity threatened, the NBA star retorted, "What do you mean?" Dave eventually gets him to admit that he probably wouldn't have "made it" with the woman if his buddy wasn't there.[112] Whether such encounters are labeled as bisexual or not, the general impression is that they are of a sort that combines male bonding with sexual performance, and such scenes aren't uncommon.

Not all athletes require an audience to perform sexually nor do they conflate eroticism and aggression, just as there are athletes who forgo the abundant opportunities for casual sexual encounters that avail themselves to celebrated young males. Indeed, one can find athletes who present themselves as monogamous and whose sexual practices remain private. These individuals stay out of the gossip columns and don't provide much fodder for locker room banter. Nonetheless, conventional sexual behavior among male athletes doesn't negate the charge that sport remains a gender-segregated milieu which harbors an ethos of enforced masculinity, denies the existence of gay athletes, and marginalizes and objectifies women. For much of history this mind-set has been tolerated, even taken for granted. However, the sports world, like society in general, is undergoing a sexual revolution. Although, *evolution* might be a better term to describe what's going on in men's sport.

THE EVOLVING STATUS OF GAY ATHLETES

Currently, some 3,500 men are active in the four major professional team sports. None of them are openly gay, as this chapter is being written. Given that more than 2 percent of men in the general population identify themselves as gay (probably underreported), it's safe to presume that there are "closets" as well as locker rooms in most male sports.[113] Only in the aesthetic sports of diving and figure skating do gay athletes routinely "come out." More often than not, professional athletes wait until they're retired to announce their homosexuality.

Men's sport continues to function as a hypermasculine culture in which heterosexuality is requisite. At the same time, this highly charged homosocial environment harbors an element of homophobia. Gay men are seen as a threat and are routinely ostracized if and when they "come out." Furthermore, men in college and professional sports remain largely segregated from women in the team clubhouses and on the playing fields. Women play a peripheral role in men's sport and often in male athletes' personal lives.

While the fraternity of male athletes remains loath to tolerate gays or accept women on equal footing, we cannot ignore the fact that sport has been on the leading edge of change in race relations following a protracted history of racism. The next chapter explores sport's racist past, it's notable progress, and the continuing problems of race. We'll consider the personal accounts of African American, Latino, and white athletes. The narrative carries us from the tribulations of Jack Johnson through the revolution crafted by Jackie Robinson and Branch Rickey to the multiethnic world of Tiger Woods.

6

TEAM COLORS: SPORT AND RACE

The battles that count aren't the ones for gold medals.

—Jesse Owens

A CENTURY OF CHANGE

No one can write about sport in America without writing about race as well. Firsthand accounts of the changing racial climate are an essential part of this record. The conventional wisdom has been that the life stories of African American and Latino athletes address race while those of white athletes do not. However, there are notable exceptions to this supposition. The NFL's Dave Meggyesy and New York Knick Bill Bradley share poignant stories about African American teammates. Their accounts supplement those of minority athletes like Roberto Clemente, Jackie Robinson, and Josh Gibson. While the reader may detect a difference in emphasis and perspective of narrators based on ethnicity, both white athletes and athletes of color address the issues of race relations, and their stories are compelling.

Sport and race have endured a troubled relationship carrying back to the 19th century. Some notable inroads toward racial integration could be detected following the Civil War. But by the closing decades of the century, sport, like most American social institutions, became infected with Jim Crow separatism. Some 30 African Americans had played with professional baseball clubs in its earlier decades, but by 1890 all the black players were gone. Their plight was indicative of the movement to resegregate American sports.[1]

The racial climate of the 1890s diminished the opportunities for African American jockeys, as well. As more white riders entered the stables, blacks were systematically excluded. Willie Simms, the leading jockey of the era was the only African American to win the Triple Crown. Despite his success, racial barriers restricted his opportunities to ride. He commented, "I did not seem able to get mounts [in America] which had any reasonable chance of winning." So he left to race in France. Tod Sloan, like most other white jockeys, went along with the color line against black riders. Sloan had no qualms about employing an African American servant to travel with him. He would refer to his "white valet" at the track and his "nigger valet" in town. His prejudices were all too typical.[2] The nation's racism was both personal and institutional.

Boxing would prove a lightening rod for racial tensions. While the sport offered a venue of social mobility for ethnic groups like the Irish and Jews, its primitive nature provoked racial passion. Boxers performed solo and nearly naked—and without gloves until 1892; just two men standing exposed in the ring fighting with their hands. When one man was black and the other white, the raw confrontational nature of the sport often provoked primitive racial impulses. However, interracial matches were becoming less common. The Irish-American bare-knuckle champion John L. Sullivan (1882–1892) refused to fight black contenders. Other white boxers followed his lead.[3]

It was in this charged environment that Jack Johnson entered the ring. The African American fighter fanned the flames of racism into a national obsession when he took the championship belt from Canadian-born Tommy Burns in 1908. Johnson's demeanor outside the ring only stoked the rage. The proud and defiant boxer refused to play the subservient role of an Uncle Tom expected by white America. His flamboyant lifestyle included his keeping company with white women. This caused an onslaught of hostile opinion to be directed at the indiscreet fighter. The sporting community set about to see the black champion defeated and threw one white boxer after another into the ring against him to no avail. After Johnson felled Jim Jeffries in a fight in 1910, all hell broke loose. The defeat of the "Great White Hope" was more than Jim Crow America could stomach. Feelings of resentment escalated into violence. Race riots broke out in towns and cities from Philadelphia to Little Rock, Arkansas. Rioting swept a mile of Pittsburgh's "black belt." In the aftermath of the outbreak, some states banned boxing. But boxing endured, as would racism. The expression "Great White Hope" could still be heard in the 1950s when Italian American Rocky Marciano challenged black fighters for the championship belt.[4]

Racism finally took its toll on the intrepid Johnson. He was, in effect, run out of his native land on trumped-up charges of trafficking in white slavery by vindictive authorities. In his autobiography, a mature Johnson reflects on a life saddled with racial prejudice:

> When I had attained distinction as a boxer and was enjoying the acclaim accorded celebrities, I found that there was much bitterness mixed with the sweetness of triumph. When prejudiced and vindictive persons and organizations began pouring their wrath upon me, and I found myself beset on every side by unjust condemnation and accusations, I sometimes wondered if there was a God. I also wondered, what after all, was the use of attaining something if its possession was to bring persecution and cause for regret.[5]

Jim Thorpe, born a decade after Johnson, fared somewhat better. Thorpe became the most famous Native American athlete of the early 20th century. By arbitrary bureaucratic measures he was one-eighth Indian. His father Hiram was the child of a Sac and Fox woman and an Irishman; his mother was part French and part Potawatomi and Kickapoo. Thorpe grew up on a reservation in Oklahoma. Like many Native Americans, he was forced into Mission schools run by whites with the purpose of assimilating him into white culture. He hated the school and ran off more than once, but was made to return by his father. Later, he enrolled at Carlisle Indian School in Pennsylvania. Here, under the influence of Coach Glenn "Pop" Warner, he developed his prodigious football and track skills. Carlisle's highly successful football teams competed against the best colleges in the country. Thorpe, an outstanding all-around athlete, went on to Olympic fame and a career as a professional football player.[6]

Thorpe's career spanned an era of widespread institutional racism, but he rarely experienced racism on a personal level. He played at a time when whites were struggling with a stereotypical view of American Indians. Following the Carlisle football team's victory over the University of Pennsylvania during the 1907 season, a reporter for the Denver *Express* commented:

> The Indian on the football field stands in the very front rank. Man for man, pound for pound, he has no superior. Through all the years of "mollycoddling" and paternalism on the part of the "dominant race" the hereditary trait in the Indian still manifests itself. He can give and take with the best of them in the severest strain the white man can put on the athletic field. In such case there is still hope. There is no "race problem" to interfere. The Indian who can stand a grilling on the football field hath his uses in the everyday strenuous life.[7]

A nation struggling with ethnic stereotypes could at least appreciate the unique athletic ability of Thorpe. His stellar performance in the Stockholm Olympic Games in 1912 would make him a national hero. Unfortunately, his life after retiring from football only reinforced the caricature of the "drunken Indian."

Meanwhile, America's "national pastime" continued to struggle with race prejudice. Jim Thorpe had played semipro ball during the opening decade of the 20th century, but African Americans had been systematically excluded. Baseball became "lily white." In an audacious attempt to bypass baseball's color barrier, Baltimore Orioles' manager John McGraw attempted to disguise black semipro player Charlie Grant as a full-blooded American Indian whom he presented as Chief Charlie Tokohama. McGraw shared his scheme with Ty Cobb, who had been roundly criticized by the African American press for his racist behavior. Characteristically, the Detroit outfielder declared, "There will never be a darky in the majors.... Darkies place is in the stands or as clubhouse help." The scheme failed anyway when Chicago fans recognized Grant.[8]

Baseball players' prejudice could reach rather extraordinary levels. The German-American Babe Ruth was a constant target of ethnic slurs. As a young player on the Boston Red Sox in 1918, his teammates rode him constantly with rough affection while his opponents jeered him and mocked him with pointed insults about his round flat nose and heavily tanned face, as well as his ignorance and crudity. They called him monkey, baboon, ape, and gorilla. Along with the simian insults were epithets employing the word "nigger." He was called "nigger-lips," nigger this and nigger that. Indeed, Ruth was called "nigger" so often that many people assumed he was partly black with an ancestor who managed to cross the color line. Players in the Negro League actually expressed beliefs or desires that the Babe was a "brother." Having grown up in southern-oriented Baltimore, Ruth considered the racial insinuations to be the ultimate insult.[9]

During one series with the New York Giants, their manager John McGraw (the same McGraw who tried to pass a black player as an American Indian) encouraged his players to "ride" Ruth to throw him off balance. A barrage of foul insults poured from the Giant dugout during the three game series. The worst insults were hurled by Johnny Rawlings whom Ruth accused of calling him a nigger. Following the final game in which the Yankees were shut out and Ruth went hitless, he burst into the Giant clubhouse and demanded, "Where's Rawlings?" "Right here," responded the diminutive infielder, some six inches shorter than the Babe. "You little bastard," Ruth blared, "if you ever call me that again I'll choke you to death." After a brief physical confrontation with some of the Giant players, Ruth retorted, "I don't mind being called a prick or a cocksucker or things like that. I expect that. But lay off the personal stuff," and walked out.[10]

Such was the climate that kept major league baseball white through the pre–World War II era, although no official ban on black players existed. Baseball Commissioner Kenesaw Mountain Landis proclaimed in 1942, "Negroes are not barred from organized baseball." Many factors were cited to explain why major league rosters included no blacks, for example, no blacks wished to play! The commissioner's remark has since been recognized as disingenuous, as have most of the reasons given for the sport's failure to integrate. Indeed, polls indicated that most white players would accept black teammates by the early 1940s.[11]

Facing institutionalized de facto segregation, African Americans organized their own separate professional teams. In 1920, Andrew "Rube" Foster, a former pitcher, assembled a group of owners and reporters from the black press who laid out plans for a league that mirrored the major leagues. Thus was born the National Association of Colored Professional Base Ball Clubs.[12] One of the stars of the "Negro League" was slugger Josh Gibson, who played for the Pittsburg Crawfords and Homestead Grays in the 1930s. His experiences and those of his teammates were a testament to the ambivalent race relations of the era. Black and white baseball fans alike turned out at Pittsburgh's Forbes Field (home to the Pirates) to watch the Negro League teams play, but the teams themselves remained segregated. Gibson did play against white major league players like Dizzy Dean in cross-country exhibition games.

Indeed, white big leaguers had played against Negro teams going back to the time of Ty Cobb. These interracial games had a distinct competitiveness about them even though they were exhibition games.[13] However, regulation games in the National and American Leagues were reserved for whites only.

Negro League teams traveled to the American South for spring training, just as the major league teams did. Only in a few Southern towns could black players feel relaxed. One was Monroe, Louisiana, a village that loved its baseball and treated visiting Negro teams like royalty. Monroe had its own Negro team, the Monarchs owned by white businessman J.C. Stovall. Stovall held the heretical view that black people were just as deserving as whites. He not only built a fine ballpark but added a swimming pool and dance area, along with bungalows for his players. At the other extreme were places like Mississippi where the players knew they might not be able to buy gas, use the washrooms, or eat a meal while on the road. They always made a point to enter Jackson, the state capital, and leave the same night.[14]

College sports—outside the American South—were somewhat more integrated than the professional ranks. Some two dozen black football players have been found on college rosters in the World War I era.[15] However, when future Olympic champion Jesse Owens matriculated at The Ohio State University in the midst of the Great Depression, he was among a small number of black athletes enrolled in American universities. Jesse soon discovered that racial integration of sports teams didn't extend beyond the stadium. He was required to live off campus with other African American students. When he traveled with the team, he had to either order carryout or eat at "blacks-only" restaurants. He often was forced to stay in segregated hotels on the road, apart from his teammates.[16]

By the end of that decade, the situation had improved slightly. When Jackie Robinson enrolled at UCLA (University of California, Los Angeles) in 1939, the school had some 50 black students along with a small group of Asian Americans. Although no official racial barriers were apparent at UCLA, black students couldn't live in the Westwood section of Los Angeles where the school was located. Jackie was forced to commute. But overall, UCLA was a racially friendly campus compared to other places. The school's struggling athletic program reached out to black athletes at a time when other schools were turning their backs on them.[17] (Two decades later UCLA would offer athletic scholarships to tennis star Arthur Ashe and future NBA standout Lew Alcindor aka Kareem Abdul-Jabbar.)

While California was on the leading edge of social change, middle America moved more slowly toward racial integration. Eventually, even in the reactionary South, college athletic programs would find it in their interest to enroll black athletes following civil rights legislation and court decisions outlawing segregation in the 1950s and 1960s. But by then, large numbers of African Americans had left the South to escape its repressive racial climate. Josh Gibson's father Mark "was possessed with no visionary impulse" when he decided he had to get his family out of Georgia in the post–World War I era. Slavery had been abolished in theory only. "Blacks continued to reap few or none of the benefits of industrial growth or economic expansion; they lived in shacks outside of white sections of towns and bore the brunt of an apartheid that knew few variances." The answer for many families was migration to Northern cities, particularly the industrial centers. Mark Gibson moved his family to Pittsburgh's North Side. It is ironic that having escaped the system of apartheid of the South, son Josh was forced to play professional baseball on segregated teams in the North.[18]

Jesse Owens had been born in rural Alabama in 1913, one of ten children in a family of share croppers. His family undertook a similar migration. They moved to Cleveland, Ohio, where Jesse, at age 10, began running competitively in the public schools. Having faced a lifetime of racial prejudice in his native country, Owens would be embraced by the nation as an athlete who shattered the Nazi myth of Aryan supremacy at the 1936 Olympic Games in Berlin. Rarely has a black athlete performed in a more racially charged setting. On the victory stand, Jesse executed the obligatory ceremonial bow to the German chancellor's box, and Hitler returned a stiff salute. But when an aide to the Fuhrer suggested that he invite Owens to his viewing box, Hitler savagely responded, "Do you think that I will allow myself to be photographed shaking hands with a Negro?"[19] The climate was more accepting on the field of competition. Owens and German rival Luz Long became fast friends. Following Owens' victory in the long jump, Long gave him a hearty hug in full sight of Hitler. In the Olympic Village, the two would remain inseparable though the German track star knew little English and Owens could speak no German. The friendship of Owens and Long was a rare symbol of hope during the racially charged Berlin Games.[20]

Back in his homeland three decades later, Owens would become embroiled in the contentious black rebellion in American sports. His mainstream political views made his role an uncomfortable one. As a member of the U.S. Olympic Committee, he toured the country in opposition to the failed black boycott of the 1968 Mexico City Olympic Games. Owens was quite disturbed by the "black power salute" offered by American sprinters Tommy Smith and John Carlos that politicized the games. This salute, which was meant to draw attention to racial inequities in the United States, set off a wave of indignation in conservative circles, and Jesse was asked to intervene with the athletes. He begged Smith and Carlos to apologize. The two young athletes looked at this man who had been a race hero at the 1936 Olympics and realized that more than a generation gap lay between them. They refused and were kicked off the team. Owens went home furious. Somehow he failed to make the connection between his performance in Berlin and the events in Mexico City.[21]

Two years later, Owens published a cowritten book *Blackthink* to make the point that not all Blacks were militants. In the book, he lashes out at civil rights leaders. The pages spew forth the anger and confusion of a middle-aged man who did not understand the changing world. One passage in particular rankled his critics. Owens proclaimed, "If the Negro doesn't succeed in today's America, it is because he has chosen to fail." After reading the book, his barber refused to cut his hair. Another reader sent Owens a copy of *Soul on Ice* by the militant Eldridge Cleaver. Dutifully, he read the book, and it opened his eyes to the prejudice and hard times of Black Americans. As a consequence, Owens wrote a second book *I Have Changed,* a sort of apology.[22] The modestly educated hero of the 1936 Olympics had been thrust into the maelstrom of racial politics in the 1960s with few of the necessary insights to understand what was going on. To his credit, he was willing to learn and change.

Joe Louis was the first black athlete to become a national hero. His fight against the Italian Primo Carnera in 1935—like Owens' performance in the Berlin Olympics a year later—was framed in the context of rising fascism in Europe. Sixty thousand patriotic fans showed up for the event. The crowd included the largest number of African Americans to ever attend a prize fight, but the applause for the American boxer from whites in the audience was just as loud. After Louis's victory, black sections of towns across the country reveled in chaotic but (significantly) nonviolent, celebrations. To these communities, Louis represented racial pride. Louis became a new phenomenon in American culture, a "race hero." White fans equally embraced Louis as a symbol of national pride. The young boxer embodied the passive traits that "good" Negroes ideally displayed unlike his predecessor Jack Johnson. White America seemed vaguely aware of the changes in racial attitudes and practices that were beginning to stir.[23]

Like Owens, Louis was poorly prepared to enter the mix of racial politics in the post–World War II era, but his views regarding discrimination would become more informed over the course of his life. In 1951, before his final retirement, he made a laudable effort to open up professional golf to African Americans. When friends invited Louis to play in the San Diego Open Golf tournament, PGA officials first refused to let him participate because of the Association rule banning Negroes. The officials then reversed themselves and allowed him to play as an amateur but barred black professional golfer Bill Spiller from the tournament. An offended Louis declared that he would fight "to eliminate prejudice from golf." He went on to say that he wanted, "The people to know what the PGA is.... We've got another Hitler to get by." The embarrassed PGA dropped its ban on Negroes. Louis responded that he had won the biggest fight of his life.[24] Fours years later the Supreme Court ordered the desegregation of public golf courses, but many private country clubs continued to bar blacks. African American golfer Charlie Sifford took on the PGA, and in 1957 became the first black golfer to win a PGA event, the Long Beach Open. That same year Althea Gibson, who had integrated women's tennis, won the women's championships at Wimbledon and Forest Hills.[25]

Clearly, the nation was still struggling with the idea and ideal of racial equality in sport. Boxing was typical of the mixed record. In the two decades following Jack Johnson's reign, no black man fought for the heavyweight championship of the world or in any big money bouts. After Joe Louis took the title, only one of the men he fought before the outbreak of World War II was black. It was in this context, that Rocky Marciano was cast as the new "Great White Hope" after he defeated Rex Layne in 1951. Marciano became the first "white" boxer to capture the heavyweight crown since 1937. The irony was that Italian American athletes were still being denied entrance to elite colleges. But in many ways sports were ahead of the rest of society in matters of race relations, and it was due primarily to the triumphs of two men: one had been Joe Louis; Jackie Robinson would become the other.[26]

Jackie Robinson inherited the mantel of race hero from Louis when he broke the color barrier in major league baseball in 1947. Civil rights advocate Roger Wilkins, 15 years old at the time, conveys the import of "race hero" in the context of sport. He proclaims that Robinson "brought pride and the certain knowledge that on a fair playing field, when there were rules and whites could not cheat or lie and steal, not only were they not supermen but we could best 'em." Robinson, he proclaimed, "became a permanent part of my spirit and the spirit of a generation of black kids."[27] Progressive Americans of that era saw Robinson as a Moses, leading his people out of the wilderness to the promised land. Baseball, after all, was the "national pastime," and its racial integration was more public and more spectacular than the integration of almost any other facet of American life. The name "Jackie Robinson" entered the lexicon as a synonym for the first to enter a field, the pathbreaker, the pioneer.[28] By challenging the caste system in baseball—an event widely chronicled in newspapers and on radio—Robinson compelled millions of white people to confront the fact of race prejudice. Notwithstanding the elements of decency and sympathetic response in some quarters, the integration of professional baseball was an act of direct confrontation that required personal courage. Robinson, for his part, was an markedly assertive individual. This characteristic encouraged him to rise to challenges where others might retreat. It also led to occasional eruptions of rage and defiance on his part.[29]

Before general manager Branch Rickey could promote Robinson to the major league roster he had to address the attitudes of his future Brooklyn teammates. A petition had circulated among some of the Dodgers to keep Robinson off the team. The core of Southern players was at the heart of the revolt including Dixie Walker, the most popular player with the Brooklyn fans. To quell the rebellion, Rickey unleashed manager Leo Durocher on them. Summoning the ringleaders to his suite in the middle of the night, "Leo the Lip" denounced the revolt in a tirade laced with obscenities. "I don't care if the guy is yellow or black, of if he has stripes like a fuckin' zebra! I'm the manager of the team, and I say he plays." Durocher admonished Carl Furillo, whose parents had come to America from Sicily, for his racist attitude. Furillo had muttered more than once, "ain't going to play with no niggers." Some of the Southern players asked to be traded rather than play with Robinson, but the uprising was put down with a show of force. Robinson joined the team without further incident.[30]

Robinson's debut with the Brooklyn Dodgers became the main attraction in baseball. The initial series with the crosstown Giants filled the Polo Grounds with 90,000 fans for the two games. Black Americans thronged to the park, and the excitement infected the white fans. While the crowd cheered Robinson, there were scattered but unmistakable boos greeting Dixie Walker. On the field, the reception was a little rougher. During his first few weeks with the Dodgers, many opposing pitchers seemed to be sending the black rookie a message. By the end of May, Jackie had been hit by pitches six times. During the previous season, no player in the National League had been hit more. But Jackie hung in. He was hit only three more times the rest of the season; he had passed the test.[31]

Much of what Robinson had to deal with from teammates suggested insensitivity rather than outright racial animosity. At mealtimes during his early years with the Dodgers, Jackie often ate alone but occasionally was joined by fellow Californian Duke Snider. On train trips, Jackie played cards with a group of teammates. Once during a game, infielder Hugh Casey breezily shared with the group his method for changing his luck at cards back home in Georgia: "I used to go out and find me the biggest, blackest nigger woman I could find and rub her teats to change my luck." Casey then rubbed Jackie's hair. In the shocked silence that followed, Jackie swallowed hard and said nothing. Ironically, Casey was one of the players who went out of his way to help Jackie in practice and backed him up in rough episodes with opposing players.[32]

The abuse from opposing teams and their fans often was unrestrained. In an April series with the Philadelphia Phillies, the team's Alabama-born manager Ben Chapman decided to make Robinson's color an issue and encouraged his team to do the same. Robinson commented later that it was one of the most unpleasant days of his life. The abuse began when Robinson came to the plate. Hateful comments poured from the Phillies' dugout: "Hey, nigger, why don't you go back to the cotton field where you belong? They're waiting for you in the jungles, black boy," and on and on. The proud and spirited Robinson got to the point where he could barely tolerate the abuse.[33] Despite his pact with Branch Rickey, he found it almost impossible to remain passive. He once protested:

What did Mr. Rickey expect of me? I was, after all a human being. . . . For one wild and crazy minute I thought, "To hell with Mr. Rickey's noble experiment. . . ." To hell with the image of the patient, black freak I was supposed to create. I could throw down my bat, stride over that Phillies dugout, grab one of those white sons of bitches and smash his teeth in with my despised black fist. Then I could walk away from it all.[34]

But Robinson rose above these feelings and maintained his nobility to a cause that was bigger than personal retaliation and bigger than the game of baseball.

The color line in baseball also had limited the opportunities of Latino ballplayers. Cuba had been sending players to the big leagues since the World War I era. "The first full-fledged Latin star was Adolfo Luque, a right hander from Havana who won 194 games during his twenty-one-year career, including 27 victories for Cincinnati in 1923. But he and his contemporaries were light-skinned Latins." They played together with their darker compatriots at home and in color segregated leagues in the United States.[35] Latin America was, and remains, a potpourri of skin colors and social nuances. In 1909, when the Detroit Tigers traveled to Cuba for off-season competition, they played against an ethnic mix of African, Spanish, Yucatec, and Jamaican ballplayers. Ty Cobb, who swore he would never step onto a field against nonwhites, refused to accompany his teammates.[36]

Caribbean cultures have been rich in their mix of ethnicities, but not totally undiscerning of skin color. In the West Indies, most of the people are dark skinned but a good 15–20 percent of the population are of lighter complexion. Where so many colors meet and mingle, status is difficult to determine. There are the white, the nearly white, the browns—who cannot pass as white and shun people darker than themselves—and the blacks. Sports reflect the prevailing social prejudice. C.L.R. James describes formation of cricket associations on the island of Trinidad along color lines in the 1930s. His club, the Old Collegians, "were a composite of the motley racial crew who attended the colleges." He notes, "With one significant exception: only one white man joined our team, and he was a Portuguese of local birth, which did not count exactly as white (unless very wealthy)." James found the social strata of other clubs interwoven with skin color. On top of the echelon was the Queen's Park Club which had its own private field. The players "were part white and often wealthy. There were a few colored men among them, chiefly members of the old well-established mulatto families. A black man in the Queen's Park was rare." Another club, Shamrock, was made up of old Catholic families, almost exclusively white. Shannon was a club consisting of black lower-middle-class members. Stingo was made up of totally black members and had no social status whatsoever. James points out that none of these color lines were absolute. A good player could occasionally cross the lines. Moreover, he notes, all the clubs played on the same fields, with the exception of the Queen's Park team.[37]

In the United States, discrimination based on skin color was much less nuanced. An incident from minor league baseball in the 1930s illustrates the barriers dark-skinned Latinos faced. Charley Graham's San Francisco Seals, in the Pacific Coast League, had a roster rich in ethnic ballplayers when Joe DiMaggio played for them. Graham's goal was to build the slumping Seals into a winning team, and he had done well with "his Latins" including Italian American Frankie Crosetti whom, along with DiMaggio, went on to play with the New York Yankees. Among the new crop of promising young ballplayers was Tony Gomez. He and Eddie Joost (another future big leaguer) formed the best double-play combination San Francisco had ever seen. The 17-year-old Gomez had quick hands, a sure throw, could hit and run. But the handsome young Latin with high cheekbones and black curly hair, had skin the color of coffee— dark enough to elicit comments. When Gomez came into camp and started taking grounders, the first thing he heard was someone in the stands, asking, "Who's that black bastard?" After ten days of sterling performance at shortstop, Gomez was called over to the grandstands by Graham who advised him, "You better quit playin' ball. You're too black." Tony Gomez was finished with the Seals.[38]

Two decades later, when the dark-skinned Latin Americans Robert Clemente and Ruben Gomez signed major league contracts, there were only 20 black players on seven major league clubs. Gomez, who signed with the New York Giants in 1953, was know as "El divino loco" (the Divine Madman). The nickname acknowledged the young pitcher's reputation for being just as wild off the mound as on it. Gomez had arrived in the States in 1948, a year after Jackie Robinson broke the color line with the Brooklyn Dodgers, only to be confronted with forms of segregation foreign to his homeland. During spring training in Florida, Gomez and the other Latin players were housed in the black section of town on the "other side of the tracks."[39] He recalls a couple of racial confrontations that, in retrospect, are chilling in their potential for escalation:

> My first year in the United States...I stopped at the Baltimore bus terminal for some coffee.... I ordered, and the man behind the counter said there was no coffee. Maybe they just ran out, I thought to myself. So I sat there wondering should I order iced tea, or should I go someplace else for coffee. Then an American guy, a white, sits next to me, orders coffee, and they serve him. I figured, maybe they didn't understand my accent, so I told the guy, "Look, I want the same kind of coffee." "I told you we don't have no coffee," he says. I was a pretty violent character in those days...I grabbed the cup of coffee from the guy next to me and gulped it down fast; it was so hot, I burned my lip. I took a coin and threw it at the waiter—hit him right in the eye! They called the police. I sat right there. When the police came I realized for the first time that I was in the South. So I refused to speak English. They spoke to me in English, cursing and everything, and I answered back in Spanish, curses and all. They finally gave up. The policeman said, "Let's leave him alone. He's not from around here."[40]

Gomez continues to relate the day's events:

> Then I went to get into the bus. I saw it said "color line," but I sat down right in the front seat, plenty angry. One lady didn't want to get into the bus because I was sitting there. The driver spoke to me and I answered in Spanish. When the lady heard me answer in Spanish, she calmed down, got in and took a seat. I didn't want to speak English to the driver, so I wrote down the address on a piece of paper and handed it to him. He took the piece of paper, nodded okay, but started abusing me verbally. I destroyed him with foul words in Spanish! When we reached Fredericksburg, he motioned to me. I got up and, as I was leaving, leaned

over and right in his ear I said in English: "You mother-fucker, come out of this bus and I'll kill you!" When he heard that, he grabbed for a tire jack and tried to get off, but the passengers held him back. I was down on the road now, yelling, "Come on down, jack and all! I'll wrap it around your neck." He drove away.[41]

Gomez fought on to eventually win 76 games over 10 major league seasons.

By the mid-1960s, Latino ballplayers were coming to the fore, including Clemente, Felipe and Matty Alou, Rico Carty, Orlando Cepeda, Juan Marichal, and Tony Oliva. By spring of 1967, their numbers in the major leagues reached 75. Even so, training camps in the American South remained problematic for dark-skinned ball players. Frank Robinson (who would become the first black manager in the major leagues in 1975) commented about the times: "Conditions in Tampa haven't changed to this day. It's downright cruel to send black rookies to places like that. A kid grows up dreaming of being a big leaguer. He's treated like a human being by the ball club, but when he steps out of the park he's lower than a mangy dog. His spirit is broken. It's a wonder he survives."[42]

Up North during the regular season, the leagues and teams treated the Latino players somewhat better; however, a sensitive Roberto Clemente claimed that a few managers and players would label the Latinos as being lazy and looking for a shortcut, while others would say that they had no guts. The young Puerto Rican and his teammates on the Pittsburgh Pirates got along well enough where they could kid each other about their ethnicity. The team doctor commented on the racial kidding: "Some of it pretty rough. It was nothing to hear somebody yell, 'Hey you nigger!' or 'wop' or 'dago.' They authentically *liked* each other, and the tougher the insult the more affection there was behind it. . . . I never heard words like that before, but by the end of '69 they started to realize that they had a good group of guys and you never so much as heard one real argument."[43]

When it came to handing out awards, however, all was not equal. Clemente was bitter at the end of the 1961 season when he hit .325 and was passed over for Most Valuable Player. His pique grew as he scanned the list of finalists and found that he came in eighth in the balloting. To him, it was a blatant example of racial prejudice.[44] That winter following the season, he told Howard Cohn of *Sport* magazine: "Latin American Negro ball players are treated today much like all Negroes were treated in baseball in the early days of the broken color barrier. They are subjected to prejudices and stamped with generalizations. Because they speak Spanish among themselves, they are set off as a minority within a minority, and they bear the brunt of the sport's remaining racial prejudice."[45]

Clemente once told a friend, "Here in America, I'm a 'double nigger,' for my skin and my Spanish heritage." These prejudices had implications off the field. A *Time* magazine article noted that "All told, Clemente has three batting titles to his credit—but nobody has ever asked him to do a shaving cream commercial."

The rebuff of ethnic ballplayers was endemic. By 1968, African Americans and dark-skinned Latins comprised 20 percent of all big league baseball rosters, 26 percent of football rosters, and 44 percent of those in basketball. But according to the Equal Employment Opportunity Commission, they appeared in only 5 percent of TV commercials that featured sports figures. Only near the end of Clemente's career did commercial offers start to come in. A lot of doors opened after the 1971 World Series. Coca Cola wanted to talk to him about a big contract and offered to set him up after retirement as a vice president for public relations. Much of the well-deserved recognition came late in his life. After his untimely death in an airplane crash, Roberto Clemente became the first Latin American player to enter the Baseball Hall of Fame.[46]

The breaking of the color line in baseball affected the integration of other professional sports like football and basketball. By 1949, black college stars could enter the nascent National Basketball Association with relative ease.[47] Once they got there, however, they had to deal with the internal racial barriers. A de facto quota system persisted into the 1960s, limiting the number of black players on each NBA team and even the number on the floor at anytime. Bill Bradley recalls his talented African American teammate Dick Barnett who, when with the Los Angeles Lakers, spent a couple years as the third guard behind Jerry West and other "white hopes," as Barnett put it. He remained "underpaid, under publicized, and unappreciated," in Bradley's words. This wasn't Barnett's initial exposure to racism. When he had left his home state of Indiana to play college ball at Tennessee State University in Nashville in 1955, he was confronted with outright segregation for the first time. Unaccustomed to the racial conventions of the South, he sat in the front of a bus. Only when everyone kept staring at him did he notice the "Whites Only" sign. Later, he would accompany a group of students to a lunch counter sit-in. He watched a white man spit in the face of one of his friends who remained motionless in response. Bradley observes, "Such incidents had a lasting effect on Barnett's view of whites and fused with his parents' advice about self-reliance and the need to be better than a white man in order to succeed."[48]

Barnett nursed long-held feelings of resentment. When businessman Jack Kent Cooke bought the Lakers basketball team from Robert Short in 1966, the former owner told the players how much he appreciated them, and that they could have a steak dinner on him. Barnett went back to the hotel and ordered 20 steak dinners from room service, and stacked them up in the hallway where Short would see them. "Man just made four million dollars and he's going to buy me a steak dinner—shit," Barnett retorted.[49]

Once African American athletes got past the quota system they were confronted with "stacking." This was the practice whereby coaches and management reserved central team positions to white players. Reserved positions in football included center and quarterback. Los Angeles Rams coach Chuck Knox was an exception to the norm. He advocated a meritocracy and practiced what he preached. Chuck promoted quarterback James Harris to the starting position on the Rams halfway through the 1974 season. Harris became the first African American to play the position regularly in the NFL. While the other players accepted him, the reaction from some of the fans got ugly. Knox received dozens of threatening letters filled with racial slurs directed at him and his quarterback. Harris recalls, "Those were supposed to be the happiest times of my life, but looking back, I don't know how I got through them. He [Knox] said he held my mail? He sure didn't hold all of it. I would get terrible letters on a regular basis. I remember one letter contained a drawing of me and Knox in a toilet, being flushed down together. I would get two or three letters like that a day." Before one of the Rams' home games, Harris got a phone call at the hotel telling him if he went out on the field that day, something bad would happen to him. He recognized it as a threat on his life. He also realized that if he gave in, his career would be over. The only person he told was backup quarterback Ron Jaworski. Harris kept his head down and played the game. Fortunately, nothing happened.[50]

Lew Alcindor would have a more positive career in college in California and in the NBA. Like most African Americans, he had experienced his share of individual acts of meanness and prejudice from whites, growing up in New York City in the 1950s. By the time he was in college in the late 1960s, he no longer believed that whites were automatically bad or all blacks were morally superior. He didn't want to be narrow-minded or eat himself up with racial hatred. This is when he decided to become a Sunni Muslim, a faith to which one of his heroes Malcolm X belonged when he was assassinated during Alcindor's senior year in high school. He was impressed with the Muslim belief that men of all colors are brothers. He rejected the racial separatism of the North American Black Muslims. Lew found a mentor, learned the Muslim prayers, chants, and ceremonies, and returned to UCLA his senior year as Kareem Abdul Jabbar. His parents who raised him as a Catholic showed understanding. So did his college coach John Wooden, who groomed the serious young player for an outstanding career in the NBA. Kareem's had found a way to deal with racism through his newfound religion.[51]

The National Football League was still working through the vestiges of racial prejudice. The climate varied from team to team. The players on the 1963 Detroit Lions team insisted that racial problems were negligible, that performance was all that counted. Both white and black players seemed to agree that, "If their prejudice got in the way, that was the end of them. You could be prejudiced against a rookie trying for your position, but prejudices in respect to race or color were violations of an unspoken code." Writer George Plimpton who sat in as backup quarterback during the preseason while writing his book *Paper Lion,* observed: "The Lions were quick to rise to any slight that involved a Negro teammate—there had been some difficulty registering in a hotel on one occasion during an exhibition swing through the South and the team had formed a bloc to force the management to back down."[52] While the relationships among players and coaches were cordial in the communal living of a training camp, some prejudice did carry onto the playing field. Plimpton relates, "One of the coaches told me that as a matter of principle he would never want to have more than six Negro players on a team," as this led to cliques and would compromise the concept of "team." There were other signs of prejudice. The social interactions between white and black players in the off-season was almost nonexistent, Plimpton recalls.[53] Racial progress seemed incremental.

During the 1967 season, the Chicago Bears decided to integrate roommates by position on road trips. When backfield coach Ed Cody approached African American running back Gale Sayers, he asked to be paired with Italian American Brian Piccolo, the lighthearted "kidder" on the team whom Sayers knew only slightly. Nobody asked Brian whom he wanted to room with. He found out when Gale walked into the room. True to his wiseass reputation, Piccolo later quipped, "Hell, I don't mind rooming with Sayers, as long as he doesn't use the bathroom." This would set the tone for a close relationship where the deeply felt affection between the two men was disguised by ethnic "digs" to break the tension. Brian was the only white guy on the team who could get away with hurling racial epithets at the black players as part of the camaraderie. When Assistant Coach Paul Patterson gave a pep talk to the black players, Piccolo would ride him with, "What are you going to do for the Italians, huh, Paul. Why don't we have a rep?"[54] Sayers noted, "Pic never badmouthed anybody. They say people who like themselves like other people, and Brian was never short on self-confidence. He truly liked people, but he was sarcastic as hell." He elaborates, "There was something about Brian. I don't know what it was. But he could call you a Nigger and you'd know—*you'd know*—he was kidding. Sometimes we made other people uncomfortable, the way we talked, because they thought even if we were just kidding, it wasn't very funny. But it was funny to us."[55] Social psychologists have written treatises on how humor breaks the tension during social and cultural change. Ethnic banter among teammates suggests a degree of comfort in accepting teammates as equals. The Bears' gesture of integrating roommates was a telling sign that things were changing in sport, but there was a long way to go before black athletes would be fully accepted.

Major League baseball's struggle with racial acceptance has been chronicled above in the experiences of Jackie Robinson and Roberto Clemente. The story of a controversial white player picks up the theme. In 1963, Pete Rose's rookie year in the major leagues, there was a residue of players, coaches, and managers who had begun their professional careers believing that they would never have to compete with or against a black player. Thus, as Rose's biographer notes, "It's not surprising that white ball players in the early sixties would have believed that a man should find his friends among his own kind." Rose, like Piccolo, violated this taboo. He preferred to hang out with black teammates Frank Robinson and Vada Pinson, and as a consequence wasn't accepted by the other white players on the Cincinnati Reds. Manager Jim O'Toole believed that the thing Rose needed to do to be accepted by the other players was to pull away from his two black teammates. He once admonished the young rookie, "I don't know who taught you the facts of life, but there are certain things you do and certain things you don't do." But the more Pete hung around the black guys on the team, the more they liked him. While they got along fine, Rose continued to be ostracized by the other white players. This upset Pinson, who remonstrated, "Frank and I had been through plenty of discrimination ourselves—having to board with black families in spring training because we couldn't stay in the team hotel, being barred from certain restaurants. The way Pete was being treated was not something we were going to go for."[56]

Even Rose's family put pressure on him to break with his black teammates. His father Harry began receiving phone calls at the bank where he worked, calling him a "nigger lover." Pete's mother LaVerne recalls that someone from the Reds' executive office called her husband and asked him if he could do something about it. Harry Rose responded by asking his son, "Aren't there any white guys you can hang out with?" The problem was exacerbated by the fact that Pete's wife Karolyn also enjoyed the company of the black couples on the team, so the white wives didn't want to have anything to do with her. Ultimately, the Reds' club president William DeWitt asked Pete to quit socializing with black players. But Rose, who marched to his own drummer, continued to hang out with whom he chose. His enduring friendship with black teammates may be one of the rare moments in Pete Rose's life when he stood for something outside of himself: "a cause unrelated to the accumulation of base hits, records, or money."[57]

Down the Ohio River from Cincinnati where Pete Rose grew up, "Louisville was still segregated in Cassius Clay's youth, much as it would remain when he returned to a hero's welcome from the Rome Olympics in 1960. The 'separate but equal' world of 'whites only' signs would leave a strong imprint on Clay, who even as a young child was quick to recognize racial injustice. As an adult he would recall crying in bed at age ten over the unfairness of racism."[58] Clay's experiences growing up helped form his intense feelings on race and segregation. These views led to his religious and social connection with the Nation of Islam led by Elijah Muhammad, identified in the media as the "Black Muslims." The radical Muslim teachings, which often referred to whites as "blue eyed devils," made it difficult for white America to accept Clay's alliance with this movement.[59]

Prior to 1964 when Clay converted to the Muslim religion and changed his name to Muhammad Ali, he seemed to fit comfortably enough within the context of white establishment values. The tall, handsome, witty, and charming young boxer's ambitions were wealth and the heavyweight championship of the world. Few whites were prescient enough to pick up on the implication of his self-evaluation "I'm so pretty," as a precursor to "black is beautiful." To white America, Clay remained little more than an celebrity oddity that could be discarded once his entertainment values had waned.[60] However, by the mid-1970s after the Foreman and Frazier fights, his public image was inextricably tied to race. Paradoxically, he remained utterly racial yet simultaneously beyond race to many of his admiring fans.

Race continued to be in the forefront from Ali's perspective. He reflects on his experience of going to Zaire in 1974 for a championship fight: "I saw black people running their own country. I saw a black President of a humble black people who have a modern country." He continues, "When I was training there before the fight, I'd sit on the riverbank and watch the boats going by and see the 747 jumbo jets flying overhead, and I'd know there were black pilots and black stewardesses in 'em, and it just seemed so nice. In Zaire, everything was black." Ali echoes the Black Muslim doctrine: "Black people in America will never be free so long as they're on the white man's land. Look, birds want to be free, tigers want to be free, everything wants to be free. We can't be free until we get our own land and our own country in North American. When we separate from America and take maybe ten states, then we'll be free."[61]

In an interview with *Playboy* magazine in 1975, the interviewer asked Ali, "What would the old Cassius Clay be doing today?" He replies that if he had retained his birth name he'd be no different than fellow boxer Floyd Patterson (whom he saw as something of an Uncle Tom). Ali expounds, "I'd probably have a white wife and I wouldn't represent black people in no way. Or I'd be like Charley Pride the folk singer…Charley stays out of controversy. It's not only him." Ali cites Wilt Chamberlain among other African American athletes who don't get involved in racial issues.[62]

A counter-persona celebrated in Black folk culture was the bad man like legendary hero Stagger Lee whose strength and style defied social conventions and the restraints of white society. Jim Croce's 1973 hit song "Bad, Bad Leroy Brown" provided a contemporary rendition of this figure. Boxer Charles "Sonny" Liston represented this persona. The term "bad nigger" was often employed by whites to describe him, echoing the sobriquet that had defined Jack Johnson—although the two men were quite different. Liston's frequent confrontations with the police and his reputed ties to the mob reinforced the image of the dangerous black man. In this sense, his image would remain distinct from that of Muhammad Ali. Following his first fight with Ali, Liston's boisterous opponent announced that he had joined the Black Muslims. This revelation, given the antagonism between the two boxers, didn't improve the latter's view of the radical religious group.[63] Sonny had been exposed to the Muslims at the Missouri State Penitentiary while they were directing their recruiting efforts at black men in prison. When Muslim proselytes hovered near Liston trying to "get his ear," he proved unreceptive. He didn't think much of their doctrine of separation of the races, and he didn't like the practice of referring to white people as "white devils." As his sidekick Foneda Cox noted with unintended mordancy, "Sonny liked white women as much as he did black women."[64]

Arthur Ashe, also a product of the American South, was altogether different. He grew up in Richmond, Virginia, in the 1950s, a city that in his words, stood for, "segregation, conservatism, parochial thinking, and slow progress toward equality." Ashe recounts the racism of his youth and how it carried over into his sport of tennis: "As a junior in Richmond, I was barred from playing on most of the public tennis courts, which were reserved for whites; and the most powerful local tennis officials had tried to kill my game by shutting me out of any competition involving whites."[65] Later in California, playing on UCLA's varsity tennis team, he would run into the prejudice of all-white tennis clubs that wouldn't admit him to play in tournaments.

In response to these experiences, Ashe became an activist. Once he achieved prominence in professional tennis, he used his celebrity clout to protest racism, in particular the apartheid policies in South Africa. He was arrested in January of 1967 in Washington, DC, while taking part in a demonstration against South Africa. When Ashe applied for a visa to visit that country and play tennis, he was turned down. The South Africans stated that Ashe's general antagonism toward South Africa's racial policies was the reason, and claimed that he might incite a riot. That's when he decided to take a more militant stand. He successfully convinced the International Tennis Federation to expel South Africa from Davis Cup competition. Later, he and white fellow player Stan Smith would tour Africa as goodwill ambassadors upon the invitation of the American government.[66] Ashe once commented, "I am *the black* tennis player." This was more than a statement of his unique status in the sport; he recognized that he was representing all black people in what he did.[67] Arthur Ashe became the "Jackie Robinson" of men's tennis.

Ashe retired from the sport in 1980. This was a decade when hostile reaction among social and economic conservatives to black progress continued to grow. The newly elected President Ronald Reagan fueled the racial and gender stereotypes of many white Americans with pointed criticism of welfare recipients, while he cut social programs that assisted African Americans. It was an era in which many neighborhoods, schools, churches, and workplaces remained segregated or resegregated. While sport as an institution stood on the leading edge of social change, athletes continued to adjust to the changing racial climate inside and outside sport.

Tim Green offers the perspective of a white athlete playing in the NFL in the late 1980s and early 1990s. He observed that players recently drafted out of college often found themselves alone in a new city. Their social habits were telling. When his team the Atlanta Falcons traveled, two large buses were needed to move them. He recalls that the black players would load onto one bus while his white teammates boarded the other. Players also would segregate themselves on airplanes. They sat with friends of the same race at the dinner table and at the tables of card players. And, race determined who roomed together. He notes that this voluntary separation of the races was so obvious that it suggested the "colored only" and "white only" signs from the era of legal segregation.[68] Despite the efforts of some coaches to break down these tendencies in training camp or on the road, they may persist among players even today.

Green's teammate Deion Sanders proved the exception. The Florida native who signed with the NFL Atlanta Falcons in 1989 personified all the racial stereotypes promulgated by whites. Green remarked: "He's got the walk, the talk, the music (he makes his own rap), the clothes, the dialect, the numerous flashy black cars, the pounds of gold jewelry." In spite of this, Green notes, you couldn't find a more racially unbiased guy in professional football. He comments that Sanders would as likely be found playing cards with his white friends as his black buddies; that he was always organizing fishing trips for the guys on the team regardless of race. The only thing that mattered was whether you liked to fish. On an occasion when Nike solicited Deion to appear in a Christmas season promotional ad dubbed "Sanderclaus," the shoe company instructed him to recruit some "brothers" to play elves in the commercial. Green recalls that Deion told them "that was fine, but he'd also be bringing some of his white brothers as well."[69]

Sanders had grown up in Fort Meyers, Florida, in the 1970s. He played street football in the projects, but his mother Connie made a point to drive him across town to play on organized teams which were made up of mostly white kids. Sanders reflects, "I could relate to Jackie Robinson even as a kid because most of the time I was the only black player in my league." He observes, "All those years I wound up playing football and baseball with guys from affluent families. Their parents owned businesses or were professional people of some kind. I was the only guy on the squad who didn't have a lot of money."[70] Race relations in Florida weren't always benign. Sanders recalls a particularly troubling incident that occurred in high school, noting they still had a lot of rednecks at North Fort Myers in those days: "I remember one afternoon after school, I was out in the parking lot talking and joking with a group of white girls, and we were having fun, telling jokes, kickn' it." He continues:

> But there was one little white girl who was just prejudiced and talking junk and giving me a hard time for no reason. She must have been thirty yards away standing there with one foot in her car, just calling me names and being obnoxious. I guess she didn't like the fact that a guy would be standing there talking to all those white girls. But I just happened to have a football in my hand, so she made one wisecrack too many and I just threw a perfect strike. The ball hit her right square in the mouth. Everybody laughed, she shut up, and we all drove home.[71]

This wasn't the end of the matter, however. A basketball game was scheduled that evening, and Sanders was the star of the team. He had forgotten about the incident that had occurred in the parking lot. But when his team came out of the locker room onto the court and looked up at the stands, he realized that practically every redneck in Florida had shown up for the game. Sanders thought, "Oh man, those guys are here to hang me!" All the blacks were on one side of the gym and the rednecks were on the other. A riot was brewing. Fortunately, the school principal and coaches figured out what was going on and called the police.

Deion was strategically escorted out the back door when the game was over. In the next few days, tempers cooled off and nothing came of the incident.[72]

Dennis Rodman grew up in Dallas' inner city. His environment changed dramatically when he transferred from junior college to rural Southeastern Oklahoma State. There he boarded with a white family, the Rich's, who virtually adopted the exotic young athlete. Mrs. Rich would often take "the scenic route" to campus to avoid the stares from neighbors at a 6 foot 8 inch black kid in her car. For an African American player to show up and dominate on the basketball court in a white rural community in the 1980s was one thing, extracurricular activities such as interracial dating were another. On the court, the racial slurs from other players and fans would wound the overly sensitive Rodman and bring on the types of self-destructive behavior that became a pattern in his life. He would threaten to quit and go home to Houston. Supporters would appease Dennis by noting that there were rednecks everywhere; they were only trying to get to the basketball player, not the person. All he had to do, they advised, was "grin and dunk."[73] He took their advice and was drafted by the Detroit Pistons in 1986, his entree to a spectacular career in the NBA.

The late 20th century witnessed a mixture of racial progress and lingering prejudice in American sport. Robert Sands, playing receiver for Santa Barbara College's football team during the 1994–95 seasons, chronicles the current racial stereotypes. It was at a time when white receivers were becoming a minority. Going against the grain, his team featured four white receivers, a black quarterback, and a black receiver's coach. One of the players jokingly referred to Sands and a white teammate as the "albino brothers." Everybody agreed that this was an uncommon sight in college football. Sands scrutinized teammates with his anthropologist's eye, noting that there was more than just color that separated them. Background and upbringing also determined perceptions. Some of his white teammates brought up in rural areas could never get completely free of their childhood prejudices. Watching a pro game on TV, one of the players commented, "More points should be given for a white guy who scores a TD." On the flip side were the black players who routinely questioned the whites' "natural abilities." "I'll tell you Doc [referring to Sands], the brothers just got the moves and the juice," observed a black teammate. "It's nobody [*sic*] fault, God just made it that way." Sands notes that lying below the surface—occasionally surfacing—are pervasive stereotypes and everybody, no matter the race, buys into them. But players usually are able to transcend these feelings and coalesce as a team.[74]

By the late 1990s four out of five professional basketball players, two out of three professional football players, and over 90 percent of track and field gold medalists were black. Athletes of color prevailed in professional boxing. One in five major league baseball players were African Americans. Yet overall, African Americans were underrepresented among individuals who made their living as athletes.[75] Notwithstanding, even the country club sports were advancing beyond token integration.

By the time Tiger Woods came along in the 1990s, the racial barriers in professional golf had long been breached. Regardless, Tiger was soon to be appropriated by African American fans as a new race hero, although he has been adamant about identifying his multiethnic roots. His mother Tina is Thai. His father Earl "Woody" is an African American with Native American, white, and Chinese blood. Woody had been a catcher for Kansas State University, the first black man to play baseball in what is now the Big Eight Conference. He had to learn to deal with the segregation of the 1950s and 1960s. He was reminded of the racial prejudice years later when he and son Tiger would walk into a golf club, and the room would go silent. They got what Earl calls, "The Look." To him, the sport epitomized the social injustice in the country. Golf was Earl's way of making a statement, to prove that the black man could play too; that he wasn't only the caddy or busboy but could walk into the front door of the clubhouse, change his shoes in the locker room, and then walk out to the first tee at a place like Shoal Creek Country Club in Birmingham, Alabama, with his head held high.[76]

Earl Woods took up golf and had a one handicap within five years, but he wasn't satisfied with his own accomplishments. He decided that his son would become a professional golfer, and began grooming Tiger to play the sport. Tiger didn't let him down. He would become the most famous golfer in America. By the mid-1990s when Tiger Woods joined the professional ranks, race relations were no longer the contentious and divisive issue that they had been. It is true that African Americans continued to be underrepresented in the traditional "country club" sports like tennis and golf, but skin color had little to do with acceptance. Athletes now played together and socialized unmindful of ethnicity. Public acceptance of sports personalities also transcended skin color.[77]

The most famous and celebrated American athlete in the 1990s was Michael Jordan. Jordan would epitomize the successful black athlete; his acceptance was the culmination of the long struggle for racial equality by African Americans in the sports arena. Michael had grown up in the postfeudal South, attending racially integrated schools in Wilmington, North Carolina, and then the University of North Carolina where he became a basketball legend. His parents raised him to be "neither blinded nor burdened by race," and he was admonished to treat everyone the same. Michael and his siblings had friends on both sides of the color line. When Michael was young and someone addressed him with a racial slur, it was more the painful exception than the rule of life in North Carolina. On these occasions, his parents instructed him that it was a sign that the other child was ignorant, "and Michael was not to lower himself to the level of ignorant people."[78]

Jordan's phenomenal success in the NBA in the late 1980s and 1990s made him the darling of the sports media and led to unprecedented opportunities to endorse a wide range of consumer products. No athlete in history accumulated such wealth or was as widely recognized because of his commercial endorsements. But celebrity came at a cost. His experience mirrored the classic dialectic between ethnic identity and assimilation of African Americans into the main-stream. Michael's image was manipulated and mediated in order to present him as a racially nonassertive, nonthreatening and asexual black male. He even provided the image for a cartoon character in a movie for children. In the opinion of some critics, Jordan had become little more than a black replication of a white model.[79] Clearly, his ethnic identity had been ameliorated to make him more palatable to white consumers—what Gerald Early refers to as "black athletes serving as all-purpose icons."[80] The less pliable Muhammad Ali had remonstrated, "I don't want to be what you want me to be, I'm free to be who I want."[81] Michael Jordan seemed more accommodating.

Basketball would play a pivotal role in the long struggle for racial equality. It had always been "the city game." As America's inner cities were reframed by "white flight," the men who excelled at the game increasingly came from the black community. The city game became the African American game, both in substance and style. The reaction in the larger society was one of ambivalence. The specter of black masculinity in the guise of the urban basketball player provided the frame for mass media accounts fed to the public.[82] The Hollywood film "White Men Can't Jump" (1992) was representative of this aggressive image. On the positive side, prominent black athletes like Michael Jordan exemplified the healthy, pure, athletic body, distanced from the threatening masculinity of the other prominent inner-city figure, the drug addict.[83]

Reservations about the manipulated image of Michael Jordan shouldn't blind us to the significant racial progress that has occurred across sports. Joe Louis and Jackie Robinson dramatically advanced the integration of American society in the World War II era. By the opening of the 1980s, this facet of popular culture had made huge strides in race relations. Chuck Knox's idea of an athletic meritocracy spread to tennis courts, the golf courses, and even to the coaching ranks. In the process, sport directly influenced the status of black people in America. As much as any other cultural institution, sport projected black Americans into white consciousness. The monolithic racial stereotypes of the pre-civil rights era have been replaced by more sophisticated images of black national figures, many of them athletes. Indeed, Muhammad Ali has become something of an American institution. Now young white kids—along with brown and black kids—unconsciously look at North American and Latino athletes of African ancestry as heroes.[84] Athletes from South America and the Caribbean dominate professional baseball, and more athletes of Asian ancestry are beginning to make their mark in baseball, basketball, and golf.

Has sport relegated racial prejudice to the dustbin of history? Not quite; we can still detect indications of lingering racism. In 1997, when Tiger Woods framed his mixture of African American, Anglo, Native American, and Asian heritage by referring to himself as a "Cablinasian," he was greeted with a backlash from the Black community who wanted him to identify with them. All the while, African Americans and other ethnic minorities have continued to be underrepresented in the ranks of team management. While this anomaly doesn't make the headlines, what did get front page coverage in 2006 was slugger Barry Bonds' quest to break Babe Ruth's career home run record. Bonds, unlike Michael Jordan, showed little interest in sanitizing his public persona. In addition, the often surly ballplayer's accomplishments have been tainted with charges of illegal steroid use. But neither of these factors explain the deluge of racist hate mail that accompanied his displacing Ruth in the ranks of home run hitters. We have a few more hurdles to clear on the road to racial equality.

7

THE ATHLETE AND HIS BODY

It's like you're not even in your own body anymore...It's like driving one
of them big earth-moving cats—your humanness, the sentimental meat and
bone of you, is high up in the cab, behind the mask, and you're scared the
sunnavabitching thing you're driving won't crank.

—James Whitehead, *Joiner*

The athlete's body isn't like his uniform. He doesn't slip into it upon entry into
the arena or hang it in his locker when the game is over. It's not an item of
equipment that he can deposit at the clubhouse for exclusive use on the field
of play. The athlete's body accompanies him into everyday life. It inspires him
with its possibilities but also preoccupies him with its demands and infirmities.
A traumatized body rudely interrupts sleep, restricts leisure activities, and
frames posture and gait. It can cry out for palliatives and lead to dependence
on pharmaceuticals. During the off-season, the body requires constant attention to maintenance. Over the course of a playing career, the athlete's body
suffers a gradual, inexorable decline.

Given this relationship, the athlete might well ask, "Do I *have* a body, or *am* I
a body?" Such feelings of ambivalence underscore the fact that the body has no
intrinsic meaning. Context determines what the body is, its value, and its utility.
Within a given situation, bodies may be beautiful or ugly, loved or hated,
respected or feared. They may be perceived as functional or dysfunctional.
As a response to these perceptions, bodies are accepted, altered, or neglected.
The current fitness movement teaches that women's bodies are to be whittled
and shaped via training for the purposes of being visibly consumed by others.[1]
Men's bodies, on the other hand, tend to be valued for performance. NFL
running back Dave Kopay's story is typical. When he developed Osgood-
Schlatter's disease as a boy, he used football to prove he had a healthy body,
a classic case of compensation.[2] The male body, fabricated through sports

and glorified by the sports media, becomes a symbol of self-mastery. Yet, we recognize instinctively that the body remains an adversary, and "that the battle is inevitably a losing one since the body eventually deteriorates and dies."[3] Thus, athletes endure a conflicted relationship with their bodies.

Throughout history, various social constructions of the body have prevailed. Plato believed that the body was a tomb; Saint Paul, that it constituted a temple. Subsequent religious scholars have viewed the body as not only physical but having spiritual and mystical dimensions. Breaking from the mystics, the French philosopher René Descartes conceived of the body as a machine.[4] This mechanistic view of the body has carried into the contemporary idiom of sport. The sentiment in the chapter's epigraph is echoed by bodybuilder Steve Michalik, who remarked: "It was like I was trapped inside a robot body, watching myself do horrible things and yelling, 'Stop! Stop! Stop!' but I couldn't even slow down."[5] Feelings of detachment and struggle emerge when the body becomes virtually a machine. Rudolf Nureyev's biographer wrote that the dancer made an instrument of his body "at the same time as his soul and his talent were revealing themselves. He was the battleground on which all this took place."[6] Athletes can empathize with this sensation.

For most of us, the body is never in question; it is beyond question, or perhaps beneath question. Our bodies are simply there. Only in situations which take away the certainty of the body, does it give us grounds to doubt it—perhaps, to lose our body in total doubt.[7] Athletes are routinely confronted with such circumstances. Michael Oriard recalls, "As early as nine years old, I began to know my own body in ways that only an athlete or dancer knows it. I discovered limits...learning to compensate for weaknesses and exploit strengths." He relates that an athlete becomes acutely conscious of any malfunction no matter how minor; he is always aware of what the body can and cannot do.[8]

NHL veteran Ken Dryden frames the athlete's body in starkly pragmatic terms as a collection of, "disembodied parts that work well or not so well, that are built up, fuelled, and conditioned, that get broken and cut, parts that wear out, sometimes from injury, sometimes from cumulative damage and age."[9] These indignities are suffered in private and in public. The sports media routinely report on the status of athletes' body parts: "He has a glass chin." "His legs are gone." "He ruined his arm."

The successful athlete must develop a highly goal-oriented personality that encourages him to exploit his body as a tool, even a weapon, appropriated to defeat an opponent. Some professional football and hockey players consciously set out to hurt players on opposing teams. NFL linebacker Bill Romanowski describes his football career as "devoted to calculatedly administering pain to other people." During one season he was fined a total of $42,500 by the league for illegal hits.[10] Boxing is exceptional among sports in that injuring your opponent constitutes an inherent strategy. Mike Tyson commented, "Every punch I threw with bad intentions to a vital area...I aimed for his ear...I wanted to bust his eardrum.... Every punch had bad intentions."[11] This mind-set has predictable consequences. A boxer doesn't avoid injuries so much as endure them. Former heavyweight champion Floyd Patterson explains, "We are not afraid of getting hurt but we are afraid of losing....a prizefighter who gets knocked out or is badly outclassed suffers in a way he will never forget," but he can accept a punctured eardrum.[12]

Notwithstanding the boxer's resignation toward injury, most athletes do fear getting hurt. The athlete's relationship with his body is most intense when it becomes dysfunctional. Mickey Mantle would burst out crying on such occasions not because of the pain but because he felt he had failed—and his body had failed him.[13] Social scientists tell us that men have two reactions to the body's failure: anxiety and denial. For those whose careers depend upon physical performance, overtly expressed fear of body dysfunction is common.[14] Romanowski confesses, "When pure passion wasn't driving me, fear and insecurity were. Believe me, at times I still don't know which was more dominant in football."[15] The obdurate Chicago Bears linebacker Dick Butkus confessed, "The only thing I'm afraid of on the football field, is injuries."[16]

Virtually, all athletes suffer dysfunctional injuries during the course of a career. Steve Bouton's diary *Ball Four* is in part a testament to the erratic nature of physical performance and the athlete's feelings of uncertainty about, and fixation on, his body. He writes paragraphs about the condition of his arm.[17] Pitchers as a breed are obsessed with their arms. Steve Howe bewails, "I couldn't believe that my arm, my security, my ultimate hedge against catastrophes, would fail me when I needed it most."[18] But it's not only dysfunctional appendages that cause apprehension. Oriard provides a comprehensive list of athletes' bodily concerns, of which the ability to execute is only one of many. Along with pain and injury, he inventories weight loss, water retention, nourishment, fatigue, exhaustion, and lack of sleep.[19]

Men learn about their bodies to a large extent through their experiences in sport. Those who continue as athletes sequentially inhabit young bodies, mature bodies, rehabilitating bodies, and aging bodies over the course of a career. Paul Merson observes, "There comes a time in an athlete's career when he realizes he will not get any better, but can only work and struggle, and hope not to get worse."[20] Athletes come to fear their own mortality; to be incapacitated by an injury is to be reminded of that mortality; it forebodes the end of a career. Floyd Patterson provides the boxer's perspective: "The losing fighter loses more than just his pride and the fight; he loses part of his future."[21] Oriard notes that each year almost a quarter of the NFL veterans fail to make the team.[22] To be an athlete is to live with an uncertain future.

The vulnerability of athletes' bodies plays out against their inherent superiority. Athletes' bodies are different from those of most people. They tend to be bigger (jockeys excepted), have more muscle tissue, superior nervous systems, and exceptionally acute sensory organs. The athlete perceives more accurately, responds more quickly, and recovers more efficiently because of

his exceptional physiology. Although a superior body is necessary, it not sufficient for success in sports. Pat Jordan's account of his baseball career (aptly
titled *A False Spring*) underlines the misleading significance of precocious
physical ability.[23] Early athletic prowess turns out to be a poor predictor of
who will make it in professional sport. Promising careers can end precipitously
with a chance injury or an inexplicable loss of the ability to perform.

However, just as surely athletes can be defeated by a poor mental attitude.
Weiss notes, "Some men are able to perform in games better than most and
yet do not seem to be dedicated at all. They are casual, irresponsible; they do
not train or get ready."[24] These types never reach their full potential despite
superior physical attributes. Physical parameters do not determine solely who
is going to be a run-of-the-mill athlete or who will become an all-star performer.
"What they do is *eliminate* the great majority of people with average physiques
and average speed and quickness from competing on a high level."[25] Then
there are the athletes who appear dedicated but are unable to become truly
great. Hard work and determination will get you only so far. Pete Rose was
the profound exception. He set an astounding number of records without any
exceptional physical abilities. Rose compensated with hustle.[26]

Notwithstanding, favorable genes provide a definite advantage in most sports.
When physiologists at the Cooper Clinic in Texas tested 16-year-old cyclist
Lance Armstrong for maximum oxygen uptake—a gauge of how much oxygen
he could utilize during exercise—they found his reading to be the highest they
had ever recorded. Armstrong also produced an extremely low amount of lactic
acid, a waste product from fatigue.[27] Quite simply, he inhabited the body of an
endurance athlete. Halberstam suggests that Michael Jordan was something of
a "genetic fluke." He "was tall, but not too tall—six foot six—with a body that
seemed eerily flawless, with wide shoulders, a slim waist, and only 4 percent
body fat" (while the average athlete is closer to 8 percent).[28] In short, a perfectly
designed NBA shooting guard. All that is required of men like Armstrong and
Jordan is to train, develop, and exploit their gifted bodies. But this is not as easy
as it sounds.

THE TOLL OF TRAINING

Performers make significant emotional and physical investments in a certain
type of body at the expense of other kinds of bodies. This holds true whether
they perform on the theatrical stage or in the sports arena.[29] Dancers and
gymnasts work to develop communicative bodies; contact-sport athletes
construct dominating bodies, track and field athletes hone resilient bodies, golfers strive to attain controlled bodies. All must cultivate disciplined bodies.
Hence, the obligation to train, to condition, to practice technique, to rehearse,
to prepare for the next performance. This requires a significant investment of
time and energy. What Oates wrote about boxing is true for most sports, that is,

that public performance is but "the final stage in a protracted, arduous, grueling, and frequently despairing period of preparation." It is the rigorous training that demands the most stamina and willpower. "To actively invite what most sane creatures avoid—pain, humiliation, loss, chaos . . ." Training in its essence constitutes the "subordination of the self in terms of a wished-for destiny."[30]

Shep Messing underscores the point about mental resolve. He notes that athletic training is less a test of physical ability than of will. He comments, "The human body is capable of amazing improvement, but its a bore for the mind. Determination must supersede pain and exhaustion. The brain must convince the muscles that it's all going to be worthwhile."[31] This is no mean feat. Dallas Cowboys running back Herschel Walker would proclaim, "My mind's like a general and my body's like an army."[32] Young Cassius Clay had this requisite sense of discipline. He'd be at the gym an hour before everyone else and be the last one to leave an hour after.[33] The same was true of Pete Rose. Teammates noted that he had a "sort of unspoken bargain with his body. His part of the deal was to give it plenty of sleep, regular meals, no alcohol, and no nicotine." He practiced harder and played with more savvy than his team-mates. His was an old-fashioned approach; no weight training, no endurance or speed training. "Rose didn't take days off during the season. When there was no game scheduled, he came to the ballpark and found someone to pitch to him." On off-days, he normally took 45 minutes of batting practice. During the off-season, he would routinely take a couple hundred whacks at a baseball in a session against a pitching machine.[34] His biographer commented, "If he was slumping at the plate, he didn't attribute it to the vagaries of the long season, as many players do, or invoke the baseball cliché that every player goes through slumps. Instead, he crunched baseball after baseball in the batting cage, sweating and grunting and working until the slump was dead."[35]

Bill Romanowski, who played for four different teams, was a training fanatic. He would try virtually anything to gain a competitive advantage. Bill never meant a training guru or a fitness "expert" he didn't like. He read their books, adopted their regimens, and took their drugs and diet supplements. During the course of his professional career, he cultivated an entourage of strength and speed coaches, massage therapists, hormone therapists, martial arts teach-ers, body builders, biomechanists, chiropractors, nutritional consultants, acupuncturists, and assorted high performance specialists. One gets the impres-sion that a veritable cottage industry of self-proclaimed training experts has arisen to offer their services to athletes. And Bill was buying; he paid one thera-pist $50,000.[36]

Unlike athletes who relied on conventional training methods, Romanowski experimented with techniques that ran from the innovative to outright quack-ery. He jumped in and out of hot and cold tubs, encapsulated himself in hyperbaric chambers, tried Muscle Activation Therapy, Chinese herb therapy, and live-cell therapy (ingesting animal embryos), purchased a $4,000 electromagnetic ring to stimulate healing, and walked into team meetings with acupuncture needles sticking out of his head and abdomen. The response of his teammates, who witnessed a succession of increasingly bizarre training regimens, was, "Romo, you're nuts!" But no matter how misguided, Bill Romanowski never lost the desire to stay in shape. This probably explains why he endured in the NFL for 16 years without ever missing a game.[37]

Sportswriter Leonard Koppett claims that one of the great clichés in sports is that "the legs go first." He is convinced it's not true. He insists that it's the enthusiasm, the desire, that goes first.[38] Psyching oneself up for the imminent ordeal of training requires no small amount of willpower. Mike Tyson struggles to explain, "The training, when you have to do things over and over again until you're sore. Deep in your mind you say, 'God, I don't want to do this no more,' and then you push."[39] It's not surprising that some athletes attempt to avoid training. Glenn Hall, who played for the Red Wings and Blackhawks, routinely informed his coaches he couldn't make hockey camp because he was painting the barn. It got to be something of a running joke in the media. Hall confesses that he never viewed training camp as necessary or essential, as there was no learning process. It was simply a way to get in shape. And he felt he shouldn't be required to show up for camp so the other guys could get in shape. He comments, "It just made me morally tired and fatigued."[40] Veteran football players have been known to announce their retirement just before training camp, and then "change their mind" when the team breaks camp.[41]

Thirty-one-year-old Jerry Kramer grumbles, "Practice starts a month from today, and I'm dreading it. I don't want to work that hard again. I don't want to take all that punishment again. I really don't know why I'm going to do it."[42] Kramer's description of a typical Vince Lombardi-directed practice helps us to understand his foreboding. In the July 17th entry of his diary he records:

> We started two-a-day workouts today, and the agony is beyond belief. Grass drills, agility drills, wind sprints... The grass drills are exquisite torture. You run in place, lifting your knees as high as you can for ten, twenty, sometimes thirty seconds. When Lombardi yells, "Down," you throw yourself forward on your face, your stomach smacking the ground, and when he yells, "Up," you get up quick and start running in place again. If he's upset, he'll keep going till someone's lying on the ground and can't get up.... We did seventy up-and-downs this morning.[43]

Kramer recounts that the morning practice session also included what was called the "nutcracker drill." A running back stands about five yards in front of a player who has to tackle him. The running back is given a head start, while the tackler has to wait to react to the runner. They run into each other repeatedly, sometimes for as long as 10 minutes. These sessions often end in exhaustion. After lunch and a nap, the Packers are back on the field for an afternoon scrimmage.[44]

Football practice can border on the abusive. Dave Kopay recalls a high school coach who used to purposely run the players into a fence to see how tough they were. He relates, "In 105-degree heat he would allow no water breaks during three-hour practice."[45] Linebacker Dave Meggyesy would lose 8–12 pounds of water during a preseason practice in the humid St. Louis climate.[46] It's only in the wake of several deaths from dehydration that coaches learned not to deny water to their athletes.

Training may incorporate rigorous weight control. Football players are among the largest of athletes; many lineman now exceed 300 pounds. They must confront the issue of body weight which is distinct from "water weight." Defensive end Tim Green claims he played his entire eight years in the NFL trying to *gain* weight.[47] Most football players (who tend to put on pounds in the off-season) are induced to lose weight. Coaches set weight limits, and players may be fined by the pound if they exceed their limit. To comply with limits, overweight athletes diet, sit in the sauna, use diuretics, wear rubber sweat suits under their pads, and ride the exercycle. In some cases they resort to subterfuge. New York Jets tackle Sherman Plunkett was so heavy that he reputedly weighed in at a feed mill. Offensive line coach Chuck Knox relates:

> He had to be kept on a constant diet during training camps. Every night at dinner, before sitting down to eat, he would smile and show [head coach] Weeb [Ewbank] his near-empty tray. After my nightly line meeting, he would go straight to bed, still smiling. But I noticed every night a rookie would follow him to his room. Always a different rookie. One night I followed the rookie. Turns out, inside his shirt the kid was stashing a sack full of hot hamburgers. Every week during his weigh-ins, when we discovered he was losing no weight, Plunkett would only shrug his big ol' shoulders and say it must have something to do with metabolism.[48]

The Jets coaches began fining the offensive lineman 25 dollars for each pound he was overweight. Plunkett requested that they donate the fines to a charity and gave them an address. Later, they found out the address belonged to his wife.

Few athletes, with the possible exception of amateur wrestlers, adopt more bizarre training regimens than jockeys in their effort to "make" weight. Traditionally, jockeys have had to keep their body weight under 114 pounds or they won't get a mount. All things being equal, the lighter a rider the greater number of horses he will ride. Many jockeys begin as teenagers but can eventually outgrow their trade. As they get older, they resort to more and more desperate measures. Some limit themselves to diets of 600 calories a day (that's one Big Mac and cream in your coffee). Red Pollard, who rode from the early 1930s to the mid-1950s, would eat nothing but eggs for days or weeks. Other jockeys would dine on lettuce, laying the leaves in the windowsill to dry before ingesting them. Water weight is the prime enemy, and most jockeys will drink virtually nothing before a race in order to make weight. They chew gum to induce salivation and constantly spit. They induce vomiting or take laxatives. Some wrap themselves in heavy clothing or rubber suits for road work and then sit for hours in Turkish baths. Jockeys desperate to make weight resort to even more extreme measures. A few of Red Pollard's contemporaries actually swallowed tape worms and then later checked into a hospital to have the parasites purged.[49]

The above-described efforts to make weight illustrate the point that not all training regimens are enforced by coaches. Often, the most cruel measures are imposed by the athlete upon himself. Lance Armstrong calls cycling a sport of self-abuse, pointing out that the rider may be on his bike for the entire day, six or seven hours at a time in all kinds of weather and under adverse conditions. The constant exposure takes its toll on the body. Indoor training can be just as taxing. Armstrong relates that cyclists are slaves to the computer, obsessed with precise calculations of cadence, efficiency, and force. He recalls being routinely propped on a stationary bike with electrodes connected to his body.[50] In contrast, Shep Messing's favorite training method was low tech. He concocted an ordeal to develop his skills and toughness as a soccer goalie and eliminate any hesitancy to go after low kicks. The routine was to toss balls hard and low off the wall at the end of the family's concrete driveway and practice diving for then. He observes, "I was pounding the hesitancy out of my body by conditioning it to make contact against the hard, gravelly concrete. By the end of the first week my hips were black and blue, my knees and elbows like chopped meat."[51] The grassy soccer field provided an inviting cushion in comparison.

Playing the other positions in soccer entails nonstop running up and down a 100-yard field. Messing recalls that it took some players a month of wind sprints before they could keep up the pace; they would run 'til they puked to get in shape. In this sense, soccer is much like basketball.[52] Bill Bradley points out that during a professional game, the players run about six miles. Not surprisingly, wind sprints are a dreaded component of preseason training in the NBA.[53] Fighters must run to get their legs in shape. Few ran more than Rocky Marciano. To prepare for a fight he would log about 450 miles of road work—the equivalent of running five miles a day for three months straight.[54] Outstanding athletes push themselves beyond the requisite. During peak training, Don Schollander would get up early in the morning to do dozens of push-ups and sit-ups before going to practice, and then swim as many as eight miles—the equivalent of running a marathon.[55]

Distance runners pound the roads and trails longer than most athletes. To train for the competitive season, college cross-country runners routinely go on 15–20 mile runs, accumulating 80–100 miles over a six-day training week. University of Colorado's champion cross-country teams are known for running in high country where the air is thin. Chris Lear describes a typical mid-August practice day. The team, both men and women, run from Balch Gym up to Chautauqua Park and then pursue a narrow trail up to the summit of Flagstaff Mountain. From U. of C. campus at 5,400-feet altitude they make a roughly 30-minute climb of some 1,400 feet at an ever-increasing grade over a distance of four miles. On the approach to the summit, the runners encounter a trail so steep that they "must scamper, bound, or, if the will is broken, walk over increasingly high steps that tax your lungs and make your quads burn and quiver." U.S. Army runner Sam Wilbur quipped that the climb to the summit of Flagstaff transforms you into "Quadzilla." In comparison, the return run seems almost leisurely. "Once the summit of Flagstaff is reached," Lear explains, "the run levels off for a quarter of a mile, allowing the runners' respiration to return to normal before they descend a fire trail that switchbacks for several miles around the other side of the mountain." Running up and down the mountain is a staple in Colorado's cross-country regimen. Coach Mark Wetmore, without irony, instructs the novice runners that the pace is to be "easy and conversational." The veterans lower their heads and chuckle.[56]

Two-hour practice sessions in bowling alleys and on golf fairways may seem easy in comparison with running up a mountain. However, bowler Carmen Salvino is quick to defend the rigor of his sport: "if somebody tells you that professional bowlers aren't athletes, you tell him...I swing that 16-pound ball maybe 200 times in my average practice session." (Hoisting an unabridged dictionary in one hand will give the reader a sense of half that weight.) Salvino trained religiously for two hours a day over the course of some 40 years, and has the calluses to show for it.[57] Ben Hogan would hit golf balls until his hands bled. The physical challenge of hitting full shots for even 45 minutes is probably lost on those who don't play golf.[58] A young Tiger Woods worked out at Gold's Gym. The 155-pound golfer would squat 250 pounds and do chest work with 65-pound dumbbells to stay in shape.[59]

Training over the course of a season gradually wears down the athlete's body. Sands observes, "In football, you start the season 100 percent and the first day is the last day you are 100 percent."[60] Athletes are willing to pay the price of training because of their love of competition. Running back Brian Piccolo waxes, "Hell, I'd play for nothin'. . . . I don't like training camp. I don't like practice. But competition, the game, it's glorious."[61] Athletes like Piccolo live to compete and recognize that training is a means to that end. The demands of competition are always on their minds. The truth is that athletes don't rely exclusively on training to ready themselves for competition. They're always looking for ways to gain an edge; a hedge against poor performance and defeat.

BETTER LIVING THROUGH CHEMISTRY

Performance aids have been a part of sport from early on. Athletes in Ancient Greece were known to add certain herbs to their diets. Some even ingested sheep testicles in an attempt to increase male hormone levels. Early 20th-century cyclists were caught mixing cocktails containing cocaine and strychnine to improve performance, and the controversy over performance-enhancing drugs continues in this sport. By the 1960s, steroids like Dianabol began to dominate the sport of weight lifting, as the East Germans provided steroids to their Olympic athletes. After warnings by the World Health Organization, the International Olympic Council banned anabolic steroids.[62] Despite attempts to regulate these drugs, steroids along with other performance aids began to infiltrate a wide range of sports. Dave Meggyesy relates that football players in the 1960s were using amphetamines, barbiturates, steroids, and/or cortisone injections not only for the purpose of recovery, but to stimulate the mind and body in order to perform more effectively and aggressively. He jibed, "NFL trainers do more dealing in these drugs than the average junky."[63] Performance-enhancing drugs had launched a "Brave New World" of athletic competition.

When Pete Rose broke into major league baseball in the early 1960s, the use of amphetamines was an aboveboard practice. So-called "greenies" were dispensed routinely by team trainers. Clubhouses might have a jar of them for players to reach into and take what they wanted, and quite a few put their hands in the cookie jar. Some took amphetamines before every game; others popped them before the second game of a double header for added energy. Another type in liquid form, the "red juice," also was available in major league clubhouses. Dave Bristol, the Red's manager from 1966 to 1969, tried to persuade Rose to stop taking the juice. He implored, "Pete, you don't need that shit. Don't drink it." But Rose drank it anyway. A new wave of better-educated trainers drove the use of amphetamines underground in the 1970s. They also stopped giving vitamin B12 shots as a "pick-me-up." But the use of amphetamines persisted. They no longer were openly dispensed but "winked at." In 1985, the year that Pete Rose overtook Ty Cobb's hitting record, Cincinnati law enforcement officers busted two local physicians who were suspected of supplying amphetamines as they were making their way into the Reds' clubhouse. Rose was believed to be one of the intended recipients.[64]

Football was the sport where the potpourri of emerging performance aids and palliatives would have their greatest impact. Bill Romanowski's autobiography reads like a pharmacopoeia. It's a testament of the extent to which contemporary athletes rely on drugs and other supplements in order to perform: mood-altering drugs, pain killers, anti-inflammatories, vitamin injections, hormones, steroids. The list is endless. As Romanowski put it, taking drugs had become as much of a pregame ritual as taping your ankles. Actually, football players were taking drugs before, during, and after competition. They utilized prescription drugs both legal and illegal, and ingested over-the-counter substances at dose levels more appropriate for a race horse. Over his 16-year professional career ending with the 2003 season, Romanowski admits to using the anti-inflammatories Felden, Naprosyn, Motrin, Supac, and Ephredrin, applying DMSO cream, taking the amino acid Creatine, the hormones Cortisol and DHEA. Early in his career he used a variety of uppers including Phentermine, an appetite suppressant with amphetamine-like effects. As a veteran, he relied more on pain killers like Toradol and would have his hip injected with Xylocaine during halftime intermissions. He also was injected with vitamin B12, and took various diet supplements in prodigious amounts. His personal tackle box, "the size of a welcome mat," was split into two levels containing well over 500 pills, mostly diet supplements. He would swallow assortments of these pills on schedule five times a day.[65]

In 1999, a friend introduced Romanowski to Victor Conte Jr., the owner of BALCO (Bay Area Laboratory Co-Operative). A kit from BALCO would arrive at his home, and he then returned it with blood, urine, and pubic hair samples. On the lab's advice he began taking ZMA, a blend of zinc, magnesium, and vitamin B6 reputed to raise testosterone and an insulin-like growth factor levels in users. During the 2001 season, Bill began intravenous injections of GSH (Glutathione) which was purported to produce energy and aid healing. Later on, he would submit to a postgame I.V. of GSH mixed with vitamin C. Eventually, Conte would recommend that Bill take what was referred to as "The Clear" (i.e., the steroid THG). At the time it was not illegal in the NFL. However, in 2003, he tested positive for THG, despite his claims he had stopped taking it. Romanowski became involved in the BALCO scandal. In 2000, a Colorado grand jury handed down a four-count indictment against Bill for unlawful possession of controlled substances. He survived the scandal and the indictment relatively unscathed; but his personal episode presaged a pattern among a growing number of athletes who were taking quasi-legal and illegal substances.[66]

Revelations of illegal use of performance aids by baseball and football players, as well as several high-profile track and field athletes, inaugurated what has been called the Steroid Era in sports. Drug tests for illegal substance became a requisite for competing at high levels. This, in turn, triggered an escalating game of "cat and mouse" between athletes and drug testing agencies.[67] Users of illegal substances found ways to sabotage the efforts to detect them. Stories floated around about urine-filled balloons stuffed into pants along with fake penises. Steroid users in the NFL would catheterize clean urine into their bladders, which they then voided in front of lab technicians.[68] But the drug problem wasn't just steroid use. Athletes have to cover all the bases, and pain killers and mood-altering drugs are part of the mix. For many athletes, drugs become a pervasive aspect of everyday life.

Getting Hurt

For athletes, injuries are the norm; they are inevitable. Injuries begin early in a career and tend to increase over time as the athlete's body wears down. They can be acute and chronic. When they do occur, they dominate the athlete's daily routine. They restrict activity and at the same time, impose a regimen of treatment. Injuries may even threaten the athlete's means of making a living. When the athlete isn't injured, he worries about getting injured. When injured, he obsesses about getting better. Some never recover. They carry their infirmities into retirement.

Unlike the weekend athlete, the serious professional or amateur must play
with and through pain and injuries. To watch professional basketball is to
watch injured athletes compete, as the sport metes out unrelenting insults to
the body over a tightly scheduled 82-game season. During one year in the
NBA, Bill Bradley suffered a jammed finger, an inflamed fascia of the arch, a
smashed nose cartilage, five split lips, injury from an elbow in the throat, a
bruised right hip, a sprained ankle, a left hip joint out of socket, and a contusion
of the left wrist. But he notes that he escaped "serious" injury that would have
prevented him from playing.[69] Some athletes are lucky when it comes to avoid-
ing injuries. In the 1985–86 season, Michael Jordan broke his left foot and was
forced to sit out almost the entire year. Remarkably, this turned out to be the
only serious injury he suffered as a professional basketball player.[70]

Pete Rose had a phenomenal record of durability. For the first two decades
of his playing career, he missed an average of about three games per year due
to injury. In eight of those seasons he played in every game. At one point he
was in 745 consecutive games, and is the only major league player to claim
two 500-game playing streaks. When he was hurt, he ignored it and kept on.
Finally, he hung up his spikes in his mid-40s. Trainer Larry Starr once
commented about Rose, "More than any athlete I've been associated with, he
just *knew* he wasn't going to get hurt."[71]

Not all athletes are this fortunate; disabling injuries and illnesses can plague
them throughout their careers. Babe Ruth was a paradox. He was big, muscular,
and strong, yet he frequently missed games due to illness and injury. During the
1920 season, he was repeatedly on the disabled list from April through September with a pulled rib muscle, strained leg, banged knee, jammed wrist, twisted
knee, and for having been hit in the forehead with a ball—in addition to a bad
cold and an infected insect sting. In the 1921 season, he had an infected arm
which had to be drained and also suffered a leg muscle tear. In 1923, Ruth
was in the hospital from April 9 to May 26 with a serious stomach ailment.
The Babe suffered from a surprising number of colds, which frequently developed into pneumonia and put him in the hospital. But he exhibited an amazing
ability to recover.[72]

We tend to view sports heroes through rose-colored glasses, focusing on
their exploits in the arena. We underplay their infirmities that routinely exile
them from the field of play and perturb their daily lives. Joe DiMaggio enjoyed
a long career of record-breaking feats, but one frequently interrupted with injuries and illnesses. Like Ruth, he was plagued with colds that occasionally developed into viral pneumonia. DiMaggio joined the New York Yankees in 1936,
but not until the 1942 season did he play all 154 games. He missed the opening day game eight times during his career because of illness or injury. In his
first season with the Yankees, he developed acute pain in his right shoulder
which kept him out of the stating lineup for over a week, followed by inflamed
tonsils which were removed along with his adenoids, keeping him disabled for
another two weeks. In his third season, he was knocked unconscious and

hospitalized after a collision with another fielder. The next year he sat out 10 days with a torn leg muscle. He wrenched his knee badly in 1940, and at end of that season, developed ulcers. In 1946, he tore the cartilage in his left knee (a recurring injury that had plagued him since his days with the San Francisco Seals) and then sprained his left ankle. DiMaggio underwent an operation on a bone spur in his heel in 1947, then was sidelined twice with a strained neck and another injured ankle. He struggled through the 1947 season, recovering from the heel operation only to face bone spur surgery on an elbow. He had three operations in two years for bone spurs and would continue to battle with spurs throughout his career. He missed the first 65 games of the 1949 season in part due to a bout with pneumonia. In 1950, the virus plagued him through June; then he was out 10 days in July with a torn leg muscle.[73]

Roberto Clemente was accused by the Pittsburg press of being a hypochondriac, a label he resented. The right fielder experienced flu attacks, a nervous stomach, infected tonsils, spasms of diarrhea and headaches (as a result of tropical diseases contracted during winter barnstorming tours), food poisoning, insomnia, and bone chips in his elbow during his tenure with the Pirates. But mostly he suffered from recurring back pain caused by an automobile accident early in his career. Once when he asked the manger to take him out of the game in the second inning, the fans booed him and accused him of not wanting to play. His teammates, as well as the press, found it difficult to believe that a trim, muscular young man with no visible injury couldn't perform. In fact, he often played with severe back pain.[74]

Catching behind home plate is an exercise in physical abuse. It was said that Josh Gibson was born to be a catcher; he had both the build and the toughness for it. Playing the position is a mental and physical challenge. It takes unusual strength, resolve, and sturdiness to endure the countless foul tips to the fingers, legs, and crotch, swinging bats catching the side of the head, wild pitches in the stomach, the collisions with base runners, plus the constant squatting and bending required to retrieve pitches and return them to the mound. Most catchers play injured, but Gibson seldom was hurt severely enough to keep him out of action. It took an appendectomy in 1932 to sideline him for a couple of days. His most bothersome injury was a shoulder that repeatedly would pop out of joint. Typically, a teammate would run on the field and jerk it back in place, and Josh would continue his catching duties oblivious of the pain.[75]

Football has to be the most physically abusive sport played with a ball. Bill Romanowski estimates he suffered almost two dozen brain concussions over his 16-year career in the NFL. His autobiography includes an appendix entitled "My Injury History," a list of sprains, strains, abrasions, contusions, dislocations, etc., that runs more than eight pages, yet he never missed a game. He remarks, "In the NFL, there are no sick days."[76] Michael Oriard observed about playing while injured: "I was amazed to discover that although I was barely able to walk at times, I could play football."[77] Indeed, an athlete's legs probably deserve the prize for the most abused body parts. A significant number of athletes find their careers ended abruptly because of a leg injury, typically a knee. Many others play for years while suffering an accumulation of trauma to their lower limbs. One of the more notorious incidents occurred in 1951 when the young Mickey Mantle's spikes caught on a rubber cover over a sprinkler fixture in Yankee Stadium's outfield, causing him to trip and tear ligaments in his knee. Mick had to be carried off the field on a stretcher. Following the injury, he under- went the first of several knee surgeries. Ten years later, Mantle caught his foot on a chain-link fence and broke his instep, again to be carried from the field on a stretcher. The rookie who could run to first base in three seconds from the left side of the plate spent most of his career playing on crippled legs.[78]

The great base stealer Ty Cobb played in an era before sliding pads were utilized. At times, his legs were so beat up he needed help pulling on his pants. He played routinely with bruised or wrenched knees and raw, infected sores acquired by sliding with his legs exposed. Before he was 28, he could count 40-odd stitch marks on his thighs, lower legs, and ankles scattered amongst an array of purplish healed-over scars. Many injuries were self-inflicted. On one occasion, Cobb spiked himself sliding into second base and had to be carried off the field. A knee injury once caused him to miss 27 games. At age 36, leg injuries had limited Cobb to playing only 137 games of the 154-game season. He retired with rheumatic knees.[79]

Soccer players also compete with exposed legs in a physical game that features tackles with spikes high, tripping, and being stepped on with spikes accidentally or on purpose. The effects are predictable. Shep Messing describes his NASL teammate Hubert Eusebio's notoriously mutilated legs:

> Never was there a more graphic illustration of the ravages of professional sport than these two limbs. They were legendary. Guys would stare at them across the locker room, unwilling to believe that a simple, nonviolent [sic] game could do that to a man. Torn tendons, surgically removed and discarded like spent rubber bands, left deep gullies on the undersides of his thighs. Long, curving scars, raised half an inch high, crisscrossed his legs. His knees were puckered and dipped like a moonscape where the flesh stretched over bone fragments and calcium deposits. On one leg you could see the outline of the bone where a chunk of muscle had been removed. His shins were a ladder of grayish-white scars, his feet scaled, calloused and gnarled.[80]

Eusebio had undergone seven surgeries by age 33. Messing himself had played with a broken ankle, as well as other serious injuries.[81]

Next to legs, hands and fingers rank among the most vulnerable parts of an athlete's body. Fingers get jammed, cut, and broken; hands are routinely bruised, and the small bones are vulnerable to fracture. For 13 years, Lou Gehrig played through 17 different fractures of small bones in his hands and fingers, suiting up for a record 2,130 straight games.[82] A seasoned Ken Dryden comments on the accumulated abuse that comes with defending a hockey goal over the years, the concussions that have left his hands sore and tender. He catches fewer shots, maybe only two or three a game. He realizes he should catch more, but the years of abuse have conditioned him to protect his lower arms. The aging goalie learns to substitute a leg or his stick to save his hands and wrists from more punishment. The physical contact of football also chews up hands.[83] Green observes that by the end of the season, a lineman's hands feel like "pouches of corned beef hash" under the skin, which itself is embellished with numerous cuts and abrasions. Finger joints are swollen; everything feels like it's been "ground up."[84] Even athletes in noncontact sports suffer trauma. Carmen Salvino's bowling hand featured fingers that widened rather than tapered at the ends from releasing bowling balls over 40 years. On the upside, he developed a grip that could crush walnuts.[85]

One can appreciate that athletes must play occasionally with their hands injured and hurting, but it seems counterintuitive that boxers would fight with injured hands. Yet, Gene Tunney once fought with a dislocated knuckle, and Rocky Marciano fought an amateur bout with a broken thumb. Early in his career, the inexperienced Marciano didn't know how to punch properly or how to tape his hands. As a result, he became a regular at the Brockton, Massachusetts, hospital for treatment of his broken or cracked knuckles.[86]

Body extremities may absorb the most trauma, but an athlete's entire body is vulnerable to injuries, and each sport seems to offer it own peculiar afflictions. Athletes in contact sports are susceptible to an array of injuries. During four years of college football, Dave Meggyesy accumulated a broken wrist, separations of both shoulders, an ankle injury that was torn up so badly it broke the arch of his foot, three major brain concussions, and a seriously infected arm.[87] Hockey is a particularly brutal sport. Chicago Blackhawk Stan Mikita had to have all his teeth replaced with prosthetics, had an ear sliced off and stitched back on, had his jaw broken and wired together, and accumulated over 400 stitches in his facial area. In addition, he broke his shoulder and suffered chronic back pain which hastened his retirement.[88] Goalie Ken Dryden could consider himself relatively fortunate among hockey players. He had stitches from being hit with a puck, pulled groins and hamstrings, broken toes and torn cartilage in a knee, but few serious injuries and none permanent.[89]

Boxing is not like other contact sports where a mediocre athlete can "get by." If you're not very, very good, you can be made over into a vegetable.[90] Even successful boxers suffer their share of serious injuries. In the 1919 Dempsey/Willard title fight, the aging Jess Willard's jaw was broken, his cheekbone split, his nose smashed, six teeth broken off at the gum, and an eye was battered shut, in addition to much damage done to his lower body. One study estimated that 87 percent of boxers suffer some degree of brain damage, no matter the relative success of their careers.[91] Muhammad Ali started boxing at age 12 and endured for 27 years. In all boxing history, only two men won the heavyweight championship at a younger age and only one prevailed in a heavyweight title bout when he was older.[92] The price he paid for such longevity was telling.

Repeated blows to Ali's head over time destroyed cells in his brain stem; the result was Parkinson's syndrome which would frame the remainder of his life.[93]

Cyclists are oft injured athletes for understandable reasons. They not only fall off their bikes but routinely collide with other cyclists in the *pelaton,* and occasionally are hit by automobiles while training. Lance Armstrong observes that he has been hit by so many vehicles, so many times, in so many places that he lost count. He references the marbled scars on both arms and discolored marks running up and down clean shaven legs. He notes that cyclists shave their limbs because when the gravel gets into your skin, it makes it easier to clean and bandage them. He adds, "I've learned how to take out my own stitches: all you need is a pair of fingernail clippers and a strong stomach."[94]

In a similar vein, riding race horses moving in dense packs at high speed is fraught with danger. There are jockeys who have taken more than 200 falls in their careers. Some are shot into the air when the horse "props" or slows its feet abruptly; others go down when their mount bolts into the rail or clips the heels of another horse and trips, sending the rider into a somersault. The typical jockey suffers career-interrupting injuries on the average of three times a year; concussions and broken bones are high on the list. Today, jockeys wear flack jackets, goggles, and high-tech helmets. In the past, they wore only skull caps with cardboard inserts. The lack of goggles caused Red Pollard to lose an eye when he was hit by a clod of dirt during a race.[95]

Riding in the era before jockeys wore effective protective gear, Pollard not only lost vision in one eye (normally a career-ending injury), he also broke numerous bones and suffered a myriad of other catastrophic injuries. When his mount Fair Knightness tripped, threw him, and then fell on top of him, Pollard suffered a crushed chest and a concussion, as well as breaking a shoulder, collarbone, and several ribs. Lying in traction in the hospital, doctors told him he wouldn't ride again for a year. But he beat the odds, and was back in the saddle within months. Later on, Pollard was riding a horse named Modern Youth who bolted during a race, broke through the outer rail, and headed for the barns. Streaking down the shed rows, the horse skidded and slammed into the corner of a barn. In the spill, Pollard's leg was nearly sheared off, the flesh ripped away and the bone exposed. Surgeons had to operate repeatedly, rebreaking the leg and resetting it. His fellow jockeys were convinced that Pollard's career was over, but again he came back to ride.[96]

Gymnastics is another sport that features bodies hurling through space—but on purpose! They leap into the air, somersault, swing from bars and rings several yards above the floor, vault over high wooden boxes, and dismount from equipment amidst a variety of contortions. Gymnasts' elbows are particularly vulnerable. Bart Conner suffered some 40 large bone chips floating in and around the elbow joint. One bone chip measured over an inch in diameter. Although the chips were eventually removed, he was no longer able to fully extend the joint. A radiologist told Bart that he had an elbow worthy of a

90-year-old man.[97] Conner's coach Paul Ziert comments, "An athlete...must have the daring, or just plain guts, to repeatedly confront the physical risk necessary to complete.... He must have tremendous courage and confidence in his own abilities."[98] A severe injury can destroy that. An athlete's self-assurance has to heal just as his body must heal.

Not all coaches are as understanding as Conner's. Dave Meggyesy notes that, "Some coaches constantly question the validity of a player's complaints, and give him the silent treatment when he has a 'suspicious' injury.... They simply stop talking to the player and the message comes across very clearly," He comments on the stigma attached to injuries: "A guy who gets hurt falls behind everybody else in learning and practicing the various offenses and defenses, and is immediately ostracized by the coaching staff. Healthy ball players don't like to fraternize with an injured man either."[99] The injured athlete can become something of a pariah, as if the condition were contagious. After a young Bill Romanowski made a hard tackle on running back Eric Dickerson, teammate Matt Millen came up and asked him if he was all right. "No," the linebacker replied, gasping for air, "I'm not all right." Millen admonished him, "Don't ever tell somebody you're not all right on the field." This is the mind-set athletes are taught.[100]

Illnesses not only interrupt sports careers, they can end them. Early in the 1939 season, Lou Gehrig's streak of 2,130 consecutive games was broken as he was benched following a mysterious deterioration in his performance. He was later diagnosed with a rare type of paralysis which would acquire his name. The "Pride of the Yankees" succumbed to Amyotrophic Lateral Sclerosis (now called "Lou Gehrig's Disease") two years after being diagnosed.[101] Arthur Ashe suffered a heart attack in 1979 after returning from a tournament in Austria and retired the following year. Three years later he would contract HIV from a blood transfusion during heart surgery. He died from complications of AIDS in 1993.[102] Brian Piccolo died in mid-career from cancer. Lance Armstrong and Dave Dravecky both contracted cancer. Armstrong fully recovered, but Dravecky's arm cancer hastened the end of his career.[103]

Deaths in the sports arena are uncommon outside of horse racing and boxing. Since 1884, there have been some 500 reported deaths in the ring. Death or serious injury is always a possibility for a jockey every time he rides. With approximately 1,000 active jockeys in the United States, on average two deaths and three catastrophic injuries occur every year.[104] A unique occurrence in major league baseball was the bean ball from pitcher Carl Mays that killed Ruth's teammate Ray Chapman in 1920.[105] From 1948 through 1981, eight professional football players died on the field or from game-related injuries.[106] Knox recalls the 1971 game in which Detroit Lions player Chuck Hughes died on the field of a heart attack (an incident the author recalls watching on television). He writes: "We all knew something was wrong when we could see from a distance, our team doctor pounding on Chuck's chest. Usually the first thing some doctors do is give a signal to the public-address announcer, to show what part of the player's body is hurt. But he didn't do it this time. All I can remember is the doctor pulling up the man's jersey and pounding on his chest."[107]

Short of career-ending injuries, much of an athlete's life off the field of competition may be spent in repair and recovery. Bart Conner's recuperation from a ripped biceps took over a year and a half.[108] The emotional toll of treatment can be just as demanding as competition. Bradley's teammate Willis Reed who had bone chips removed from his ankle, an operation on his left knee for tendonitis, and an operation on his right knee for a torn cartilage, comments: "You got to be up for an operation—emotionally up just like for a game."[109] Recovery from an injury can be a daunting prospect.

THE THREE R'S OF INJURIES: REPAIR, REHAB, AND RECOVERY

Bill Bradley lists whirlpool baths, diathermy, ultrasound, ice packs, elastic wraps, aspirin, cold pills, vitamins, and sleeping pills all as a part of an athlete's life.[110] He could have added needles and scalpels. The former NBA forward's observation underscores the point that injured athletes have been subjected to a variety of remedies that run from state-of-the-art to primitive. Indeed, effective treatment of injuries wasn't routine for much of the 20th century. And when it was available, the quality was erratic.

Minor league baseball in the 1930s offered no guaranteed contracts; if you got hurt you lost your job, simple as that—and often times the doctor bills were yours too. DiMaggio's teammate Charley Wallgren was cut from the 1933 San Francisco Seals for a bad case of jock itch![111] Before penicillin, even minor cuts and abrasions could become infected and escalate into blood poisoning. Serious infections could end a career or even prove fatal. Babe Ruth's manager Miller Huggins died during the 1929 baseball season from complications of an infected carbuncle on his face.[112] Notre Dame's George Gipp received a neck injury that was reinjured in the Northwestern game at the end of the 1920 season. It was thought to have weakened his resistance. The young halfback caught a cold following the game; then got a sore throat which escalated into strep throat at a time when there was no effective treatment for streptococcal infections. Gipp figured he'd be in the hospital for about a week. He never left alive.[113]

In times past, injured athletes were less likely to be treated by a medical doctor than by the team trainer. Earl V. "Doc" Painter, trainer for the Yankees in the 1930s, was all too typical of the practice in that era. Painter's regimen of treatments included cups of sweet tea with lemon before dinner, tepid salt water as a cure for indigestion, and laxatives for players who were "constipated through over exercise." To treat Joe DiMaggio's bruised foot, Painter put it into a diathermy machine, a new gadget at the time. He commenced to cook the foot until it looked like a broiled red pepper. Joe suffered first-degree burns and was a month recovering from the "treatment."[114]

While trainers often were given free reign to treat athletes, the coaches of yesteryear were mistrusting of doctors and hospitals. George Strickler, the NFL's first public relations director, recalls playing football for Knute Rockne at Notre Dame in 1924. In those days "Rock" wasn't keen on operations. Strickler relates, "About the second day of practice [Rockne] caught me going down on passes. Well, my knee would lock, but I would just hit it and it would be okay. Rock caught me doing it and sent me into Doc Glimstead. He examined it, and after practice that day Rock told me, 'Turn in your uniform. You're through.'" Strickler knew he was in trouble because without football he wouldn't get any financial aid. So he told Rockne, "Well, I'll go down to Indianapolis...and let them operate on it." He recalls that Rockne hit the roof, replying, "No operation! Positively not! You might get an infection and have a stiff leg for the rest of your life, and football isn't worth it." Rockne eventually changed his view about orthopedic surgery, as did most coaches.[115]

When penicillin became available in the 1940s, infections were less lethal. However, the quality of treatment provided to athletes continued to be unreliable, and penicillin proved no cure-all. Following surgery for a bone spur, DiMaggio showed up for spring training in 1947 with a five-and-a-half inch gash around his heel, raw, infected, and oozing fluids. Every day team doctors would cut away more diseased flesh as the hole in his heel continued to grow. Penicillin had almost no effect on the wound. Maggots were sown into the heel to eat away the dead skin. Finally, doctors took a piece of his thigh the size of a postage stamp and grafted it onto his heel.[116]

While playing football for Syracuse University in the early 1960s, Dave Meggyesy tore open his elbow on a piece of blocking equipment. Sent to the training room to see the team doctor, he lay down on the training table while the physician took the cover off a pan of medical instruments in which all the fluid had evaporated. The doctor pried out the instruments with his fingers as the needle holder flew loose onto the floor. He picked it up, took out some surgical thread and began to sew up the two-inch gash in Meggyesy's elbow without anesthetic. Meggyesy was sent back to practice with 10 stitches and a bandage. He later developed a staphylococcus infection in his arm which was treated inappropriately by the same doctor with penicillin. The arm almost had to be amputated because of the improper medical treatment.[117] In 1961, Mickey Mantle's hip had to be lanced when a botched injection by a medical doctor turned into an abscess, leaving a surgical wound four inches long and two inches wide. The unfortunate encounter with a hypodermic needle caused Mantle to miss 16 games at the end of the season.[118]

Clemente would regularly eschew the services of the team trainer and doctors in favor of treatment by a semiretired chiropractor in Puerto Rico, whom he believed was helping his pain from dislocated discs. The elderly doctor would treat athletes by rubbing them down with a potent orange ointment called Atomic Balm, "cauterize" their tendons with a black plastic cylinder that emitted crackling purple sparks, and heat their aching muscles with an infrared lamp. The local newspaper wrote an article about the "magic hands" of this healer who resorted to electric shock and "cyclo-therapy," as well as physiotherapy. Clemente swore by him.[119]

Eventually, coaches and trainers learned to practice "preventive medicine." They viewed the athlete as an investment to be protected. Taping became a regular part of pregame preparation. Joe DiMaggio listed the places where he had to be taped during the 1948 season: his Charley horse thigh, the cinch around his midriff, a patch on his hip for a strawberry, and a bandage on his left hand. He reacted, "I feel like a mummy."[120] No one in baseball was wrapped in more tape than Mickey Mantle. Each day before a game, the Yankee trainer would massage Mantle's legs and then Mick would tape himself from low on his shin to the top of his thigh.[121] Football players are not only taped but encapsulated in an array of protective gear. Tim Green notes that in addition to his helmet and mouthpiece, he normally wore double X shoulder pads, a tailbone pad, forearm pads, hand pads, elbow pads, thick thigh pads, and a neck roll. Running backs and quarterbacks also wear flak jackets or rib pads. Some football players even wear eye goggles. Yet, they still get injured on a routine basis.[122]

The current uses of technology to shape, protect, and repair the athlete's body stand in stark contrast to the treatments used in the days of Red Pollard and Ty Cobb. Today's athletes may be attired in aerodynamically designed and padded clothes as well as locked into ankle, knee, arm, and neck braces. In addition, athletes are nourished with high-calorie foods, vitamins, and carbohydrates, and administered multiple analgesics. When an athlete's body is damaged, efforts are geared to quickly repair and return it to its function. Increasingly, damaged body parts are thrown away and replaced by Teflon articulations.[123] We are approaching the era of the bionic athlete.

In the meantime, human parts continue to break down or just wear out. Few veteran athletes avoid orthopedic surgery over the course of a career. The record for most surgeries may be held by former Kansas City Chief center E.J. Holub who underwent more than a dozen operations. His carved-up joints caught the attention of teammate Michael Oriard:

> When I first saw them, E.J. [Holub]'s knees looked like well-marbled meat at the butcher shop. Or, as a magazine article about the most operated-on knees in sport said a couple of years ago, as if he'd lost "a swordfight with a midget." Simply to count the elegant "S's" swirling around his kneecaps, and the more brutal slashes and short arcs of his various incisions, could not reveal the true number of E.J.'s operations. Some of these incisions had been reopened more than once. He had had his first knee operation in high school in 1956, and his ninth during the off season.... He had two more before he retired in 1971, and was looking ahead to several more in the future, as doctors attempted to keep him from becoming totally crippled.[124]

In addition, Holub underwent five other operations on his hands, elbows, and hamstring muscle. Oriard observes that it was as if he had donated his body to science *before* he became a cadaver. E.J. routinely drained his own knees by slitting them open with a razor, wearing a feminine napkin over them to absorb the seepage. Yet, he never complained of pain.[125]

Green enlightens us on the textbook approach to this grisly pregame procedure. "If you have never had your knee drained, you should know that it's not as easy as turning on the tap of a keg and letting the contents spill out." He describes the method of extraction in some detail. A very large needle is inserted into the side of a player's knee and forced under the kneecap. Then the plunger is pulled back so that the yellow, blood tinged fluid that has accumulated slowly fills the syringe. The players who undergo this procedure report excruciating pain.[126]

Green's teammate Bret Clark would have his swollen knee drained every Sunday morning before a game. Immediately after the draining, smaller needles would be used to inject Xylocaine to mercifully numb the knee. Clark would endure this ritual week after week, while his limp became noticeably worse. Eventually, the syringe withdrew nothing but a "viscous red goop." The swelling in Clark's knee could no longer be controlled. Green recounts that "Bret took the needle once again and tried to gimp out there with the rest of the team, it was no use. The swelling in the joint would not permit him to perform. His body had finally defeated the wiles of modern medicine."[127] That was the end of Bret Clark's NFL career. He went into retirement badly crippled.

For athletes like Clark, pain killers become a requisite to competing. Steve Howe recalls, "I could pitch only if the pain [from a bone chip] was deadened. I must have had thirty Novocain shots in my ankle during the season." Pain killers can be a "mixed blessing." Howe acknowledges, "When I reported the soreness to the team trainer, he put me on Darvocet, a painkiller that was supposed to be nonaddictive. I began taking four to eight 100-milligram pills a day." Howe had trouble getting off the pain killer and graduated to cocaine. Following his suspension and drug rehab, he submitted to another ritual that has become a part of sport. Howe reveals, "I had urinated in hundreds of specimen containers to prove I was (or wasn't) clean."[128]

Pain killers may mask the sensation of injured body parts, but the parts themselves have to be rejuvenated if an athlete is to continue his career. "Rehab" following an injury makes up the daily routine for an injured athlete. Dave Dravecky recalls recovering from arm surgery: "Every morning, starting about nine o'clock, I did forty-five minutes of exercises.... Soon as I gained strength, we added routines with weights. Three days a week I threw a ball. Every day I did an aerobic workout on the stationary bike. It was a tough day's work.... Typically, I'd get home from the clinic about one in the afternoon, absolutely exhausted. For at least an hour I'd sink into my chair and say nothing.... For one month I did nothing but pedal the stationary bike."[129]

Following a serious auto accident, Ben Hogan required a three-and-a-half hour preround ritual in order to continue playing golf. For the first hour out of bed, he soaked in a tub full of hot water and salts; the second hour he rubbed on liniment and wrapped his legs in elastic bandages. He would arrive at the locker room an hour and a 20 minutes before starting time, hit practice shots for 40 minutes, then back to the locker room, to soak his wounds in hot water, and finally on to the first tee.[130]

Bart Conner describes therapy and rehabilitation after surgery on his arm. The immediate regimen consisted of CPM (Continual Passive Motion), a device consisting of cables, pulleys, and a motor which lifted his swollen arm up and down continuously for three days (even during sleep) while he lay in a hospital bed recovering. Following CPM, Bart began ice therapy.[131] He recalls:

> Of all the treatments, the worst was being soaked in ice. I would sit for forty or fifty minutes in this hydro-therapy room while my elbow and shoulder were resting in a large stainless steel vat filled with chipped ice. A motor swirled in the bottom of the vat and it sounded like you were stirring ice cubes in a tall glass. The rest of my body was wrapped in warm blankets, but some days that wasn't enough. I would get so cold that I couldn't stop my teeth from chattering. It felt like I was standing in a blizzard in my swimming suit.[132]

If pressed, most athletes would admit that ice is the best treatment for aches and pains, although Shep Messing was of the same mind as Conner. He judged the cure to be far worse than the ailment.[133]

When rehabilitation ends, the athlete must then face the long difficult task of regaining his pre-injury strength, endurance, and feel for competition. Conner remarks that during his long therapy he forgot what parallel bars felt like and that he had lost all the calluses on his hands. The things that were accomplished effortlessly before, now required a laborious effort.[134] Most athletes aren't prepared for how hard it is to return following an injury. The discomfort experienced during rehab may accompany the return. There's discomfort and then there's outright pain.

No Pain, No Gain

For career athletes, pain can be a constant companion. It follows them home and accompanies them on road trips. Athletes describe a variety of ways they experience pain in their respective roles whether football player, boxer, gymnast, or cyclist. For hockey goalies, pain has an identifiable cause. Dryden observes that the pain from getting hit by pucks is constant and cumulative. When a shot hits a player's shins or forearms, the ache spreads. He compares its effect with that of "a long slow battering from a skillful boxer, gradually wearing you down." Pain is experienced by athletes not only during competition but before the game, after the game, and between games. The veteran goalie wakes up in the morning following a game sore, aching, moaning with each move.[135] He is not alone.

The omnipresence of pain in sport might lead one to think of it as something like background noise that can be "tuned out." This would underrate its gnawing effects. Boxing writer Tom Boswell places pain in context: "Pain is the most powerful and tangible force in life. The threat of torture...is stronger than the threat of death...pain is corrosive, like an acid eating at the personality. Pain, as anyone who has had a toothache knows, drives all other emotions and sensations before it. Pain is a priority. It may be a man's strongest and most undeniable reality."[136]

"I hurt, therefore I am." quips Robert Sands. He chose to play football for Santa Barbara College at age 38 as part of a participant observation study for his graduate degree in anthropology. The volunteer guinea pig grouses about the perils of a pass receiver: "Look at my hands, fingers, and wrists. I know I am going to start feeling pain there from jamming them all the time.... My fingers hadn't been their normal size for two years." Over the course of a season, Sands became convinced that there is something crucial derived from pain, that pain is the essential ingredient in creating the sum of what it means to be a football player, a vital element in constructing a cultural identity as a stud as opposed to a wimp.[137]

His view echoes that of Michael Oriard who relates tolerance of pain to what he labels the "limits of toughness." He recalls: "Through grade school, high school, and college—I had defined myself in relation to football largely by my toughness. I created a sense of my own powerfulness and of control over my own life in large part through knocking other people down, never allowing any physical fear to inhibit me, and being able to play with pain."[138] In a similar vein, Romanowski claims, "One thing I realized in high school was that, somehow, I could absorb an enormous amount of pain. I would get neck stingers on a regular basis, but I never wanted to come out of the game, and I never did."[139] For the professional football player, as for most athletes, pain cannot be avoided. Oriard points out, "It is as much a part of the football player's everyday world as inky fingers are to the printer's.... If football players did not play with pain, no NFL club could field a team on Sunday."[140] Pain may be an element in the identity of an athlete, just as it is an occupational necessity.

The psychology of dealing with pain is a topic which draws comments from athletes as well as those who study sport. It's probably true that some athletes play with physical pain because the emotional pain of not playing would be even greater. Athletes must learn to normalize pain as part of the sport experience. Lance Armstrong is convinced that equal elements of denial and masochism enter into the equation; that all athletes, especially cyclists, are in the business of denial. "You deny all the aches and pains because you have to in order to finish the race. It's a sport of self-abuse." Someone once asked Armstrong what pleasure he took in riding for so long. "'Pleasure?' I said. 'I don't understand the question.' I didn't do it for pleasure. I did it for pain." He would boast, "I'm the guy who can take it."[141] Don Schollander describes the mind-set of competitive swimmers:

> In a race, at the threshold of pain, you have a choice. You can back off—or you can force yourself to drive to the finish...a champion pushes himself on into agony. Is it masochistic? In a way, yes. When it comes it is oddly satisfying

because you know it had to come and now it is there, because you are meeting it, taking it without backing down—because you enjoy the triumph of getting through it, knowing it is the only way you can win.[142]

He elaborates on the swimmer's relationship with the discomfort that accompanies extreme effort:

You learn the pain in practice and you will know it in every race. As you approach the limit of your endurance it begins coming on gradually, hitting your stomach first. Then your arms grow heavy and your legs tighten—thighs first, then knees. You sink lower in the water because you can't hold yourself up; you are actually swimming deeper in the water, as though someone were pushing you down on your back. Your stomach feels as though it's going to fall out—every kick hurts like hell—and then suddenly you hear a shrill, internal scream.[143]

Bart Conner observes that pain is "of two types: constructive and destructive. A gymnast, for example, is constantly adjusting and extending the movements of his body . . . overextension results in pain. . . . The pain of the ripped muscle was of the second type."[144] The competitive athlete has to determine when the necessity of playing with pain has crossed the line to jeopardizing his physical well-being.

Messing notes that the most intensive use of drugs in sports is for coping with pain. He recalls teammate Keith Eddy who suffered a pulled groin muscle. "Sitting on the training table naked, beside an arsenal of hypodermic needles, he squeezed a washcloth in one hand as the doctor inserted the first needle into the tender skin of his thigh. His face a mask of pain, Keith waited a moment for the Novocain to take effect and then ran his hand over the area. 'No good, doc,' he said, 'I can still feel it.'" The process is repeated a second and third time. By the fifth needle both Messing and Eddy realize that the shots aren't going to do any good, and they both exit for the playing field. Messing comments that from the stands Keith Eddy probably looked normal; only those who got close to him on the field saw the agony on his face. Eddy retired to accept a coaching position.[145]

There is no mandatory retirement age in sports. More often than not, the body determines when a career is over. And the accumulated injuries and discomforts continue to take their toll. For most athletes, the infirmities don't disappear when they hang up their uniforms for the last time. E.J. Holub and Bret Clark still walked with painful limps following the end of their careers. When asked at age 70 if a visible wound were painful, Ty Cobb replied testily, "What the hell do you think?"[146] The aging ballplayer's retort brings us full circle. If it hadn't been for the legendary feats performed by his body in its youth, no journalist would have bothered to ask the question. The body is first a gift and then a burden. Cobb entered his twilight years like the soldier in Shakespeare's "Seven Ages of Man" (*As You Like It,* II.vii), "Full of strange oaths," "Jealous in honor, sudden and quick in quarrel," wistful for "the bubble reputation" of his playing days. He wasn't the only ex-athlete to play the final act as tragedy.

8

RETIRING FROM SPORT

Now you will not swell the rout
Of lads that wore their honours out,
Runners whom renown outran
And the name died before the man.

—A.E. Housman

The day came when the great Joe DiMaggio took his final bow as a ballplayer. In the Yankees' Fifth Avenue suite amidst the newsreel and television cameras, he thanked the team, the game, and the fans; then he posed for pictures and answered questions from the press for almost an hour. Unexpectedly, the newsreel spotlights blew a fuse and plunged the suite into darkness. When the lights came back on, DiMaggio was gone.[1] But the Yankee Clipper didn't disappear for long. Indeed, he seldom escaped the public's attention during his retirement. He would remain a much sought-after national icon until his death at age 84.

DiMaggio's retirement was both exceptional and unexceptional. He was retired from baseball for more than 47 years, over half his life and a decade longer than Lou Gehrig's entire life.[2] It is unusual for former athletes to live until their mid-80s, but most like DiMaggio face a retirement that greatly exceeds the length of their sports careers. In the so-called youth sports of swimming and gymnastics (where the typical competitor is a teenager), athletes will spend three or four times as many years retired from their careers as active. Don Schollander alluded to fighting the "enemy of age" at 20, following a decade of swimming competitively. He later quipped, "I suppose it's funny to be considered an old man at twenty-two," the age he retired.[3] Boxing may not be a youth sport, but no athletes age more rapidly and visibly. Most boxers are "old" by age 30.

Athletes' careers generally start and end early. Tod Sloan began riding professionally at age 13 and rode until he was 32.[4] Michael Oriard retired from football at age 26 after playing at the amateur and professional levels for 18 years.[5]

Sloan's tenure as a paid athlete was unusual. Most professional sports careers are brief. The average major league baseball player lasts about five years; the average stint in the National Football League is about four years. In the National Basketball Association, a career averages some three and a half years, about the same as for hockey players in the NHL. Thus, athletes' careers come to an end when most men's careers are beginning to take off. The majority retire in their 20s, fewer in their 30s, and a handful in their 40s. It's a matter of attrition.[6]

The end of a sports career can approach gradually or with shocking sudden-ness. An athlete's future can be erased in a matter of minutes due to catastrophic injury. Football players routinely are carried off the field into early retirement. Bill Romanowski recounts an incident in training camp his rookie year in the NFL: "I was standing next to our starting linebacker Todd Shell when he ran out-side to defend a sweep play, engaged the tight end, and then suddenly fell to the ground, limp."[7] Shell had fractured his neck. He would never play football again. Baseball pitchers seem particularly vulnerable. Every year some 15 percent suffer serious injury. More often it's not catastrophic injury that ends a career but the gradual accumulation of minor "nagging" afflictions that takes a toll: a pulled groin, a bad knee, a "crick" in the neck.[8] The upshot is a career shortened due to repeated poor performance. "You're only as good as your last game," they say. And there's always an eager rookie in the wings waiting to take your job.

Moreover, managers tend to see the strengths of rookies and the shortcom-ings of veterans. When Branch Rickey took over the Pittsburgh Pirates in 1950, he instituted a "crash program" of bringing up green young recruits. So ruthless was this "sink or swim" strategy that one local reporter commented, "A pitcher who was knocked out of the box didn't know whether to take a shower or catch a train."[9] For other athletes, a professional career is a steady downhill journey accompanied by the gradual awareness that it is ending. Pat Jordan pitched in the minor leagues for several seasons, never realizing his dream to play in the majors. He describes his last stop in professional base-ball at Palatka, Florida:

> I began pitching regularly again. That was all there was to it, I told myself, although I knew that the Braves did not share this belief. Why else would they have sent me to "The Elephants' Burial Ground?" That's what we called Palatka during spring training. It was the lowest of the Braves' Class D teams, a receptacle for aging veterans playing one last season; for all those faceless "Lefties" and "Studs" who were used to fill out a roster until midseason, when they were released.[10]

Jordan notes that the ballpark where the Palatka Braves played was misnamed the Azalea Bowl, for most of the aging veterans who played there would not bloom again.[11] The town's main street is Lemon Street. He allows that mockery to pass without comment.

Sports reflect the American fear of failure which carries over into fear of retirement. For the athlete, the end of a career is haunted by trepidations. It's

not like retiring from an office job at a predetermined age after a long, successful tenure. Instead, he leaves because he can't perform any more. It may feel
more like getting "fired" than being retired. Oriard frames the end of the
athlete's career: "The major occupation and preoccupation of his life, for which
he has prepared himself through a childhood and adolescence of developing
his skills and for which he has committed himself intensely and risked serious
injury over and over again—is suddenly taken from him. 'The coach wants to
see you in his office.' The equivalent of the 'pink slip.'"[12]

The overriding theme in this chapter is that terminating a lifelong relationship
with sport is distinct from most retirements. It can be uniquely difficult and unset-
tling. Although some negotiate the adjustment from athlete to ex-athlete without
major difficulty, many deny and delay the inevitable end of their careers. What is
it about sport that makes this transition so difficult? Participation in sport develops a sense of mastery and resilience, instills pride and competitiveness—traits
that should contribute to success in subsequent vocations and avocations. Yet,
other aspects of the athlete's experience conspire against a successful transition
into the "real world." The following section explores these factors.

ONE GAME AT A TIME

Sport by its nature may set up the athlete for problems when his career ends.
For one thing, it is a world of greater certainties than he will find after he
retires. The athlete becomes accustomed to a life governed by simple rules,
and stripped down to the essentials.[13] Pursuing a career in sports means letting
others organize your everyday affairs. Team athletes are handed an itinerary
which lays out their schedule in detail. On the road, they are carried between
the airport, hotel, and arena; curfews are set; dress standards are established.
In effect, management makes all the decisions so that the athletes can concen-
trate on the game.[14] Former NHL wingman Ted Irvine comments on the
narrow parameters of responsibility among professional hockey players. His
perception was that he had to do two things: keep in shape and compete to
win. That was his idea of a career. He didn't consider his responsibilities for
making a life with his family or how he would make a living after he retired.
He recalls, "I did what I thought I was supposed to be [sic], an NHL hockey
player who went to banquets, signed autographs and did charity work."[15]

Oriard points out that sport offers an escape from life, but no return
passage.[16] It's a lesson that eludes many athletes. The ex-athlete must adjust
to a wider world of much greater ambiguity and complexity. Dave Meggyesy
reflects on retiring from football:

> Before I could quit playing football I had to learn what it was to be an individual.
> This won't seem very momentous to people who have grown up outside the
> world of athletics. But for a jock, becoming somebody real, getting involved in life
> off the playing field, is a significant problem. I imagine that in some small way it

resembles what a priest who has always lived in a cloister must feel after he goes out, gets married, and tries to go on from there.[17]

Les Costello, who played with the Toronto Maple Leafs, actually went from professional hockey directly into the seminary to study for the priesthood.[18] But Father Costello was exceptional in knowing exactly what he wanted to do when he hung up his skates. Journalist Johnette Howard observes that 99 percent of the guys in the NHL have been playing hockey since they were five years old and have no idea what else they would do when their playing careers end.[19] She could have been writing about baseball, basketball, or football players, as well. Sports don't encourage a focus on the future. Athletes are vaguely aware that any game could be their last, but few of them look beyond next season. More-over, coaches don't encourage their players to think about their long-range plans or their retirement. Athletes are routinely admonished to take things "one game at a time" and focus on "the task at hand."

The first 20 or 30 years of an athlete's life are devoted almost exclusively to his sport at the cost of neglecting the acquisition of skills or credentials necessary to move into other occupations when the inevitable end arrives. Moreover, athletes tend to block awareness of the pattern assumed by most all careers that depend on skilled performance: that there is an ascent, plateau, and descent. For sports careers, the descent typically arrives early due to the vicissitudes of high-level competition. Ken Dryden notes that in about 10 short years an athlete goes from "boy wonder" to "emerging star" to "middle-age problem" to "aging veteran."[20] Retirement from sport may perpetuate the descent.

It's easy to see why the "hothouse" environment of sport contributes to diffi-culties adjusting to life after sport. Most athletes begin competing during their school days. Their participation is sanctioned and reinforced by significant others, not only parents and coaches but leaders in the community. Success leads to prestige on the local, state, and regional levels: name and picture on the sports page and on the local television channel, maybe even mention in national publications like *Sports Illustrated.* This heady experience escalates as the star athlete is courted by prominent college coaches and then by profes-sional scouts. Once established as a professional athlete, public recognition can approach that afforded film and music celebrities. Even in sports without a pro-fessional venue, the young athlete is acclaimed and doted on. Eighteen-year-old Don Schollander won four Olympic gold medals and was voted best athlete in the world. He spoke at hundreds of banquets, assemblies, and press conferences, and became an international celebrity and world traveler before his 20th birth-day.[21] To Schollander's credit, he was able to adjust to private life. But many athletes struggle with this transition, whether it comes in their 20s or later.

Veterans tend to live in a state of denial. They hang on as long as they can. The social milieu of sport reinforces this mind-set. They may be unaware of the coach's plan to cut them from the team. Although their teammates usually see the "axe" approaching, the player concerned is often surprised and shocked. An athlete may suspect his career is in jeopardy by the nonverbal communications coming from the coaching staff or management. However, some degree of pretense is maintained (shared by the athlete himself). Ultimately, there is open acknowledgment that the career has ended.[22] Invariably, the athlete seems surprised. An Australian football player relates, "I was called into the clubhouse to meet with the coach and club manager; they told me that my services were no longer required. I was so shocked I couldn't say anything. They asked me if I was OK and I never heard from them again."[23]

Too much can be made of the athlete's early retirement. History professor Morris Mott—who played professional hockey in North America and Europe for 10 years—suggests that professional athletes are no different than other people who have to make career transitions. He points out that when people don't get admitted to law school or their business goes bankrupt, they learn to start all over. Mott has little sympathy for athletes who feel sorry for themselves because they have to begin a new career. "There are lots of people who start over," Mott notes.[24] Nevertheless, veteran athletes often delay making this transition as long as they can; they try to hang on for another year or two. As for starting over, the first thing many retired athletes think about is making a comeback.

"ONE-MORE-YEAR" SYNDROME

Before the final game of the 1971 World Series as Roberto Clemente was lacing his shoes; he called trainer Howie Haak to his side. Roberto confided, "Howie, you have been a good friend of mine over the years and I want you to be one of the first to know something. If we win today's game, I'm going to quit baseball." But a couple of hours later as the 37-year-old Clemente ran in from right field, he changed his mind. He rushed over to the stands and embraced his wife Vera who was crying with tears of joy. "Roberto," she said, "don't quit baseball. Please don't quit now, it's your life." His wife's words were portentous. Clemente decided to play for one more year.[25] He was killed in a plane crash three months after the end of the season. Tragedy had eclipsed his retirement.

Oriard compares athletes struggling with the "one-more-year syndrome" to compulsive gamblers who convince themselves that one more hand will make their fortune. He cites baseball players like Willie Mays and Mickey Mantle who played too long.[26] Josh Gibson was another case of someone not knowing when to quit. In 1946, the 35-year-old catcher was playing on ravaged knees, 40 pounds under his playing weight, a hollow image of his former self. He was drinking too much, suffering from chronic hypertension, and had spasms of dizziness. But Gibson tried to hold on, haunted by the specter of becoming a "has been."[27] It's a syndrome that infects athletes in all sports. Sands refers to athleter who, "play until they can't walk anymore, till their joints resemble leggos and they can't get through a day without painkillers."[28] Alcohol was Gibson's painkiller. He would die in his 30s.

The veteran Mickey Mantle, hobbled by aging, injured legs most certainly played too long. He should have taken his bow following the 1964 season. As his biographer put it, "Looking for a last hurrah, The Mick met old age coming 'round the bend. The result was not pretty."[29] Mantle would play another four years, but they were seasons of struggle. He batted .237 with 18 home runs in 1968. He was used as a sometimes first baseman to spare his beat-up legs while the fans continued to pay their tribute, but it made him uneasy. "It's all sentiment," he said. "I'm not sure I like that. They sure as hell aren't cheering me for my batting average." Mantle turned up at the Yankee's spring training camp in 1969 hoping for one more year, but it was evident that the legs were gone. Reluctantly, he conceded the obvious and retired before the season opened.[30]

Babe Ruth refused to give it up after 21 years of professional baseball. Following a contract dispute with the Yankees, he signed to play with the Boston Braves in 1935. The Babe didn't look good during spring training. He was fat at 245 pounds, almost 20 pounds overweight. The combination of weight and age made him almost immobile in the outfield, so they put him at first base. He had some early success during the season but then nothing more happened. He was slow on the bases and bad in the field. Not once did he play an entire game. The Braves lost game after game, and settled into last place. Booing from the stands became more audible. Ruth was angry and chagrined. He realized he was through, and in early May asked management to put him on the voluntary retirement list. "I made a mistake," Ruth conceded, "I never should have signed." It was a rather sad ending to a great career.[31]

Veteran ball players fall victim to the one-more-year syndrome; for boxers, it's always one more fight. They keep pursuing another victory in the ring until they have been punched silly. Muhammad Ali was typical of the fighter who didn't know when to quit. He retired reluctantly at age 39, "old" for a boxer. When he fought Larry Holmes in the Fall of 1980 he had nothing left, no jab, no legs, no reflexes. Ali suffered the first knockout of his career, quitting on his stool. One wag commented, "Ali still had his million-dollar punch. He got paid $8 million and threw eight punches all night."[32] Undeterred by this fiasco, Ali finally ended his career with an inglorious loss to Trevor Berbick in 1981.

Tennis is a less physically demanding sport, but most players have peaked by their early 30s. Bill Tilden was intent upon beating the odds. At age 60, he could be found most every day on the Southern California courts teaching and getting ready for the next tournament. In the weeks leading up to the 1953 U.S. pro championship in Cleveland, the gaunt old veteran worked diligently on his game even while suffering from a terrible cough that rattled his whole body. The coughing became so severe at times that he had to put down his racket and lean against the canvas for support. But there was no time or money for a doctor, so he "toughed it out." The night before the tournament some friends, the Andersons, invited Bill over for a going-away dinner. When Tilden didn't

show, the concerned host went to his apartment across town and had the land-
lady let him in. He found Big Bill dead across his bed, his bags packed.[33]

There's something about performing in front of the public that makes quitting seem unthinkable. Seventy-year-old singer Willie Nelson could be found
"on the road again" still performing for his fans. Stand-up comic Don Rickles
was doing 70 gigs a year in his 70s. Athletes share with stage performers a
reluctance to retire, but an athlete's talents fade early. Septuagenarians might
play the guitar and sing or tell jokes, but they can't run up and down a basketball court or a football field for two hours. It's true that Andy Varipapa was still
bowling at age 78, but he was the glaring exception to the rule.[34] The same
may be said for Satchel Paige, the 42-year-old major league rookie who continued to pitch into his 50s. Ben Hogan played in an occasional golf tournament in
his late 50s; but golf like, bowling, is relatively forgiving of age. Forty-year-old
athletes remain an anomaly.

Comebacks are a corollary to the one-more-year syndrome. Pitcher Dave
Dravecky titled his autobiography *Comeback,* to highlight his return to baseball
following cancer surgery on his arm.[35] Dravecky's effort seems heroic, as does
golfer Ben Hogan's return following his automobile accident;[36] just as often
comebacks are a matter of an athlete simply not knowing when to "hang it
up." Longtime Pittsburgh sportswriter Al Abrams lamented the great boxers
who attempted too many comebacks: "Sugar Ray Robinson fighting somebody
nobody knew, and Willie Pep fighting somebody nobody knew. Now here
were two of the greatest fighters of all time in their classes being degraded:
250 people in the crowd. They were fighting for a two-hundred and three-
hundred dollar purse. One comeback is okay. Maybe two. Not four or five."[37]

Thirty-six-year-old Joe Louis came out of retirement in 1950 in an attempt
to square his account with the U.S. Treasury Department in the matter of back
taxes. He won eight fights before a final humiliating defeat at the hands of a
young Rocky Marciano.[38] Marciano was one of those rare exceptions: a champion who retired from boxing in his early 30s at the peak of his career with the
title. He never seriously entertained the idea of a comeback. But for every
Marciano, there are a dozen Sugar Ray Robinsons. For the aging Jack Dempsey,
it was as if getting his "brains beat out" seemed better than living the life of a
"forgotten man." He reluctantly hung up his gloves in his mid-30s after a brief
flirtation with a comeback.[39]

As this chapter was being finalized, baseball pitcher Roger Clemens decided
to "unretire" for the fourth time and join the New York Yankees. It's a familiar
phenomenon in sports. Baseball scholar Neil Isaacs concludes: "When men's
lives are devoted to boys' games . . . to give them up is to acknowledge the end
of youth. . . . The recognition of mortality comes with greater force when maturity itself has been long postponed. The longer it takes to graduate from the
brotherhood, to put away the childish things—the stronger will be the pull to
stay or the shock of having to go."[40] But the reality finally sets in. Bill Bradley
observed that when an athlete's career is over, he can sense that his youth is

gone, along with the innocence that characterizes all games which at their root promote a prolonged adolescence. Now the athlete must face a world where awkward naiveté can no longer be overlooked.[41] Ken Dryden echoes Bradley's comment: "If it is true that a sports career prolongs adolescence, it is also true that when that career ends, it deposits a player into premature middle age. For while he was always older than he seemed, he is suddenly younger than he feels."[42]

The aging athlete doesn't so much *retire* from sport, as he *disengages* from it. This process of disengagement, the transformation from athlete to becoming something else, can be challenging, often disorienting, occasionally traumatic. Some make the transition better than others.

TRANSITION AND ADJUSTMENT

Athletes who retire voluntarily adjust better than those who try to hang on. However, the overwhelming majority of athletes are forced out by coaches or management. One study found that about 5 percent of professional hockey players retire voluntarily.[43] Most athletes fight it out to the bitter end. The NFL's George Blanda was forced to retire from football at age 48! Such tenacity is not surprising given that one of the signature traits of a successful athlete is refusing to be a "quitter." This ethic is instilled from an early age and explains why so few quit voluntarily when their careers are winding down. Even when they can get past the stigma of giving up sports, athletes lacking education or "real-world" job skills postpone retirement because they see no other options available.[44]

However, there's little doubt that the most agonizing aspect of making the transition from athlete to ex-athlete is accepting that one's life in sport is over. The figures of speech employed by athletes facing the end are telling. The NHL's Gary Dornhoefer remarks, "When the bubble bursts, you became very quickly just like everyone else. It's the feeling of having your feet hacked out from under you."[45] Ken Dryden reflects on his last playoff series: "I kept looking back, for I needed a guide. Nothing in the present was making sense. I felt like a chess player at a scrambled board."[46] Tim Green recalls, "I saw the end of football as kind of like a cliff that I would either jump or be pushed off of."[47] Robert Sands describes the end of his college football career: "I experienced a free fall that plunged me deep into a natural state of competitive withdrawal."[48] Sportswriter Jimmy Cannon sums it up: "[A] lot of times famous men quit baseball and it's like they fell off the rim of the world."[49]

Indeed, retirement is experienced as a kind of death. Kubler-Ross's five-stage model of a dying person's progression toward acceptance of impending death has been applied to ending a sports career: *denial*: "No, it's not true, I'm still fit." *anger*: "Why me, why now?" *bargaining*: "I'll do anything to stay in the game." *depression*: "I can't bear the thought of not playing." And finally, *acceptance*: "It's happened, my sport career is over, what now?"[50] Bradley notes that by age 35 something in the athlete dies, a fundamental passion dies. The athlete rarely recuperates. He approaches the end of his playing days the way old people approach death. He puts his affairs in order.[51] But the athlete differs from the octogenarian on his deathbed; he must recover from the loss and go on living.

When athletes give up their careers, they deal with intense feelings of separation from teammates and from the crowd. Their reaction may resemble a combination of home sickness and withdrawal. Following his final season, Babe Ruth haunted spring training camp. He was uncomfortable being anywhere else. But he finally realized that no one wanted him around.[52] Most athletes eventually come to this realization. A retired Gary Dornhoefer observes, "You develop relationships with your teammates but I find that they are very shallow. Once your career is over, everyone goes their separate ways. For the most part, the only thing you have in common was hockey."[53]

Former teammates and management often treat the recently retired athlete like a nonperson. Dornhoefer remembers, "Phone calls didn't get returned, so-called friends were too busy with their own problems...the doors that were open were suddenly closed."[54] A retired Australian football player comments, "When the club decides they no longer need you, they just don't want to know you; in fact, no one wants to know you."[55] As if to punctuate his point, he is quoted anonymously. The intense bond among athletes often cannot survive retirement. Only teammates share it; others, including former players, are outsiders.[56] Jim Bouton put it bluntly, "When a guy got cut, we'd say he died."[57]

Boxers don't have teammates. Muhammad Ali missed the crowds. In retirement, he couldn't give up the public attention (and the public couldn't give him up). Despite suffering from Parkinson's syndrome, he continued to make numerous public appearances. The private audiences also persisted. Lonnie Ali commented that the most difficult thing about being his wife was the stream of strangers in their lives. "Muhammad loves people and loves having people around him." She rationalizes, "Muhammad belongs to the World." But clearly Lonnie resents the imposition. She protests, "When we're traveling, they're always up in our hotel room. Of course, Muhammad lets them in. And I don't care if it's a suite or a single room, either I have to stay in the bedroom with the door closed or be in the same room, and I lose all my privacy and freedom." At home it was the same story. Ali maintained an open-door policy. Whoever showed up, he invited them in.[58]

Identity as an athlete is heavily socialized, and much of this social network disappears when an athlete retires. At that point, athletes may rely heavily on the women in their lives for support during disengagement from sport. Arthur Ashe was fortunate in this regard. He describes how his wife Jeanne helped him through the transition:

> She had been listening and watching me and anticipating my feelings through the many signals of distress I was obviously sending out, even if I was not fully aware

of...most of them. In the fall of 1978, on a date that had no special significance for us, she presented me with a gift of a book, *The Seasons of a Man's Life....* She inscribed it, "For my husband, with love, Jeanne." It was a timely gift.[59]

For married athletes, family can fill the space that was occupied by teammates and fans. The relationship should be reciprocal; there's no longer any excuse for being an absentee husband and father. Retired hockey player Ted Irvine acknowledges, "My wife and son paid the price for my hockey career. I was irresponsible as far as leading a family life. I'm getting closer to my son and now we relate to each other more and more. My family life is better."[60] But not all athletes make this adjustment. Mickey Mantle's wife Merlyn hung onto the idea that retirement from baseball meant that her husband would become more of a homebody. But Mickey wasn't cut out for domestic life. He would grow restless and bored. It's as if he had no practice being a family man during all those years on the road. His four sons rarely saw a father who was on the golf course more than he was in the house.[61]

Dave Dravecky accepted his retirement with less resistance than most. His view of sport and life had been tempered by a serious bout with cancer, and in some ways adversity made the transition easier. Two days before announcing his official retirement from baseball, he sat at home with his wife Janice and caught the end of the movie *The Natural* on television. Actor Robert Redford, playing an old ballplayer, comes back for one last game and dramatically hits a towering home run high off the outfield wall, striking the light pole, and shattering the bulbs so that sparks rain down like fireworks. The ball keeps traveling in a segue through space and time into the mitt of the ballplayer's son who is playing catch with him. Dravecky realizes, "That's me. That's my career. I'd had a chance to hit one last home run, so to speak. Now I would be playing catch with my kids, just as my dad had done with me."[62]

Dravecky's experience underscores that point that as ex-athletes make adjustments in their relationship with others, they also must deal with the infirmities and health problems that accompany them into retirement. Gary Dornhoefer is a textbook case. The former Boston Bruin earned a reputation for sacrificing his body on the ice. Indeed, he never played a full season due to injuries. A retired Dornhoefer comments, "Today, I have difficulty walking 18 holes of golf or playing tennis or racquetball because of my knees. Year after year, the knees get worse." He reflects, "The experiences from fifteen years of playing professionally I wouldn't trade. But if I had a choice of doing it all over again, I wouldn't do it. Maybe I'd try the golf tour; you don't break legs doing that."[63]

A legacy of injuries isn't the only impairment that retired athletes face; they may "let themselves go" through inactivity, overeating, and indulging in alcohol or drugs. Mickey Mantle got his only exercise in a golf cart, gained weight, developed ulcers, and finally destroyed his liver due to heavy drinking.[64] Mantle wasn't the only athlete who used alcohol to deaden the pain that accompanies disengagement from sport. Baseball retiree Ty Cobb drank too much; so did Jim Thorpe. Mark Heaslep drank and used cocaine after his career in the NHL ended. This only added to his problems. He notes, "At one time I had a criminal lawyer, a divorce lawyer, and a tax lawyer." Eventually, he entered drug rehab to deal with his addictions. Only then did life after sport begin in earnest.[65]

Other facts of life make the transition into retirement challenging. A career in sport offers unique working hours and a generous salary. Former athletes have to adjust to a regular job and a normal workday. Jean Pronovost who played professional hockey for Pittsburgh, Atlanta, and Washington explains, "The biggest adjustment has been the time. As a hockey player, I spent about two hours at the rink and then it was free time. And in the summer, you had four or five months off." Now retired, Jean works an eight-and-a-half-hour day all year round.[66] Commenting on his early posthockey career, Ted Irvine concedes, "I never accepted responsibility when I quit the game because I didn't know what responsibility was. I didn't know how to get up every day and go to work. I felt that if I worked one day and sold something, I took three days off and patted myself on the back. I didn't know how to handle being out of hockey."[67]

There are related adjustments to a job outside of sport. Former Philadelphia Flyer Don Saleski notes that in hockey, "After every game you could evaluate yourself, the coaches and fans let you know where you stood. In the business I'm involved in, you close possibly four or five deals a year. So, there was a long wait between report cards." Saleski was placed in a training program running a vending route. He recalls, "I remember being out at Honeywell Corporation in my first week. People walked by looking at me filling vending machines and saying, 'Isn't that Don Saleski?' I had to swallow a little pride." Ex-athletes must make financial adjustments along with the loss of status. Ending a sports career usually means a cut in pay and a lower standard of living. Saleski jokes about his new job, "When I got my first paycheck, I thought it was meal money for a road trip!" [68]

Few athletes are able to live off their accumulated earnings when they retire. Throughout most of the 20th century only a tiny percentage of major league baseball players were what could be called "set for life" at the end of their playing careers. The idea that sport in and of itself will lead to upward mobility, socially or professionally, is largely a myth.[69] Many athletes have to go out in the world and scrap for a living at something usually less pleasant than playing sports. Few have postponed retirement longer than Satchel Paige, who pitched his last game at age 60. When writer William Price Fox visited him for an interview in 1965, the retired pitcher was out of work, out of money, and looking for another gig to keep the kids fed. He gladly accepted a loan to get his car out of hock.[70]

The great majority of athletes don't play as long as Satchel Paige, but many of them attempt to maintain contact with their sport when their playing days end. They try to find a way "back into the game." Retired athletes look for positions as coaches, scouts, or in management. A retired Babe Ruth coached briefly with the Dodgers. Other retired athletes take positions with the media covering sport. DiMaggio did a short stint as a batting instructor and a broadcaster for the

Yankees. ESPN hired Bill Romanowski as a draft-day analyst. Deion Sanders is prominent among recent ex-athletes who have become successful TV sports commentators. Of 32 former members of the 1980 champion Philadelphia Phillies located by *Sports Illustrated* 25 years later, among those still working, two out of three had careers connected in some way with sport.

Ron Ellis played for the Toronto Maple Leafs for 15 years. He reflects on his disengagement from professional hockey. Ellis recalls that the hardest part was trying to find a part of him that enjoyed doing something other than playing hockey. He remembers saying to himself, "I need to find that thing that's going to give me that same amount of satisfaction, the same drive and willingness to get up each morning and work at it."[71] Making the adjustment to the world outside sport even affects those who have never played at the professional level. Meggyesy remarks, "You see a lot of guys whose life actually stopped after their last college game. They hang on by becoming insurance salesmen and the like, selling their former image as a football player."[72] The label "Rabbit Run syndrome" derives from John Updike's series of novels about a fictional high school basketball star "Rabbit" Angstrom. Rabbit represents those athletes who reach the top when they are young and then have nowhere to go. They continue to live in the past—school sports heroes who spend the remainder of their lives in fatal decline.[73]

Not all athletes become Rabbit Angstrom. Many are able to make the transition to ex-athlete with a minimum of angst. The veteran striker Pelé talked to his young teammate Shep Messing about adjusting to life without soccer. He reflects on what it will be like to stop playing after 22 years in the game: "That part will die. But it's okay, because another life is born. In my mind, it will be hard. I think someday I will wake up and get my things and go to the stadium, because this is what I do all of my life. Now, I must remember to go to the office. I don't know how I will like this...because...my life is soccer."[74]

Jackie Robinson found it easier than most to hang up his uniform and "go to the office." In his own words, he "never looked back." The former Dodger went on to become a successful business executive. He made the adjustment from performing in front of a crowd to satisfying a corporate board. In this regard, the ex-athlete is like a butterfly caught in reverse metamorphosis; he must shed his brilliant identity and take on a new less flattering one.

THE EX-ATHLETE IN SEARCH OF IDENTITY

Retirement isn't inevitable in all professions. Pablo Picasso spent virtually his entire life painting. He was never an "ex-painter," just as the prolific Henry James was never an "ex-writer." Ludwig van Beethoven continued to compose music even when he lost his hearing. He completed the Ninth Symphony at age 54, three years before he died. A clever joke has it that Beethoven spent his entire life *composing* and his entire death *decomposing*. For athletes, the decomposing may commence this side of the grave. By definition, an athlete becomes an ex-athlete when he can no longer perform. Rare are the Bill Tildens who die with their bags packed for the next tournament. Most athletes are left to find a new identity beyond the sports arena.

Tim Green proclaims, "I can *be* an attorney until the day I die, but I can't *be* a football player. You either play football or you do not play football."[75] A recently retired Green relates an incident at a coffee shop when he was approached by a young boy who came up to him holding a football card to be autographed. "Are you Tim Green?" he asked, "the football player?" The former defensive end recalls, "I felt that pocket around my heart filling with adrenaline.... 'I used to play football,' I heard myself say to the boy as I scratched out my name. As I handed the card back to that boy I took one more fleeting look at the image of myself, the ferocious one, and realized that I would never be that again, never be that football player." "They say that football players die two deaths," Green reflects. "The first death comes when their career finally ends.... And in that moment, with those words, I think I died my first death."[76]

Pat Jordan gave up a baseball career in his late 20s and became a professional writer. He admits, "I still think of myself not as a writer who once pitched, but as a pitcher who happens to be writing."[77] An ex-athlete may continue to identify with his sports career; he most certainly will be identified with it by others. A retired Jackie Robinson, despite his intentions to establish a new identity, was routinely introduced as "the former Brooklyn Dodger." DiMaggio remained "Joltin' Joe" and "The Yankee Clipper" even in his obituaries.

Retiring athletes differ widely in how they adjust to the change of identity. Three former Cincinnati Reds provide a study in contrasts. In an interview with *Newsday*, infielder Joe Morgan made the following comment about Pete Rose: "At the end, I don't want to be around him when it comes. I know what it will do to him." Morgan continues, "When I'm through I'm still Joe Morgan. He won't be Pete Rose.... You know the movie where the guy sold his soul. Pete would do it over and over again." Catcher Johnny Bench echoed Morgan's remarks. "You soon learn that you can only play so long, then you've got to live the other half of your life. But with Pete, you wonder if he could do anything outside of baseball and be happy." Reds trainer Larry Starr observed, "I don't think Johnny could visualize why anyone would want to play baseball for twenty-five years. To him, baseball was his job. It was his business. And Pete couldn't visualize how anyone could feel that way."[78]

From the time they are in Pee Wee league, athletes are immersed in their sport to the exclusion of other activities. They develop an identity composed almost entirely from their involvement in sport. When their sports career ends, they have lost the one activity through which they have built a lifelong sense of identity. The role of athlete is never totally eclipsed.[79] The past vies with the present for the soul of the erstwhile gladiator. Pat Conroy found a new identity as a successful writer. Yet he always carried a torch for the incarnation of his former self—the young man in basketball shorts. In his memoir, he writes about the reunion of his college basketball team during homecoming at The Citadel:

> On Saturday evening, we gathered in the dining room of the Lodge Alley Inn, well dressed, successful, and middle-aged. It was the first time we had come together as a team since our final meal in Charlotte when we lost to Richmond in overtime. I went to the middle of the room...putting a cassette in the VCR. We sat with the women in our lives to watch the only piece of film I had discovered of my team in action during that dismal year.... In the grainy film of a handheld camera, the year suddenly materialized as my team, so beautiful in their prime, were seen running up and down the court.[80]

Conroy's book is extraordinary in its ability to bridge the dual (and dueling) identities that grip the aging former athlete. In contrast, most sportswriting skirts the issue of retirement and the identity crisis that accompanies it. Few athletes write about their careers after the fact, and the great majority of sports biographies are published *during* an athlete's career, often in mid-career or following a championship season. Arthur Ashe's *Days of Grace* is that rare book from an athlete who reflects on his postsports life. The book was published a dozen years after Ashe's playing career had ended at age 37 and following his diagnosis with AIDS (and as fate would have it, the year of his death).[81] Likewise, Al Stump's *Cobb* offers an unforgettable firsthand account of a retired ball player in his twilight years.[82]

The interview format has been successfully exploited by Michael A. Smith in *Life After Hockey*.[83] While an assistant manager with the Winnipeg Jets, he surveyed 22 former hockey players. The retired athletes talk about their playing careers, their transition from the hockey world to the "real world," and their posthockey careers. Successes and failures are discussed honestly and candidly. The following section owes a debt to sports writers and athletes who have written candidly about life after sport.

REPRESENTATIVE RETIREMENTS

The narratives of athletes in retirement are suggestive of a Sergio Leone film title: some are good, some are bad, and a few are downright ugly. The specter of Joe Louis has haunted boxers nearing the end of their careers. The popular heavyweight retired from the ring in 1949, followed by a brief comeback terminated in 1951. Louis's 30 years in retirement were riddled with major and minor tragedies, including a little-known drug problem and episodes of paranoia. The ex-champ's chronic financial difficulties ranged from an embarrassing court appearance for back traffic fines to tax liens filed by the federal government that eventually reached $1 million. His efforts to make a living became an ongoing misadventure. After attempting some rather inept business deals, Louis entered the professional wrestling circuit where he suffered intermittent humiliations and a career-ending chest injury. Two decades later he was employed as an official "host" at Caesar's Palace, the Las Vegas casino.[84] The former champ was then appropriated as a "rented celebrity" by political campaigns when this author met him in the mid-1970s. Louis's financial problems followed him to the grave; he died insolvent a month before his 67th birthday. Former ring opponent and friend Max Schmeling paid for his funeral.

Jim Thorpe could just as well serve as the "poster boy" for failed retirements. The man who could do almost anything on an athletic field had few coping skills for dealing with the world beyond. His early schooling and college experience had done little to prepare him for a job outside sport. He wasn't a student-athlete at Carlisle College, but simply an athlete. He routinely cut classes and acquired few vocational or academic skills. Despite his achievements in track and field at the Stockholm Olympics and an impressive career in professional sports—including appointment as president of the American Professional Football Association—his athletic career became increasingly marginal. Stints in the minor leagues devolved into exhibitions and demeaning personal appearances such as fronting for American Indian dancers. He allowed himself to be exploited for publicity by various causes. There seemed to be no end to such ventures to trade on his past. Thorpe toured the desultory professional wrestling circuit for a while. These enterprises offered him diminishing financial returns over the remainder of his life. The jobs available to him fell on a descending scale. When he was photographed digging ditches in Los Angeles, the newspapers referred to him as "poor Jim." A lack of steady employment plunged him into financial distress.[85]

Thorpe's personal life was equally ruinous; his habits self-destructive. When a Los Angeles Judge fined him for drunk driving, he was reprimanded and reminded that he was "a legend to our youth." His continuing bouts with drinking only reinforced the uncomplimentary stereotypes. Back in Shawnee, Oklahoma, the police had to rope and tie him to get him to jail. Saloons also had a tendency to expose his streak of gullibility, leaving him as easy mark for a loan if he had money on him. Thorpe's later years played out in a dismal sequence of odd jobs, unpaid bills, bar fights, and broken homes. He passed through three marriages. His favorite pastimes of hunting and fishing with his sons appear to be singular positive elements in his retirement.[86]

Another Olympic hero would cope somewhat better with retirement from sport. For Jesse Owens, the transition came in his early 20s. His career as a competitive runner was virtually ended when he was banned from amateur competition by a vindictive Amateur Athletic Union. It was one thing to harness his formidable talents to win four gold medals; testing himself against the demands of the workaday world would prove more challenging. In the months following his return from Berlin, Owens was offered national tours and movie contracts. He traveled all over the United States, trading his fame for whatever money he could make. No single job amounted to much, but the total added up. He bounced around from banquet to radio broadcast to endorsement opportunities for consumer products. Other promotions like racing against horses seemed demeaning, but he did it for the money. He might earn a $1,000 check at some promotional events, but even these offers soon faded. A permanent career proved harder to come by. Owens observes, "After I came home from the 1936 Olympics with my four medals, it became increasingly apparent that everyone was going to slap me on the back, want to shake my hand or have me up to their suite. But no one was going to offer me a job."[87]

Owens continued on the road in a variety of barnstorming adventures. Despite a lack of musical education or talent, he toured the country as a band leader under the patronage of entertainer Bill "Bojangles" Robinson in the late 1930s. He then organized several touring sports teams (basketball, softball) which would play exhibition games. During breaks in the games, he would run races against the local town's speedster. In 1940, Owens lost his dry cleaning business when the IRS demanded payment of back taxes. At age 27, he returned to Ohio State to finish his degree; however, poor grades kept him from ever receiving a diploma. He worked in the personnel department of Ford Motor Company during World War II, and then went back to barnstorming, this time with the Harlem Globetrotters in 1950.[88]

And so it went. Owens held public relations positions for clothing factories, insurance companies, and dry cleaners while plugging a variety of products on radio and television. These commercial ventures eventually led him to form his own public relations company. Later, he would find a niche in public service. Jesse worked for the Chicago Boys Club and served as a goodwill ambassador for the U.S. State Department. He seemed to find his professional legs as life progressed. Unlike Thorpe's retirement, Owens' had something of a silver lining.[89]

Babe Ruth was almost twice as old as Owens when he retired, having played his last season with the Boston Braves at age 41. He entered retirement with a show of optimism. An upbeat Babe phoned sportswriter and friend Grantland Rice and bellowed, "Get out your golf clubs, kid. I'm ready for you now." The Babe told his friends that he planned to play a lot of golf, but also hinted that he would like to manage. He wanted to stay close to the game. However, baseball executives were leery of hiring a man to manage a team who had always struggled to manage himself. For a brief period in 1938, the Brooklyn Dodgers hired him as a coach mostly to stimulate attendance, but the reality was that he was finished with baseball, and baseball with him.[90]

Away from baseball, Ruth played cards, bowled, hunted, and fished, but he normally could be found hanging out at the golf club. Often, he took his meals there. His biographer writes:

> Golf became something of a passion...and he played as often as he could.... Often, he would leave his apartment in the morning, stop at the butcher's on Ninth Avenue, pick up a nice steak, drive to the course, give the steak to the cook at the

club and have two or three drinks over the steak at lunch and then play golf. [Following the ninth hole] Ruth's foursome would usually pause at the bar where Ruth would have one or two more. And then go on to complete the round.[91]

Bitter about being snubbed by baseball, Ruth went to relatively few games. He became increasingly discontent with retirement. At home, he listened to the radio a great deal and worked at being a husband and father to Claire and his daughters, but he wasn't used to domestic life. He missed baseball, and it hurt that no one wanted him any more. He never seriously tried to find something meaningful to do outside the game. The Babe's health continued to deteriorate following a life of hard living. He held on for a decade before succumbing to cancer at age 53.[92]

Many athletes experience withdrawal when they are forced by age or infirmity to leave the game. An ailing Lou Gehrig retired at age 36. The former Yankee "hangs around" for a while, sitting in the dugout watching the game with his old teammates. But he soon feels out of place and pursues other interests. Lou "takes up music," his wife's passion. The two attend concerts and the opera. The couple go on drives in the countryside entertaining friends and family. For a vocation, Gehrig tries his hand as a customer's man for a brokerage firm, but it didn't work out. Everyone seems to want to help. Endorsement deals are offered to him; syndicated newspaper articles are published under his name. But Gehrig never seems to find comfort in his brief retirement, haunted by a degenerative disease that inevitably took its toll. Lou died prematurely in the fourth decade of his life.[93]

During Joe DiMaggio's long retirement, the ex-Yankee slugger was able to make a living off his name. This began in public relations jobs with business interests and on golf tours. Joe took a position with a company that supplied merchandise to U.S. Army posts. His job essentially was to play golf with colonels and generals so that they could drop his name to their friends, while he enticed them to turn their business to his employer. There were more lucrative opportunities ahead. By 1989, DiMaggio was commanding $40,000–50,000 a day for autograph shows and memorabilia sales. He would sign baseball cards, baseballs, and pictures at $150 each, occasionally netting up to $100,000 for his appearance. He also did television ads for Mr. Coffee. In short, the retired Joe DiMaggio "went into the business of being Joe DiMaggio."[94]

While DiMaggio had a reputation for being tightfisted with money, the retired Tod Sloan spent it faster than he could make it. The flamboyant jockey still had some $300,000 in "ready money" when he was banned from racing in Britain and the United States. He soon lost $100,000 of it on an ill-advised scheme to set up an automobile factory. By 1903, still in Europe, he found himself hard up for cash in great part due to his gambling. He had to borrow from a friend to enter a trap shooting tournament, his current passion. He then tried buying and selling horses, something that he knew, but found that there was little money to be made. In 1904, he returned to the United States to make a career on the vaudeville stage. He enjoyed a brief success with help from George M. Cohan and Oscar Hammerstein. He married an actress, soon was working as a bookie and hustling money at billiard parlors. There were lawsuits and further financial disasters. Sloan's retirement brought on one scheme—and one calamity—after another. Few ex-athletes endured a more colorful life. He was "Yankee Doodle Dandy" with the final act alternating between farce and tragedy.[95]

The inability to handle money has framed the retirement of more than a few athletes. While they are competing, their finances often are handled by wives, managers, or agents. There's little in their backgrounds to suggest they are prepared to become accomplished financial managers in retirement. Boxers are notorious for making millions of dollars in the ring, only to find that all the money is gone when they retire. Ballplayers can be equally susceptible to this failing. Mickey Mantle was "taken" by a con man who persuaded him to invest in a nonexistent insurance company. It was the first of a series of investment adventures that followed him into his retirement. In 1969, Mantle and New York Jets quarterback Joe Namath invested in a personnel agency called, "Mantle Men and Namath Girls" which went belly up after three years, as did a chain of apparel stores in which Mantle had invested. Several real estate investments also fizzled.[96]

Ty Cobb was the exception among ballplayers in managing money. The Tiger outfielder made his fortune through astute investments and held on to most of it. Cobb began buying stock and commodity futures during his playing days. In his retirement, he continued to watch the Dow-Jones average and would phone financial experts around the country to determine good buys on the stock market. Notably, his holdings included 20,000 shares of Coca Cola. According to *Sporting News,* Cobb was worth $12 million when he died in 1961.[97] If only money could buy happiness.

Cobb had a rather miserable retirement despite his wealth. The irascible recluse spent his latter years in an isolated 10-room lakeside lodge near Lake Tahoe, California, honing his image for his biographers and railing against the Fates. Time grew so heavy for the retired ballplayer that he would wad up newspaper and toss it from a distance into a wastebasket by the hour. No one could stand to live with him for very long. Two wives left him, as did several butlers, housekeepers, chauffeurs, nurses, and mistresses. His health suffered from his own neglect and indulgences. He continued to drink between a pint and a quart of whiskey on a daily basis in spite of doctors' warnings. He also downed a large collection of pills for his various maladies including diabetes and ultimately the cancer which ended his life at age 74.[98]

Josh Gibson never had to face the challenges of retirement, having died of a stroke at 35. But there was every indication that he would have reacted poorly to a life away from baseball. He was coping badly with his fading years, drinking too much and letting himself get out of shape. Two of Gibson's teammates would endure their retirements with mixed success. Sammy Bankhead was

Gibson's closest friend during their playing days in the Negro League and the Latin American winter league. Sammy went on to manage several teams after his playing career ended, and became the first black manager in white organized baseball. Finally he left the game and retired to Pittsburg, where he worked for the city for some 20 years. He was an avid reader who would devour the magazines and books he could get his hands on. But mostly, Sammy drank. He spent a lot of his leisure time with his buddies at the local tavern on Wylie Avenue. Much of the conversation revolved around the old days of baseball, with Sammy as the self-appointed arbiter of disputes. Although Sammy enjoyed talking about the game, the old shortstop stayed away from ballparks no matter what the occasion or how compelling the invitation. It seemed that watching a major league game was too painful, something he couldn't bear. He feigned disinterest. The antipathy was so ingrained that on one occasion after obtaining tickets for a Pirates game for himself and some friends, he left after the first inning and quietly went home.[99]

Satchel Paige was another sports hero who attempted to live off his reputation in retirement. After his short stint in the major leagues beginning in the late 1940s (when he was in his early 40s), he drifted in and out of baseball as a player and coach on minor league teams or with barnstorming clubs like the Indianapolis Clowns (the club he was with when this author saw him play). As he got older, he would make token appearances on the mound. His retirement had its high points and its lean periods. He got a part in a Western movie and ran unsuccessfully for state office. Mostly, he was left looking for another gig to tide him over. By 1965, he was out of work and out of money. His induction into the Baseball Hall of Fame in 1969 briefly led to more lucrative popularity. He spoke at dinners and conventions, made television appearances and did endorsements, and now could ask for up-front money for interviews. But his reborn fame proved less than sustaining. Satchel was always coy about how old he was. When asked, the ageless wonder would reply with his classic quip, "Age is a question of mind over matter. If you don't mind, it doesn't matter." Stoicism seemed a fitting disposition for a man who could no longer live off his talent or his name.[100]

The above accounts reinforce the general impression that ex-athletes struggle with retirement. The reality is more nuanced. The majority of professional hockey players that Smith interviewed experienced a relatively smooth transition from sport into a second career and quickly got on with their lives.[101] Michael Oriard who went from the NFL to a successful career in academia, observed that many of his former teammates were remarkably successful in developing their lives after football.[102] One does find accounts of successful retirements among athletes.

Jackie Robinson retired at age 37 while he still was able to play competitively. He was contemplating his future in baseball when offered the position of personnel director for a popular chain of coffee shops. He decided to accept the position and purchased a home in Connecticut. Robinson had already taken on an assignment with the NAACP to chair their Fight for Freedom Fund. Despite his failing health from complications of diabetes, and the personal tragedy surrounding Jackie Jr., his 16 years of retirement were fulfilling. Jackie was a devoted husband and father who found time to be with his wife Rachel and his three children despite a demanding schedule. He initiated several entrepreneurial ventures including a successful bank and insurance company. He devoted an inordinate amount of time to the civil rights campaign. In addition, he did volunteer work for charities, wrote newspaper columns, and worked on national political campaigns. He never looked to baseball with nostalgia or regrets, although he did a short stint as a game commentator for ABC television and often spoke out on baseball's reluctance to hire black managers.[103]

Robinson was unusual among athletes of his era in having gone to college. Of all athletes, boxers tend to be the least educated and this often leads to problematic retirements. However, even this sport can boast of successful retirees. After his release from prison following a trumped-up conviction of the Mann Act, a resilient Jack Johnson described his retirement years from boxing as "modestly successful and happy ones." The ambitious and talented Johnson went on lecturing tours, became a small investor and sold stocks and bonds for a while, devoted a portion of his life to theatrical work, and acted as an advertising representative. He was a fanatic about personal fitness and couldn't stay away from boxing entirely. On occasion, he would engage in exhibition matches outside the United States up into his late 40s. For a man who had led such a tumultuous public and private life during his boxing career, he was able to endure his retirement with a surprising amount of equanimity.[104]

After heavyweight champion Jack Dempsey reluctantly gave up on his career in the ring, he found work as an occasional actor and part-time wrestling referee. These occupations kept a roof over his head during the Great Depression. He then joined the Coast Guard while in his middle 40s. Later, he would spend much of his time at his prominent restaurant opposite Madison Square Garden until it closed in 1974. Jack seemed to enjoy his later years hobnobbing with his prominent Broadway patrons.[105] Dempsey's ring opponent Gene Tunney was the first heavyweight champion to retire with the title. After hanging up his gloves in 1928, Tunney married, went into business, traveled widely, and studied art and literature. He remains extraordinary among retired athletes in cultivating such refined tastes.[106]

Although he retired tardily, former heavyweight champion Muhammad Ali made the best of his retirement amidst failing health. Despite suffering from Parkinson's Syndrome, the gregarious boxer found it difficult to step out of the public eye. He would spend as many as 200 days per year on the road, and made a substantial income through public appearances and by attending autograph and sports memorabilia shows. In 1996, he was invited to light the torch at the Summer Olympic Games in Atlanta. Later, he would appear before U.S. Congress to help lobby for research money for Parkinson's.[107] Eventually, his public appearances became less frequent because of his physical deterioration. The aging champion's decline brings to mind the epigraph offered by boxing aficionado Norman Mailer: "Hard training as a fighter grows older seems to speak of the dull deaths of the brightest cells in all the favorite organs."[108] Ali would retire with his fourth wife Lonnie to a comfortable life on their farm in southern Michigan.

Tennis champ Arthur Ashe devoted much of his retired years to a variety of political and social causes including justice for African Americans, opposition to South Africa's apartheid, and the U.S. policy toward Haitians seeking asylum. In 1988, he discovered he had been infected with HIV from a blood transfusion during heart surgery. He utilized this personal tragedy to enlighten the public about the mounting AIDS epidemic. Ashe's schedule during retirement was full to the point of being frenetic, packed with speaking engagements, business enterprises, and the forming of foundations—in addition to days on the golf course. Indeed, the reader of his memoir suspects that the busyness may be a defense against the void of contemplating his fragile mortality. He is the rare athlete who entered into psychotherapy for a short time after retiring. Ashe lived with a sense of purpose and equanimity that eludes many former athletes.[109]

Golfer Ben Hogan stands in contrast to the gregarious Ashe. The inveterate workaholic was forced to quit playing full time in his 40s because of a heart condition. He is among those athletes who seemed to adjust to the end of his professional career with a degree of resignation. The introverted Texan kept up his business interests but abhorred his "ceremonial" status in the golf world. He avoided travel and remained the "loner" he always had been. Hogan's daily routine followed a well-worn path. He would spend two hours in the office from 10 to noon; then lunch at Shady Oaks Country Club, eating alone at a table for eight overlooking the greens. This was followed by a game of golf or practice if the weather was warm. On the weekends, Hogan would come to the course in his golf clothing and watch football games on TV.[110]

Tolstoy wrote, "Happy families are all alike; every unhappy family is unhappy in its own way." The opposite seems true for retired athletes. Happy retirements can be as dissimilar as those of ring opponents Jack Dempsey and Gene Tunney, as antipodal as the lifestyles of the gregarious Arthur Ashe and the introverted Ben Hogan. Unhappy retirements, on the other hand, reveal common elements. These include the lack of a meaningful vocation or avocation, a sense of aimlessness, abuse of alcohol or other drugs, and failure to adjust to a more modest standard of living. Living off of one's name proves a dicey proposition. Married retirees err in adopting the golf course or the local bar as their home, and choosing the company of male cronies or fawning young women over their families.

The truth is that retirement from sport is distinct from that of most every other profession. The obvious difference is that it occurs 30–40 years earlier. In this sense, it is less a retirement than a transition to the next phase of adult life. Retirement from sport also means making the conversion from public life to private life. The shift from the limelight to the twilight can be disorienting. Team sport athletes have to adjust to life outside the organization; they must break with teammates and the paternalistic reach of management. Finally, the ex-athlete, like all retirees, must deal with the assault on personal identity which is so closely tied to vocation in American society. The effort required to make these adjustments may be heroic, but there is nothing heroic about retirement itself.

The traditional hero accepted an early death because his life, consecrated and magnified by death, passed into immortality. In contrast, contemporary sports heroes live on to reappear sporadically in Old Timers Games and at Hall of Fame ceremonies. The heroic image from their playing days is muted by the reality of decline into middle age and senescence. The sleek, trim champion is replaced by the paunchy imitation of his former self. As Tim Morris observes, the sports hero has a history and he has (ominously) a future. From the moment he has no future, he is history.[111] Novelist and sport biographer William Brashler expresses it more poetically: "Old ballplayers do die, over and over again, in ninth innings past and future. Somehow the last man is always retired, the field empties, and the shouting ends."[112]

The author's generation savors the romantic image of film actor Gary Cooper portraying Lou Gehrig, crippled by a disease which would carry his name, taking his final bow with superhuman dignity and grace as the camera pans the adoring crowd in Yankee Stadium. In *The Quiet Hero,* biographer Frank Graham glosses over the clinical details of Gehrig's decline.[113] The impression instilled by popular movies and books is that sports heroes don't have an afterlife. Like General MacArthur's old soldier, they just "fade away." The reality proves more stark.

The ex-athlete tends to make one of three choices. He places his athletic accomplishments in perspective and moves on to the next phase of his life much as Jackie Robinson did; or he adds to his normal misery and that of others in one of two ways: he retreats into the past and thrives on the glory of yesteryear *a la* Satchel Paige, or he overestimates his intellect and ignores his limitations, while attempting to capitalize on his heroic achievements in sport in the manner of a young Jesse Owens. A more mature Owens was able to adjust to the realities of retirement; Paige never did.[114]

A career in sport can be a hurdle or it can be a launching pad. A retired Jim Thorpe floundered like a fish out of water; Pete Rose spent the first season of his retirement in a prison cell; Mickey Mantle dedicated this chapter of his life to drinking himself into an early grave. In contrast, yachtsman Ted Turner docked his sailboat and founded a national television network; Bill Bradley left the NBA, entered politics, and became a U.S. Senator; Ken Dryden rose from hockey goalie to Minister of Social Development for the liberal government in Canada. Arthur Ashe found in tennis the key to living and dying with dignity.

9

CONCLUSIONS

Baseball executive Branch Rickey once exclaimed to his son, "I am an educated man. . . . And I like to believe that I am an intelligent man. . . . Then will you please tell me, why in the name of common sense, I spent four mortal hours today conversing with a person named Dizzy Dean?"[1] It probably goes without saying that Mr. Rickey wasn't interested in reading the life story of his star pitcher. Apparently others have been, as Dean's exploits on and off the ball fields inspired five biographies.

The St. Louis Cardinal manager's question goes to the heart of this book: why are we so interested in the lives of athletes? These individuals don't appear particularly profound in the insights they offer, as most postgame interviews will attest. Rarely have they changed the world in any meaningful way, Jackie Robinson excepted. It would be difficult to maintain that, as a group, they lead exemplary lives or that they're "role models," to borrow the current mantra. However, given the number of sport biographies published every year, it's fair to say that the reading public is fascinated with the lives of athletes.

Among the readers are admitted "jock sniffers" who enjoy basking in the shadow of greatness. Their primary interest lies in accomplishments on the fields of competition. They want to know more about their favorite ballplayer than can be found on the sports page of the local newspaper. Sports biographies written for popular consumption focus on athletic performance. Bill Gutman has made a career of writing such books. His, *Bo Jackson: a Biography,* is typical. Barely, a fifth of the 130-page paperback touches on the former NFL and MLB star's life out of uniform. Open the book to virtually any page and you find accounts like, "Bo gained 121 yards on 19 carries, including a 67-yard jaunt for a touchdown. He also caught 48 yards' worth of passes as the [Auburn] Tiger won 24-10."[2]

The attraction to heroic feats shades over into fascination with celebrity culture. Historian Daniel Boorstin remarked that a celebrity is someone who is famous because he has a famous name.[3] This sardonic comment suggests that all the attention paid to celebrities is self-serving, if not shallow. I would argue that sports celebrities are the exceptions; their fame is tied directly to accomplishments. Regardless, athletes make up a prominent contingent among celebrities. Sports stars like Lance Armstrong and Tiger Woods appear routinely in the print and electronic media; their images are connected with the marketing of commercial products; they are guests on talk shows and in the sports broadcasting booth. Fans want to know more about what their lives are like beyond the TV cameras. This desire spawns biographies that focus on the private lives of public personalities.

The inquisitive reader wants to know what in the famous athlete's life accounts for his ability to run faster or jump higher, to hit or kick a ball farther; what triggers his fierce competitiveness, determination, and perseverance. The feat becomes less important than the man. One corollary of celebrity culture is that an athlete's life off the field may compete with or even upstage his athletic accomplishments. We expect the athlete's private life to be juicier. Sometimes it is (Babe Ruth, Dennis Rodman) and sometimes not (Lou Gehrig, Ben Hogan). But we can find out only by plunging into their biographies. Can a mediocre athlete have a more interesting life story than a star athlete? Who is the real person behind the heroic image? Is there any correlation between public and private life?

We expect accomplished men in sport to have exceptional personal lives, and more often than not they do. Baseball writer Leonard Koppett offers an explanation:

> Those who live high-intensity lives in brief and hazardous careers, for great rewards, in businesses that require constant traveling and considerable loneliness and disorientation, will produce among their number a certain proportion of people who seek relief in drugs. Such people also have a higher rate of sexual promiscuity, divorce, tax problems, and gossip-column mentions than a similar number of middle-class office workers who seldom travel, have stable family lives, and tune in to Monday night Football.[4]

Moreover, there's reason to believe that men who lead physical lives provide particularly interesting life stories: adventures and explorers like Sir Richard Burton, dancers like Rudolf Nureyev.[5] Athletes clearly fall into this mold. They captivate us with their physical exploits and their appetites. Compare biographies of athletes with those whose subjects lead a life of the mind. The late science-fiction writer Isaac Asimov reputedly wrote and edited more than 400 books, and penned several thousand personal letters. He spent most of his life at his writing desk. Dizzy Dean and Babe Ruth probably didn't read a hundred books between them, but their life stories make for considerably more interesting reading—and we probably learn more about human nature therein.[6]

In *Living Out of Bounds*, I've drawn on the lives of some six dozen men who competed in a range of sports over the course of the last 100 years. The book traces their lives from initiation into sport, through their careers, into retirement. The focus is on their everyday lives, at home and on the road, at work and at play; their relationships with family, coaches, teammates, buddies, journalists, fans, and lovers. From these accounts, we can arrive at some general conclusions.

Foremost, there's no single representative experience in sport and no typical athlete. This realization is significant, given that we routinely employ stereotypical labels like "jock" to describe men in sport. Athletes come from a wide variety of backgrounds and acquire their interest in sports under a wide range of circumstances and at various stages of life. As a group, their personalities vary widely; we find both introverts and extroverts, ascetics and Epicureans, the urbane and the vulgar, world citizens and an occasional sociopath.

Despite the differences among these men's lives, we can identify common themes that have persisted over time and across sports. The career of an athlete is distinct from most other professions. Few jobs are so physically and emotionally demanding. Athletes are under constant pressure to perform, and do so in the public arena. Moreover, they describe a profoundly disjointed existence, an on-again, off-again regimen of competition, workouts, travel, and intermittent leisure—a perpetual waiting for the next game or recovering from the last. At the same time, the athlete's life appears uniquely insular, set apart from the outside world and often from reality. Sport constitutes a singularly authoritarian environment, and most athletes capitulate to authority. The critics suggest that a life in this environment delays maturity. It most certainly can lead to traumatic adjustment when a sports career ends.

Equally notable is the hypermasculine culture of men's sport, reliant upon strong homosocial bonds yet infused with homophobic anxiety. One detects elements of latent homosexuality that coexist with overt heterosexual performance expectations. Too often, women are objectified and marginalized. Young athletes discover and reinforce their identities largely by learning to please older males: fathers, surrogate fathers, and coaches. These men exert significant power over athletes and coerce them to perform to their standards and expectations. Coaches often vie with the women in athletes' lives for control. It's ironic that sport has been on the leading edge of racial progress, while sexism and gay bashing remain salient among male athletes.

Fame and fortune arrive at a tender age for many athletes. It's the rare individual who can deal with the instant notoriety, just as it is an exceptional athlete who can manage large sums of money. Celebrity sports stars have been around since the 1920s, while millionaire athletes are a more recent phenomenon. But the stories of profligate lives run through history. Jockey Tod Sloan had gone through several hundred thousand dollars by the late 1920s; boxers Mike Tyson and Muhammad Ali went through several millions two generations later. Ty Cobb's and Michael Jordan's prudent investing of their money remains the exception to the rule. The professional athlete's life might be characterized as "too much, too soon."

If handling notoriety and money are an athlete's most daunting challenges, gambling and use of recreational drugs run a close second. There's something about highly competitive individuals that attract these types to making wagers. Most athletes keep their gambling within reasonable limits at the horse tracks or card tables (and avoid betting on their own sport), but more than a few lives have been damaged by the compulsion to gamble. Likewise, addiction to drugs has curtailed the careers of several prominent athletes. The overwhelming physical and emotional demands of competing on a regular basis predispose athletes to seek relief through drugs. The fact that athletes increasingly are given, and self-treat with, performance-enhancing drugs and pain killers often carries over to recreational drug use, and often, abuse.

In summary, it becomes clear that outstanding physical talent can be both a blessing and a curse. The superior athlete experiences moments of joy and exaltation that escape the common man; but the demands and expectations that accompany a sports career can be overwhelming. The gift of exceptional physical ability is ephemeral. It declines over time and can perish with the snap of a tendon. Competing in sports at a high level means being able to accept this reality. Equally daunting is the task of shaping a meaningful life outside the sports stadium. Legendary sportswriter Grantland Rice got it right; the thing that matters most is how these men "played the game," not only on the fields of competition, but the game of life.

NOTES

INTRODUCTION

1. Cashmore, E. (Ed.) (2000), *Sports Culture: An A–Z Guide,* London: Routledge, pp. 32–39.

2. Duncan, M.C. (1998), "Stories We Tell Ourselves about Ourselves," *Sociology of Sport Journal,* 15(2), p. 106.

3. Ibid.

4. Duncan, 1998, op. cit., p. 100.

5. Johnson, J. (1992), *Jack Johnson—in the Ring and Out,* reprint, New York: Citadel Press.

6. Oriard, M. (1982), *The End of Autumn: Reflections on My Life in Football,* New York: Doubleday, pp. 33–34.

7. Salvino, C. with Klein, F. (1988), *Fast Lanes,* Chicago: Bonus Books, insert facing p. 111.

8. In Johnson, J. (1992), op. cit., pp. 14–15.

9. Hauser, T. (1991), *Muhammad Ali: His Life and Times,* New York: Simon & Schuster, pp. 343, 464.

10. Knox, C. and Plaschke, B. (1988), *Hard Knox: The Life of an NFL Coach,* San Diego: Harcourt Brace Jovanovich, p. 7.

11. Woodward, S. (1949), *Sports Page: The Story behind Newspaper Writing,* New York: Simon & Schuster, p. 123.

12. Vaughan, R. (1975), *The Grand Gesture: Ted Turner and the America's Cup,* Boston: Little, Brown, pp. 97*ff.*

13. Kopay, D. and Young, P. (1988), *The David Kopay Story,* New York: Primus.

14. Morris, J. (1971), *Brian Piccolo: A Short Season,* Chicago: Rand, McNally.

15. Stump, A. (1994), *Cobb: The Life and Times of the Meanest Man Who Ever Played Baseball,* Chapel Hill, NC: Algonquin Books.

16. Bickley, D. (1997), *No Bull: The Unauthorized Biography of Dennis Rodman,* New York: St. Martin's Press.

17. Sanders, D. with Black, J. (1998), *Power, Money & Sex: How Success Almost Ruined My Life,* Nashville: Word Publishing.

18. Romanowski, B. with Schefter, A. and Towle, P. (2005), *Romo: My Life on the Edge,* New York: William Morrow.

19. Ashe, A. with Deford, F. (1993), *Arthur Ashe: Portrait in Motion,* New York: Carroll & Graf, p. 112.

20. Kramer, J. (1968), *Instant Replay: The Green Bay Diary of Jerry Kramer,* Edited by Dick Schaap, New York: New American Library.

21. Bouton, J. (1970), *Ball Four: My Life and Hard Times Throwing the Knuckleball in the Big Leagues,* New York: World Publishing Co.

22. Tosches, N. (2000), *The Devil and Sonny Liston,* New York: Little, Brown.

23. DeGregorio, G. (1981), *Joe Dimaggio: An Informal Biography,* Princeton, NJ: Townhouse Publishers.

24. Cramer, R. (2000), *Joe DiMaggio: The Hero's Life,* New York: Simon & Schuster.

25. Rosaforte, T. (1997), *Tiger Woods: The Makings of a Champion,* New York: St. Martin's, p. xv.

26. Schecter, L. (1970), *The Jocks,* New York: Paperback Library, p. 135.

27. Epstein, E. (1997), *Born to Skate: The Michelle Kwan Story,* New York: Random House, p. 9; Rosaforte, op. cit., pp. 20–21.

28. Cohen, N. (1992), *Jackie Joiner-Kersee,* Boston: Little, Brown, pp. 13–14; Stravinsky, J. (1997), *Muhammad Ali,* New York: Park Lane Press, pp. 12–13.

29. Friedman, S. (1996), *Swimming the Channel: A Memoir of Love, Loss, and Healing,* New York: Farrar, Straus and Giroux.

30. Ryan, J. (1995), *Little Girls in Pretty Boxes,* New York: Doubleday.

31. Richards, R. with Ames, J. (1983), *Second Serve: The Renee Richards Story,* New York: Stein and Day.

32. Merson, P. with Ridley, I. (2000), *Hero and Villain,* London: Collins Willow.

33. Messing, S. with Hirshey, D. (1978), *The Education of an American Soccer Player,* New York: Dodd, Mead & Co.

34. Dryden, K. (1983), *The Game,* Toronto: Macmillan.

35. James, C.L.R. (1983), *Beyond a Boundary,* New York: Pantheon Books.

36. Rhodes, R. (1988), *The Making of the Atomic Bomb,* New York: Simon & Schuster, pp. 138*ff.*

37. James (1983), op. cit.

38. Vaughn (1975), op. cit.

39. Oriard (1982), op. cit., p. xvii.

40. Messing (1978), op. cit.

41. Schollander, D. and Savage, D. (1971), *Deep Water,* New York: Crown Publishers, pp. 4–5.

42. Rosaforte (1997), op. cit.

43. Cramer, R. (1999), "What Do You Think of Ted Williams Now?" In Halberstam, D. (Ed.), *The Best American Sports Writing of the Century,* Boston: Houghton Mifflin, pp. 58–89.

44. Menand, L. (2004, March 1), "Game Theory," *The New Yorker,* from http://www .newyorker.com/archive/2004/03/01/040301crbo_books1.

45. Salvino and Klein (1988), op. cit., pp. 88, 121.

46. James (1983), op. cit., pp. 192–93.

47. In Casper, S. (1999), *Constructing American Lives: Biography and Culture in Nineteenth-Century America,* Chapel Hill, NC: Univ. of North Carolina Press, p. 208.

48. Bradley, B. (1995), *Life on the Run,* New York: Vintage Books.

49. Brashler, W. (1978), *Josh Gibson: A Life in the Negro Leagues,* New York: Harper & Row.

50. Messing (1978), op. cit.

CHAPTER 1: THE ATHLETE'S FAMILY AND YOUTH

1. Piersall, J. and Hirshberg, A. (1955), *Fear Strikes Out: The Jim Piersall Story,* New York: Grosset & Dunlap, p. 8.

2. Sokolove, M. (1990), *Hustle: The Myth, Life and Lies of Pete Rose,* New York: Simon & Schuster, p. 33.

3. Stravinsky, J. (1997), *Muhammad Ali,* New York: Park Lane Press, p. 5.

4. Cawardine, R. (2003), *Lincoln,* Essex, UK: Pearson Longman, p. 1.

5. Rosaforte, T. (1997), *Tiger Woods: The Makings of a Champion,* New York: St. Martin's, pp. 7, 14–17.

6. Jordan, P. (1975), *A False Spring,* New York: Dodd, Mead & Co.

7. Bickley, D. (1997), *No Bull: The Unauthorized Biography of Dennis Rodman,* New York: St. Martins, p. xii.

8. Wagenheim, K. (1973), *Clemente!* New York: Praeger Publishers, p. 161.

9. Gentry, T. (1990), *Jesse Owens: Champion Athlete,* New York: Chelsea House Publishers, pp. 20–21.

10. Goertzel, M, Goertzel, V. and Goertzel, T. (1978), *Three Hundred Eminent Personalities,* San Francisco: Jossey–Bass Publishers.

11. Calhoun, D. (1987), *Sport, Culture, and Personality,* Champaign, IL: Human Kinetics, p. 211.

12. Vaughan, R. (1975), *The Grand Gesture: Ted Turner and the America's Cup,* Boston: Little, Brown, p. 254.

13. Ashe, A. and Rampersad, A. (1993), *Days of Grace: A Memoir,* New York: Knopf.

14. Sampson, C. (1996), *Hogan,* New York: Broadway Books.

15. Armstrong, L. with Jenkins, S. (2000), *It's Not About the Bike: My Journey Back to Life,* New York: Putnam's Sons, p. 14.

16. Fleischer, N. (1931), *Gene Tunney—Enigma of the Ring,* Springfield, MA: The Ring, Inc.; Evensen, B. (1996), *When Dempsey Fought Tunney: Heroes, Hokum, and Storytelling in the Jazz Age,* Knoxville: Univ. of Tennessee Press, pp. 35–42.

17. Hillenbrand, L. (2002), *Seabiscuit: An American Legend,* New York: Ballantine Books, pp. 60–63.

18. Creamer, R. (1974), *Babe: The Legend Comes to Life,* New York. Simon & Schuster, pp. 29–33.

19. Newcombe, J. (1975), *The Best of the Athletic Boys: The White Man's Impact on Jim Thorpe,* New York: Doubleday, pp. 38–43.

20. See Overman, S. (2004), "Male Athletes and Their Fathers through the Lens of Auto/biography," *Auto/Biography,* 11(1 & 2), pp. 5–13, for a discussion of the influence of siblings on young athletes.

21. DeGregorio, G. (1981), *Joe Dimaggio: An Informal Biography,* Princeton, NJ: Townhouse Publishers, pp. 13–18, 83.

22. Wagenheim (1973), op. cit., pp. 23–35.

23. Sanders, D. with Black, J. (1998), *Power, Money & Sex: How Success Almost Ruined My Life,* Nashville: Word Publishing, pp. 115.

24. Gutman, B. (1991), *Bo Jackson: A Biography*, New York: Pocket Books, pp. 3–4, 9–12.

25. Deford, F. (1976), *Big Bill Tilden: The Triumphs and the Tragedy*, New York: Simon & Schuster, p. 204.

26. Berger, P. (1998), *Mickey Mantle*, New York: Park Lane Press, p. 16.

27. Sokolove (1990), op. cit., p. 13.

28. Stowers, C. (1971), *The Randy Matson Story*, Los Altos, CA: Tafnews Press, pp. 8, 9, 14–18.

29. Armstrong and Jenkins (2000), op. cit., pp. 22–24, 30.

30. Sanders and Black (1998), op. cit., pp. 16–42.

31. Graham, F. (1942), *Lou Gehrig: A Quiet Hero*, Eau Claire, WI: E.M. Hale & Company, pp. 6–11.

32. Salvino, C. with Klein, F. (1988), *Fast Lanes*, Chicago: Bonus Books, pp. xviii, 9–19.

33. Brashler, W. (1978), *Josh Gibson: A Life in the Negro Leagues*, New York: Harper & Row, pp. 1–3, 6–11.

34. Stravinsky (1997), op. cit., pp. 12–16.

35. Tosches, N. (2000), *The Devil and Sonny Liston*, New York: Little, Brown, pp. 19–34, 50.

36. Johnson, J. (1992), *Jack Johnson—in the Ring and Out*, reprint, New York: Citadel Press, pp. 27–39.

37. Sanders and Black (1998), op. cit.

38. Oriard, M. (1982), *The End of Autumn: Reflections on My Life in Football*, New York: Doubleday, p. 11.

39. Conroy, P. (2002), *My Losing Season*, New York: Doubleday, p. 6.

40. Schollander, D. and Savage, D. (1971), *Deep Water*, New York: Crown Publishers, p. 16.

41. Messner, M. (1992), *Power at Play: Sports and the Problem of Masculinity*, Boston: Beacon Press.

42. Gutman, B. (1998), *Brett Favre: A Biography*, New York: Pocket Books, pp. 6–8.

43. Conner, B. with Ziert, P. (1985), *Winning the Gold*, New York: Warner Books, pp. 5–6.

44. Sokolove (1990), op. cit., pp. 28, 33–39.

45. Rosaforte (1997), op. cit., pp. 13–14, 18–24.

46. Ibid., pp. 21, 23–25.

47. Ibid., pp. 58, 63, 167, 236.

48. Ibid., pp. 176, 192, 240.

49. Berger (1998), op. cit., pp. 4–11, 14–15, 60.

50. Piersall and Hirshberg (1955), op. cit.

51. Schollander and Savage (1971), op. cit.

52. Cohen, J. (1971), *Big A: The Story of Lew Alcindor*, New York: Scholastic Books.

53. Messing, S. with Hirshey, D. (1978), *The Education of an American Soccer Player*, New York: Dodd, Mead & Co.

54. Kopay, D. and Young, P. (1988), *The David Kopay Story*, New York; Primus.

55. Morris, J. (1971), *Brian Piccolo: A Short Season*, Chicago: Rand, McNally, pp. 42*ff.*

56. See Overman (2004), op. cit.

57. Richards, R. with Ames, J. (1983), *Second Serve: The Renée Richards Story,* New York: Stein and Day.

58. Armstrong and Jenkins (2000), op. cit., pp. 19*ff.*

59. Sanders and Black (1998), op. cit.

60. Sampson (1996), op. cit.

61. Bickley (1997), op. cit., pp. 2–6.

62. Rampersad, A. (1997), *Jackie Robinson: A Biography,* New York: Knopf, p. 29.

63. Ibid.

64. Sanders and Black (1998), op. cit., pp. 25–27.

65. Armstrong and Jenkins (2000), op. cit., pp. 17–18, 20, 40.

66. Heller, P. (1995), *Bad Intentions: The Mike Tyson Story,* New York: De Capo Press, pp. 6–21, 78.

67. Creamer, R. (1974), *Babe: The Legend Comes to Life,* New York. Simon & Schuster, pp. 24–40.

68. Ibid.

69. Bickley (1997), op. cit., pp. 2, 59*ff,* 82, 85.

70. Cashmore, E. (Ed.) (2000), *Sports Culture: An A–Z Guide,* London: Routledge, p. 237; Cole, C. and King, S. (1998), "Representing Black Masculinity and Urban Possibilities: Racism, Realism, and *Hoop Dreams,*" In Rail, G. (Ed.), *Sport and Postmodern Times,* Albany, NY: SUNY Press, p. 55.

CHAPTER 2: THE NARROW WORLD OF SPORTS

1. Koppett, L. (1981), *Sports Illusion, Sports Reality: A Reporter's View of Sports Journalism and Society,* Boston: Houghton Mifflin, p. 181.

2. Kopay, D. and Young, P. (1988), *The David Kopay Story,* New York: Primus, p. 47.

3. Romanowski, B. with Schefter, A. and Towle, P. (2005), *Romo: My Life on the Edge,* New York: William Morrow, p. 2.

4. Armstrong, L. with Jenkins, S. (2000), *It's Not About the Bike: My Journey Back to Life,* New York: Putnam's Sons, p. 88.

5. Richards, R. with Ames, J. (1983), *Second Serve: The Renée Richards Story,* New York: Stein and Day, pp. 30, 42.

6. Pryor, A. with Terrill, M. (1996), *Flight of the Hawk: The Aaron Pryor Story,* Sun Lake, AZ: Book World, pp. 19–20.

7. Ibid., p. 60.

8. Oates, J. (1987), *On Boxing,* London: Pan Books, p. 29.

9. Oriard, M. (1982), *The End of Autumn: Reflections on My Life in Football,* New York: Doubleday, p. xvii.

10. Deford, F. (1976), *Big Bill Tilden: The Triumphs and the Tragedy,* New York: Simon & Schuster, p. 191.

11. Ibid., pp. 43, 47–48, 59.

12. Conroy, P. (2002), *My Losing Season,* New York: Doubleday, p. 32.

13. Pryor and Terrill (1996), op. cit., pp. 15–17.

14. Bradley, B. (1995), *Life on the Run,* New York: Vintage Books, pp. 114, 169.

15. Bickley, D. (1997), *No Bull: The Unauthorized Biography of Dennis Rodman,* New York: St. Martins, p. 106.

16. Romanowski (2005), op. cit., pp. 34, 202.

17. Pryor and Terrill (1997), op. cit., 37.

18. Heller, P. (1995), *Bad Intentions: The Mike Tyson Story*, New York: De Capo Press, p. 111.

19. Cramer, R. (2000), *Joe DiMaggio: The Hero's Life*, New York: Simon & Schuster, p. 106.

20. In Holtzman, J. (1995), *No Cheering in the Press Box*, New York: Henry Holt, p. 347.

21. Howe, S. with Greenfield, J. (1989), *Between the Lines: One Athlete's Struggle to Escape the Nightmare of Addiction*, Grand Rapids, MI: Masters Press, pp. 116, 148, 188.

22. In Kopay and Young (1988), op. cit., p. 225.

23. Merson, P. with Ridley, I. (2000), *Hero and Villain*, London: Collins Willow, p. 74.

24. Jordan, P. (1975), *A False Spring*, New York: Dodd, Mead & Co., p. 17.

25. Armstrong and Jenkins (2000), op. cit., p. 203.

26. Conroy (2002), op. cit., p. 36.

27. Oriard (1982), op. cit., pp. 17, 154.

28. Sands, R. (1999), *Gutcheck!*, Carpinteria, CA: Rincon Hill Books, p. 191.

29. Romanowski (2005), op. cit., p. 3.

30. Edmundson, M. (2002), *Teacher: The One Who Made the Difference*, New York: Random House, p. 54.

31. Ibid.

32. Meggyesy, D. (1970), *Out of Their League*, Berkeley, CA: Ramparts Press, p. 217.

33. Sands (1999), op. cit., 192.

34. Morris, T. (1997), *Making the Team: The Cultural Work of Baseball Fiction*, Urbana: University of Illinois Press, pp. 131–32.

35. Richards and Ames (1983), op. cit., p. 103.

36. Bradley (1995), op. cit., p. 26.

37. Oriard (1982), op. cit., pp. 310–11.

38. Pryor and Terrill (1996), op. cit., p. 17.

39. Howe (1989), op. cit.; Sanders, D. with Black, J. (1998), *Power, Money & Sex: How Success Almost Ruined My Life*, Nashville: Word Publishing.

40. Oates (1987), op. cit., p. 13.

41. Wiggins, D. (1995), "Victory for Allah: Muhammad Ali, the Nation of Islam, and American Society," In E.J. Gorn, *Muhammad Ali: The People's Champ*, Champaign: University of Illinois Press, p. 90.

42. Romanowski (2005), op. cit., 29.

43. Ibid., pp. 33, 38.

44. Armstrong and Jenkins (2000), op. cit., p. 88.

45. Richards and Ames (1983), op. cit., p. 347.

46. Dryden, K. (1983), *The Game*, Toronto: Macmillan, p. 11.

47. Bradley (1995), op. cit., p. 70.

48. Ashe, A. with Deford, F. (1993), *Arthur Ashe: Portrait in Motion*, New York: Carroll & Graf, p. 60.

49. Messing, S. with Hirshey, D. (1978), *The Education of an American Soccer Player*, New York: Dodd, Mead & Co., p. 24.

50. Conroy (2002), op. cit., p. 17.

51. Sands (1999), op. cit., p. 113.

52. Cramer (2000), op. cit., pp. 107, 290; DeGregorio, G. (1981), *Joe Dimaggio: An Informal Biography*, Princeton, NJ: Townhouse Publishers, p. 99.

53. Morris, J. (1971), *Brian Piccolo: A Short Season,* Chicago: Rand, McNally, pp. 37–38.

54. Conroy (2002), op. cit., pp. 17–18.

55. Oriard (1982), op. cit., p. 252.

56. Meggyesy (1970), op. cit., p. 36.

57. Gershberg, Z. (2001), "Abandon Sport Clichés for Real Life Struggles." *The Ithacan Online,* 74(11), available from http://www.ithaca.edu/ithacan/articles/0109/27/sports/0press_box.htm.

58. In Betts, J. (1974), *America's Sporting Heritage: 1850–1950,* Reading, MA: Addison-Wesley, p. 95.

59. Deford (1976), op. cit., p. 108.

60. Ibid., p. 22.

61. Bickley (1997), op. cit. pp. xiv, xvii, 154–56, 167.

62. Ibid., p. 258.

63. Deford (1976), op. cit., pp. 22, 48–49, 59, 90.

64. Armstrong and Jenkins (2000), op. cit., pp. 62–64.

65. Creamer, R. (1974), *Babe: The Legend Comes to Life,* New York. Simon & Schuster, pp. 139, 265*ff.*

66. Cramer, R. (1999), "What Do You Think of Ted Williams Now?," In Halberstam, D. (Ed.), *The Best American Sports Writing of the Century,* Boston: Houghton Mifflin, pp. 58–89.

67. In Will, G. (1998), "Pete Rose's Chromosomes," In *Bunts: Curt Flood, Camden Yards, Pete Rose, and Other Reflections on Baseball,* New York: Scribner, p. 119.

68. Sokolove, M. (1990), *Hustle: The Myth, Life and Lies of Pete Rose,* New York: Simon & Schuster, pp. 11, 291.

69. Howe (1989), op. cit., pp. 68–70.

70. Morris (1971), op. cit., p. 118.

71. Howe (1989), op. cit., p. 66.

72. Berger, P. (1998), *Mickey Mantle,* New York: Park Lane Press, pp. 28–30.

73. Oriard (1982), op. cit., pp. xvii, 168.

74. Dryden (1983), op. cit., pp. 8–11, 33.

75. Green, T. (1996), *The Dark Side of the Game: My Life in the NFL,* New York: Warner Books, pp. 22–23, 191.

76. Oriard (1982), op. cit., p. 315.

77. Bradley (1995), op. cit., pp. 122–23.

78. Halberstam, D. (1999), *Playing for Keeps: Michael Jordan and the World He Made,* New York: Random House, p. 387.

79. Jordan (1975), op. cit., p. 192.

80. Armstrong and Jenkins (2000), op. cit., pp. 73–74.

81. Rampersad, A. (1997), *Jackie Robinson: A Biography,* New York: Knopf, p. 66.

82. Heller (1995), op. cit., pp. 1–90 passim.

83. Ibid., pp. 71–72.

84. Ibid., pp. 72, 393–94.

85. In Howe (1989), op. cit., p. 205.

86. Sands (1999), op. cit., pp. xi, 13, 121, 159.

87. Green (1996), op. cit., p. 48.

88. Meggyesy (1970), pp. 11–12, 72, 154–55.

89. Stowers, C. (1971), *The Randy Matson Story,* Los Altos, CA: Tafnews Press, pp. 20, 22.

90. Oriard (1982), op. cit., pp. 193–95.

91. Sullivan, R. (2002), *Rocky Marciano: The Rock of His Times,* Urbana, IL: University of Illinois Press, p. 26.

92. Ibid., pp. 63–64.

93. Kramer, J. (1968), *Instant Replay: The Green Bay Diary of Jerry Kramer,* Edited by Dick Schaap, New York: New American Library, p. 31.

94. Knox, C. and Plaschke, B. (1988), *Hard Knox: The Life of an NFL Coach,* San Diego: Harcourt Brace Jovanovich, p. 244.

95. Creamer (1974), op. cit., pp. 192, 219.

96. Cramer (2000), op. cit., p. 92.

97. Green (1996), op. cit., pp. 191–92.

98. Newcombe, J. (1975), *The Best of the Athletic Boys: The White Man's Impact on Jim Thorpe,* New York: Doubleday, pp. 107–8, 111–12.

99. Ibid., pp. 115, 120, 137, 180.

100. Gentry, T. (1990), *Jesse Owens: Champion Athlete,* New York: Chelsea House Publishers, p. 43.

101. Green (1996), op. cit., p. 192.

102. Creamer (1974), op. cit., pp. 110–11.

103. Smith, R. (1999), "And All Dizzy's Yesterdays," In Halberstam, D. (Ed.), *The Best American Sports Writing of the Century,* Boston: Houghton Mifflin, p. 164.

104. Sokolove (1990), op. cit., pp. 268–69.

105. Bradley (1995), op. cit., p. 147.

106. Pryor and Terrill (1996), op. cit., p. 158.

107. Edmonds, A. (1973), *Joe Louis,* Grand Rapids, MI: Wm. B. Eerdmans, pp. 69–71, 102–4.

108. Heller (1995), op. cit., pp. 282–86, 424.

109. In Johnson, J. (1992), *Jack Johnson—in the Ring and Out,* reprint, New York: Citadel Press, pp. 1–2.

110. Stravinsky, J. (1997), *Muhammad Ali,* New York: Park Lane Press, pp. 143–51.

111. Oriard (1982), op. cit., p. 324.

112. Schollander, D. and Savage, D. (1971), *Deep Water,* New York: Crown Publishers.

113. Kopay (1988), op. cit., p. 95.

114. Stafford, T. (1990), *Dave Dravecky: Comeback,* New York: HarperCollins, p. 41.

115. Armstrong and Jenkins (2000), op. cit., pp. 99, 156, 163.

116. Ibid., p. 202.

117. Bradley (1995), op. cit., p. 72.

CHAPTER 3: PUBLIC LIFE, PRIVATE SPACE

1. Johnson, J. (1992), *Jack Johnson—in the Ring and Out,* reprint, New York: Citadel Press, p. 230.

2. Stuart, O. (1995), *Perpetual Motion: The Public and Private Lives of Rudolf Nureyev,* New York: Simon & Schuster, 1995, p. 12.

3. Cramer, R. (2000), *Joe DiMaggio: The Hero's Life,* New York: Simon & Schuster, p. 60.

4. Armstrong, L. with Jenkins, S. (2000), *It's Not About the Bike: My Journey Back to Life,* New York: Putnam's Sons, pp. 219ff; Edmonds, A. (1973), *Joe Louis,* Grand Rapids, MI: Wm. B. Eerdmans, p. 37.

5. Malamud, B. (2003), *The Natural,* New York: Farrar, Straus & Giroux.

6. Sokolove, M. (1990), *Hustle: The Myth, Life and Lies of Pete Rose,* New York: Simon & Schuster, p. 147.

7. Edmonds (1973), op. cit., pp. 33–39.

8. Cramer (2000), op. cit., pp. 175–77.

9. Evensen, B. (1996), *When Dempsey Fought Tunney: Heroes, Hokum, and Storytelling in the Jazz Age,* Knoxville: Univ. of Tennessee Press, p. ix.

10. Schollander, D. and Savage, D. (1971), *Deep Water,* New York: Crown Publishers, p. 87.

11. Ashe, A. and Rampersad, A. (1993), *Days of Grace: A Memoir,* New York: Knopf, p. 20.

12. Rosaforte, T. (1997), *Tiger Woods: The Makings of a Champion,* New York: St. Martin's, pp. 17, 184.

13. Conroy, P. (2002), *My Losing Season,* New York: Doubleday.

14. Bradley, B. (1995), *Life on the Run,* New York: Vintage Books, p. 35.

15. Jordan, P. (1975), *A False Spring,* New York: Dodd, Mead & Co., p. 23.

16. Dizikes, J. (2000), *Yankee Doodle Dandy: The Life and Times of Tod Sloan,* New Haven, CT: Yale University Press, pp. 88, 119, 183–85.

17. Sanders, D. with Black, J. (1998), *Power, Money & Sex: How Success Almost Ruined My Life,* Nashville: Word Publishing, pp. 69, 125.

18. Dryden, K. (1983), *The Game,* Toronto: Macmillan, p. 159.

19. Evensen (1996), op. cit., p. 53.

20. Knox, C. and Plaschke, B. (1988), *Hard Knox: The Life of an NFL Coach,* San Diego: Harcourt Brace Jovanovich, p. 236.

21. Rampersad, A. (1997), *Jackie Robinson: A Biography,* New York: Knopf.

22. Gentry, T. (1990), *Jesse Owens: Champion Athlete,* New York: Chelsea House Publishers, pp. 61–62.

23. Schollander and Savage (1971), op. cit., pp. 82–87, 131.

24. Rosaforte (1997), op. cit., p. 218.

25. Wagenheim, K. (1973), *Clemente!* New York: Praeger Publishers, pp. 172–73.

26. Ibid., p. 209.

27. Sullivan, R. (2002), *Rocky Marciano: The Rock of His Times,* Urbana, IL: University of Illinois Press, pp. 199–200.

28. Messing, S. with Hirshey, D. (1978), *The Education of an American Soccer Player,* New York: Dodd, Mead & Co., 223.

29. Dizikes (2000), op. cit., p. 116.

30. Edmonds (1973), op. cit., p. 77.

31. Armstrong and Jenkins (2000), op. cit., pp. 260, 266, 272.

32. Gentry (1990), op. cit., p. 98; Sokolove (1990), op. cit., p. 135.

33. Sokolove (1990), op. cit., p. 169.

34. Morris, J. (1971), *Brian Piccolo: A Short Season,* Chicago: Rand, McNally.

35. Salvino, C. with Klein, F. (1988), *Fast Lanes,* Chicago: Bonus Books, p. 75.

36. Hauser, T. (1991), *Muhammad Ali: His Life and Times,* New York: Simon & Schuster, pp. 40, 343.

37. Heller, P. (1995), *Bad Intentions: The Mike Tyson Story,* New York: De Capo Press, p. 163.

38. Ibid., p. 256.

39. Oriard, M. (1982), *The End of Autumn: Reflections on My Life in Football,* New York: Doubleday, pp. 293–95.

40. Wagenheim (1973), op. cit., pp. 221–22.

41. Dryden (1983), op. cit., p. 159.

42. Jordan (1975), op. cit., p. 29.

43. Bradley (1995), op. cit., p. 120.

44. Patterson, F. and Talese, G. (1998), "In Defense of Cassius Clay," In Early, G. (Ed.), *The Muhammad Ali Reader,* New York: Rob Welch Books, p. 65.

45. Bradley (1995), op. cit., p. 103.

46. Green, T. (1996), *The Dark Side of the Game: My Life in the NFL,* New York: Warner Books, p. 130.

47. Richards, R. with Ames, J. (1983), *Second Serve: The Renée Richards Story,* New York: Stein and Day, pp. 90*ff.*

48. Ashe and Rampersad (1993), op. cit., p. 250.

49. Cramer (2000), op. cit., p. 122.

50. Halberstam, D. (1999), *Playing for Keeps: Michael Jordan and the World He Made,* New York: Random House.

51. Ibid., p. 305.

52. Sokolove (1990), op. cit., pp. 127, 131.

53. Berger, P. (1998), *Mickey Mantle,* New York: Park Lane Press, p. 84.

54. Sokolove (1990), op. cit., pp. 124–25.

55. Bradlye (1995), op. cit., pp. 22–23.

56. Wagerheim (1973), op. cit., p. 53.

57. Sokolove (1990), op. cit., pp. 18, 123, 139–42.

58. Ibid., p. 283.

59. Creamer, R. (1974) *Babe: The Legend Comes to Life,* New York. Simon & Schuster, p. 220.

60. Messing (1978), op. cit., p. 2.

61. Sokolove (1990), op. cit., pp. 237–39, 281.

62. Salvino and Klein (1988), op. cit., p. 75.

63. Cramer (2000), op. cit., p. 247; DeGregorio, G. (1981), *Joe Dimaggio: An Informal Biography,* Princeton, NJ: Townhouse Publishers, p. 192.

64. Green (1995), op. cit., pp. 211–12.

65. Berger (1998), op. cit., pp. 82–86.

66. Creamer (1974), op. cit., pp. 2, 13, 250, 325.

67. Cramer (2000), op. cit., pp. 122, 177.

68. De Gregorio (1981), op. cit.

69. Halberstam (1999), op. cit., pp. 306–7, 318, 417.

70. Messing (1978), op. cit., p. 6.

71. Sullivan (2002), op. cit., p. 213.

72. Rampersad (1997), op. cit.

73. Cramer (2000), op. cit.

74. Rampersad (1997), op. cit., pp. 354–56*ff.*

75. Bickley, D. (1997), *No Bull: The Unauthorized Biography of Dennis Rodman,* New York: St. Martins, pp. 180–85.

76. Brosnan, J. (1960), *The Long Season,* New York: Dell Publishing, p. 12.

77. Jordan, P. (1975), op. cit.

78. See Sands, R. (1999), *Gutcheck!,* Carpinteria, CA: Rincon Hill Books, p. 127.

79. Richards, R. (1983), op. cit.

Chapter 4: In the Arena's Shadow

1. Oriard, M. (1982), *The End of Autumn: Reflections on My Life in Football,* New York: Doubleday, p. 190.

2. Meggyesy, D. (1970), *Out of Their League,* Berkeley, CA: Ramparts Press, p. 190.

3. Romanowski, B. with Schefter, A. and Towle, P. (2005), *Romo: My Life on the Edge,* New York: William Morrow, p. 259 *passim.*

4. Messner, M. (1993), "The Meaning of Success: The Athletic Experience and the Development of Male Identity," In Eitzen, D.S. (Ed.), *Sport in Contemporary Society,* New York: St. Martin's Press, p. 409.

5. Ashe, A. with Deford, F. (1993), *Arthur Ashe: Portrait in Motion,* New York: Carroll & Graf, pp. 169–70.

6. Bickley, D. (1997), *No Bull: The Unauthorized Biography of Dennis Rodman,* New York: St. Martins, p. 99.

7. Ashes and Deford (1993), op. cit., pp. 20–22.

8. Bradley, B. (1995), *Life on the Run,* New York: Vintage Books, p. 65.

9. Oriard (1982), op. cit., p. 211.

10. Jordan, P. (1975), *A False Spring,* New York: Dodd, Mead & Co., p. 98.

11. Armstrong, L. with Jenkins, S. (2000), *It's Not About the Bike: My Journey Back to Life,* New York: Putnam's Sons, pp. 244, 249.

12. Messing, S. with Hirshey, D. (1978), *The Education of an American Soccer Player,* New York: Dodd, Mead & Co., pp. 119–20.

13. Sampson, C. (1996), *Hogan,* New York: Broadway Books; Cramer, R. (1999), "What Do You Think of Ted Williams Now?" pp. 58–89, In Halberstam, D. (Ed.), *The Best American Sports Writing of the Century,* Boston: Houghton Mifflin.

14. Morris, J. (1971), *Brian Piccolo: A Short Season,* Chicago: Rand, McNally, p. 154.

15. Dryden, K. (1983), *The Game,* Toronto: Macmillan, pp. 46–47.

16. Schollander, D. and Savage, D. (1971), *Deep Water,* New York: Crown Publishers, pp. 13, 228–30, 246.

17. Merson, P. with Ridley, I. (2000), *Hero and Villain,* London: Collins Willow, pp. 58–59.

18. Dryden (1983), op. cit., p. 70.

19. Meggyesy (1970), op. cit., pp. 110, 149, 150–54.

20. Kramer, J. (1968), *Instant Replay: The Green Bay Diary of Jerry Kramer,* Edited by Dick Schaap, New York: New American Library, pp. 27–28.

21. Fleischer, N. (1931), *Gene Tunney—Enigma of the Ring,* Springfield, MA: The Ring, Inc.

22. Ibid.

23. Sullivan, R. (2002), *Rocky Marciano: The Rock of His Times,* Urbana, IL: University of Illinois Press, pp. 36, 178.

24. Stravinsky, J. (1997), *Muhammad Ali,* New York: Park Lane Press, p. 70.

25. Sampson, C. (1996), op. cit., pp. 37, 67.

26. Oriard (1982), op. cit., p. 84.

27. Bickley (1997), op. cit., p. xiv.

28. Stowers, C. (1971), *The Randy Matson Story,* Los Altos, CA: Tafnews Press, p. 176.

29. Dryden (1983), op. cit., pp. 91–93.

30. Ibid.

31. Sampson (1996), op. cit., pp. 35–36, 48, 64.

32. Salvino, C. with Klein, F. (1988), *Fast Lanes,* Chicago: Bonus Books, p. 67.

33. In Holtzman, J. (1995), *No Cheering in the Press Box,* New York: Henry Holt, p. 301.

34. Stump, A. (1994), *Cobb: The Life and Times of the Meanest Man Who Ever Played Baseball,* Chapel Hill, NC: Algonquin Books, p. 115.

35. Graham, F. (1942), *Lou Gehrig: A Quiet Hero,* Eau Claire, WI: E.M. Hale & Co., p. 119.

36. Isaacs, N. (1995), *Batboys and the World of Baseball,* Jackson, MS: Univ. of Mississippi Press, p. 83.

37. Howe, S. with Greenfield J. (1989), *Between the Lines: One Athlete's Struggle to Escape the Nightmare of Addiction,* Grand Rapids, MI: Masters Press, p. 56.

38. Jordan (1975), op. cit., pp. 100, 253–54.

39. Sokolove, M. (1990), *Hustle: The Myth, Life and Lies of Pete Rose,* New York: Simon & Schuster, pp. 173–74.

40. Brashler, W. (1978), *Josh Gibson: A Life in the Negro Leagues,* New York: Harper & Row, pp. 15–16, 65–68.

41. Jordan (1975), op. cit., p. 191.

42. Ibid., pp. 87, 93.

43. Bradlye (1995), op. cit., pp. 29–31, 41, 58, 293.

44. Sokolove (1990), op. cit., p. 49.

45. Cramer, R. (2000), *Joe DiMaggio: The Hero's Life,* New York: Simon & Schuster, pp. 58–59.

46. Salvino (1988), op. cit., p. 79.

47. Rosaforte, T. (1997), *Tiger Woods: The Makings of a Champion,* New York: St. Martin's, pp. 179, 197.

48. Vaughan, R. (1975), *The Grand Gesture: Ted Turner and the America's Cup,* Boston: Little, Brown, pp. 113–14.

49. Ashe and Deford (1993), op. cit., pp. 28–29, 202, 255.

50. Ibid.

51. Messing (1978), op. cit., p. 213.

52. Wagenheim, K. (1973), *Clemente!,* New York: Praeger Publishers, p. 136.

53. Sullivan (2002), op. cit., pp. 199–200.

54. Gentry, T. (1990), *Jesse Owens: Champion Athlete,* New York: Chelsea House Publishers, p. 102.

55. Ashe and Deford (1993), op. cit., *passim.*

56. Brosnan, J. (1960), *The Long Season,* New York: Dell Publishing, p. 12.

57. Stump (1994), op. cit., p. 104.

58. Dizikes, J. (2000), *Yankee Doodle Dandy: The Life and Times of Tod Sloan,* New Haven, CT: Yale University Press, p. 148.

59. Cramer (2000), op. cit., p. 303.

60. Sampson (1996), op. cit., p. 36.

61. Armstrong and Jenkins (2000), op. cit., p. 59.

62. Ashe and Deford (1993), op. cit., pp. 21, 182.

63. In Holtzman (1995), op. cit., p. 2.

64. Jordan (1975), op. cit., p. 191.

65. Merson (2000), op. cit., p. 145.

66. Dryden (1983), op. cit., p. 76.

67. Bradley (1995), op. cit., p. 31.

68. Salvino and Klein (1988), op. cit., p. 95.

69. Schollander and Savage (1971), op. cit., p. 163.

70. Armstrong and Jenkins (2000), op. cit., p. 234.

71. Jordan (1975), op. cit., p. 245.

72. Sampson (1996), op. cit., p. 46.

73. Messing (1978), op. cit., p. 22.

74. Tosches, N. (2000), *The Devil and Sonny Liston,* New York: Little, Brown, pp. 134–36.

75. Halberstam, D. (1999), *Playing for Keeps: Michael Jordan and the World He Made,* New York: Random House, p. 318.

76. Hauser, T. (1991), *Muhammad Ali: His Life and Times,* New York: Simon & Schuster.

77. Bouton, J. (1970), *Ball Four: My Life and Hard Times Throwing the Knuckleball in the Big Leagues,* New York: World Publishing Co.

78. Creamer, R. (1974), *Babe: The Legend Comes to Life,* New York. Simon & Schuster, pp. 192, 221–22.

79. Pryor, A. with Terrill, M. (1996), *Flight of the Hawk: The Aaron Pryor Story,* Sun Lake, AZ: Book World, Inc., p. 235.

80. Stafford, T. (1990), *Dave Dravecky: Comeback,* New York: HarperCollins, pp. 5–6.

81. Bradley (1995), op. cit., pp. 69, 102.

82. Dryden (1983), op. cit., pp. 49, 79.

83. Oriard (1982), op. cit., pp. 24, 306–7.

84. Schollander and Savage (1971), op. cit., p. 234.

85. Dryden (1983), op. cit., pp. 18–19.

86. Dizikes (2000), op. cit., pp. 16, 123.

87. Merson (2000), op. cit., pp. 12, 28.

88. Bickley (1997), op. cit., p. 189.

89. Bradley (1995), op. cit., pp. 93, 102.

90. Conner, B. with Ziert, P. (1985), *Winning the Gold,* New York: Warner Books, pp. 69, 128.

91. Schollander and Savage (1971), op. cit., pp. 25, 42.

92. Salvino and Klein (1988), op. cit., pp. 18–25, 38, 51.

93. Deford, F. (1976), *Big Bill Tilden: The Triumphs and the Tragedy,* New York: Simon & Schuster, pp. 43, 48, 273.

94. Armstrong and Jenkins (2000), op. cit., pp. 174, 196, 200.

95. Ibid., pp. 224–25.

96. Lear, C. (2000), *Running with the Buffaloes,* Guilford, CT: The Lyons Press, p. 21.

97. Oriard (1982), op. cit., p. xvii.

98. Messing (1978), op. cit., pp. 119–20.

99. Salvino and Klein (1988), op. cit., p. 116.

100. Morris (1971), op. cit.

101. Sokolove (1990), op. cit, p. 49.

102. Merson (2000), op. cit., pp. 51, 56–57, 89, 115, 145, 196, 255.

103. Rosaforte (1997), op. cit., p. 201.

104. Halberstam (1996), op. cit., pp. 319–20.

105. DeGregorio, G. (1981), *Joe Dimaggio: An Informal Biography,* Princeton, NJ: Townhouse Publishers, pp. 50, 100, 169–70.

106. Armstrong and Jenkins (2000), op. cit., p. 91.

107. Sokolove (1990), op. cit., p. 233.
108. Rubin Jr., L. (Spring 1993), "Babe Ruth's Ghost," *Sewanee Review,* 101(2), p. 246.
109. Parr, J. (1976), *The Superwives,* New York: Coward, McCann & Geoghegan.
110. Kramer (1968), op. cit., p. xii.
111. Hillenbrand, L.(2002), *Seabiscuit: An American Legend,* New York: Ballantine Books, pp. 59, 101.
112. Wagenheim (1973), op. cit., pp. 58–59.
113. Green, T. (1996), *The Dark Side of the Game: My Life in the NFL,* New York: Warner Books, pp. 113–14.
114. Conroy, P. (2002), *My Losing Season,* New York: Doubleday, p. 181.
115. Bouton (1970), op. cit.
116. Oriard (1982), op. cit., p. 173.
117. Wagenheim (1973), op. cit., p. 158.
118. Messing (1978), op. cit., p. 145.
119. Halberstam (1996), op. cit., p. 320.
120. Deford (1975), op. cit., p. 47.
121. Sokolove (1990), op. cit., pp. 207–8.
122. Sampson (1996), op. cit., p. xi.
123. Mathewson, C. (1977), *Pitching in a Pinch,* reprint, New York: Stein & Day, p. 50.
124. Messing (1978), op. cit., p. 124.
125. Salvino and Klein (1988), op. cit., pp. 19, 46, 49.
126. Dizikes (2000), op. cit., pp. 89, 93–94.
127. Sokolove (1980), op. cit., pp. 209–10.
128. Newcombe, J. (1975), *The Best of the Athletic Boys: The White Man's Impact on Jim Thorpe,* New York: Doubleday, pp. 229, 242.
129. Plimpton, G. (1966), *Paper Lion,* New York: Pocket Books, p. 16.
130. Rosaforte (1997), op. cit., p. 21.
131. Bickley (1997), op. cit., pp. xviii, 161.
132. Halberstam (1996), op. cit., pp. 317–20.
133. Sokolove (1990), op. cit., pp. 194–258 passim.
134. Ibid., pp. 248–68, 284–93.
135. Green (1996), op. cit., p. 118.
136. Merson (1999), op. cit., p. 71.
137. Howe (1989), op. cit., p 192.
138. In Holtzman (1995), op. cit., p. 222.
139. Brashler (1978), op. cit., pp. 125–43.
140. Berger, P. (1998), *Mickey Mantle,* New York: Park Lane Press, pp. 71, 88–89.
141. Anonymous (2007, Oct. 15), "La Russa DUI Hearing Postponed," *St. Louis Post-Dispatch,* from http://www.wpbf.com/sports/14341084/detail.html; Nightengale, B. (2007, May 7), "Hancock's Death Leads Cards to Ban Booze in Clubhouse," *USA Today,* available from http://www.usatoday.com/sports/baseball/nl/cardinals/2007-05-07-alcohol-ban-hancock_N.htm.
142. Howe (1989), op. cit., pp. 4, 91–141 *passim.*
143. Pryor and Terrill (1996), op. cit., pp. 140–80 *passim.*
144. Merson (2000), op. cit., pp. 10*ff.*
145. Dizikes (2000), op. cit., pp. 148, 165.

146. Johnson, J. (1992), *Jack Johnson—in the Ring and Out,* reprint, New York: Citadel Press.

147. Creamer (1974), op. cit., pp. 229, 260–63, 314–19.

148. Sullivan (2002), op. cit., p. 196.

149. Sanders, D. with Black, J. (1998), *Power, Money & Sex: How Success Almost Ruined My Life,* Nashville: Word Publishing, pp. 65, 86–87.

150. Sokolove (1990), op. cit., pp. 16, 224.

151. Rosaforte (1997), op. cit., p. 213.

152. Armstrong and Jenkins (2000), op. cit., pp. 4, 7.

153. Conner (1985), op. cit., pp. 75, 90, 105, 122–24.

154. Vaughn (1975), op. cit., p. 232.

155. Heller, P. (1995), *Bad Intentions: The Mike Tyson Story,* New York: De Capo Press, pp. 163, 188, 232, 282–86.

156. Parr (1976), op. cit., p. 262.

157. Brashler (1978), op. cit., pp. 187–88.

158. Bradley (1995), op. cit., pp. 173–74.

159. Morris (1971), op. cit., pp. 117*ff.*

160. Messing (1978), op. cit., p. 203*ff.*

161. Armstrong and Jenkins (2000), op. cit., pp. 46, 55.

162. Morris (1971), op. cit.

163. Conner (1985), op. cit., p. 88.

164. Sands, R. (1999), *Gutcheck!,* Carpinteria, CA: Rincon Hill Books, p. 131.

165. Oriard (1982), op. cit., p. 258.

166. Kramer (1968), op. cit.

167. Green (1996), op. cit.

168. Oriard (1982), op. cit., pp. 70–71.

169. Green (1996), op cit. p. 24.

170. Stafford (1990), op. cit., p. 71.

171. Meggyesy (1970), op. cit., pp. 203–7.

172. Ibid., pp. 139, 193–201.

173. Dryden (1983), op. cit., p. 4.

174. Stafford (1990), op. cit., p. 28.

175. Jordan (1975), op. cit., p. 121.

176. Scholander and Savage (1971), op. cit., pp. 15–16.

177. Stump (1994), op. cit.; See Creevy, P. (2002), *Tyrus: A Novel,* New York: Tom Doherty Associates, for a compelling fictional account of Cobb's life.

178. Dizikes (2000), op. cit., p. 124.

179. Cramer (2000), op. cit., p. 251.

180. Sokolove (1990), op. cit., pp. 150, 191, 197.

181. Ibid., pp. 15, 49, 52.

182. Berger (1998), op. cit., pp. 85–89, 114, 134.

183. Merson (2000), op. cit.

184. Ashe and Deford (1993), op. cit, p. 20.

185. Hillenbrand (2001), op. cit.

186. Schollander and Savage (1971), op. cit., p. 39.

187. Sanders and Black (1998), op. cit., p. 162.

188. Pryor and Terrill (1996), op. cit., p. 79.

189. Ibid., p. 86.

190. Heller (1995), op. cit., pp. 388, 433.

191. Stravinsky (1997), op. cit., pp. 126–27.

192. Halberstam (1999), op. cit., pp. 322–23.

193. Weiss, P. (1969), *Sport: A Philosophic Inquiry*, Carbondale: Southern Illinois Univ. Press, p. 27.

194. Kramer (1968), op. cit., p. xii.

195. Oriard (1982), op. cit., p. 188.

196. Schollander and Savage (1971), op. cit., p. 246.

CHAPTER 5: SEX AND SEXUALITY

1. In Edwards, H. (1973), *Sociology of Sport*, Homewood, IL: Dorsey Press, p. 15.

2. Betts, J. (1974), *America's Sporting Heritage: 1850–1950*, Reading, MA: Addison-Wesley, p. 182.

3. Ibid., p. 183; Lee, M. (1983), *A History of Physical Education and Sports in the U.S.A.*, New York: John Wiley and Sons, p. 145.

4. Cramer, R. (2000), *Joe DiMaggio: The Hero's Life*, New York: Simon & Schuster, p. 59.

5. Oriard, M. (1982), *Dreaming of Heroes: American Sports Fiction, 1868–1980*, Chicago: Nelson-Hall, p. 57.

6. Cramer (2000), op. cit.; Oriard, M. (1993), *Reading Football: How the Popular Press Created an American Spectacle*, Chapel Hill, NC: Univ. of North Carolina Press, p. 250.

7. Oriard, M. (1982), *The End of Autumn: Reflections on my Life in Football*, New York: Doubleday, p. 227.

8. Edmonds, A. (1973), *Joe Louis*, Grand Rapids, MI: Wm. B. Eerdmans, p. 20.

9. Messner, M. (1993), "The Meaning of Success: The Athletic Experience and the Development of Male Identity," In Eitzen, D.S. (Ed.), *Sport in Contemporary Society*, New York: St. Martin's Press, pp. 409–11; Sparkes, A. and Smith, B. (2002), "Sport, Spinal Cord Injury, Embodied Masculinities, and the Dilemmas of Narrative Identity," *Men and Masculinities*, 4(3), pp. 262–63.

10. Morris, T. (1997), *Making the Team: The Cultural Work of Baseball Fiction*, Urbana: University of Illinois Press, pp. 4, 43–44, 67.

11. Oriard (1982), *The End of Autumn*, pp. 22–23, 29.

12. Kopay, D. and Young, P. (1988), *The David Kopay Story*, New York: Primus, pp. 39, 42.

13. Sparkes and Smith (2002), op. cit.

14. Kaufman, K. (2003, Jan. 8), "Football: America's Favorite Homoerotic Sport," *Salon*, from http://www.salon.com/news/sports/col/kaufman/2003/01/08/homoerotic/.

15. Kopay and Young (1988), op. cit., pp. 50–51.

16. Morris (1997), op. cit., p. 79.

17. Deford, F. (1976), *Big Bill Tilden: The Triumphs and the Tragedy*, New York: Simon & Schuster, pp. 18, 49.

18. Kopay (1988), op. cit.

19. Louganis, G. (1995), *Breaking the Surface*, New York: Random House.

20. Vox, D. (2007, Sept. 20), "Four Amazing Sports Stars Join 'Advocate' List of Top Gay Heroes"; ——— (2007, Feb. 7), "Basketball's John Amaechi comes out," available from http://gaywired.com/article.cf?section=70&id=16540.

21. Perkins, C. (2007, Sept. 28), "Hardaway Learns from His Mistake," PalmBeachPost.com. Available from http://www.palmbeachpost.com.

22. Bickley, D. (1997), *No Bull: The Unauthorized Biography of Dennis Rodman,* New York: St. Martins.

23. Bouton, J. (1970), *Ball Four: My Life and Hard Times Throwing the Knuckleball in the Big Leagues,* New York: World Publishing Co., p. 233.

24. Kowet, D. (1977), *The Rich Who Own Sports,* New York: Random House, p. 128.

25. Morris (1997), op. cit., p. 4.

26. Ibid., p. 66.

27. Schollander, D. and Savage, D. (1971), *Deep Water,* New York: Crown Publishers.

28. Graham, F. (1942), *Lou Gehrig: A Quiet Hero,* Eau Claire, WI: E.M. Hale & Company, pp. 158*ff.*

29. Conroy, P. (2002), *My Losing Season,* New York: Doubleday, pp. 314–15.

30. Meggyesy, D. (1970), *Out of Their League,* Berkeley, CA: Ramparts Press, p. 22.

31. Ibid., p. 73.

32. Kopay and Young (1988), op. cit., pp. 53–54.

33. Sands, Rt. (1999), *Gutcheck!,* Carpinteria, CA: Rincon Hill Books, p. 261.

34. Meggyesy (1970), op. cit., p. 181.

35. Knox, C. and Plaschke, B. (1988), *Hard Knox: The Life of an NFL Coach,* San Diego: Harcourt Brace Jovanovich, pp. 108–9.

36. Conroy (2002), op. cit., p. 81.

37. Green, T. (1996), *The Dark Side of the Game: My Life in the NFL,* New York: Warner Books, p. 72.

38. Meggyesy (1970), op. cit., pp. 182–83.

39. Parr, J. (1976), *The Superwives,* New York: Coward, McCann & Geoghegan, p. 56.

40. Salvino, C. with Klein, F. (1988), *Fast Lanes,* Chicago: Bonus Books, p. 66.

41. Howe, S. with Greenfield, J. (1989), *Between the Lines: One Athlete's Struggle to Escape the Nightmare of Addiction,* Grand Rapids, MI: Masters Press, p. 135.

42. Creamer, R. (1974), *Babe: The Legend Comes to Life,* New York. Simon & Schuster.

43. Morris, J. (1971), *Brian Piccolo: A Short Season,* Chicago: Rand, McNally, p. 112.

44. Heller, P. (1995), *Bad Intentions: The Mike Tyson Story,* New York: De Capo Press, pp. 164–65.

45. Salvino and Klein (1988), op. cit., p. 83.

46. Armstrong, L. with Jenkins, S. (2000), *It's Not About the Bike: My Journey Back to Life,* New York: Putnam's Sons, pp. 73–74.

47. Ashe, A. with Deford, F. (1993), *Arthur Ashe: Portrait in Motion,* New York: Carroll & Graf, p. 78.

48. Parr (1976), op. cit., p. 285.

49. Rampersad, A. (1997), *Jackie Robinson: A Biography,* New York: Knopf, p. 143.

50. Vaughan, R. (1975), *The Grand Gesture: Ted Turner and the America's Cup,* Boston: Little, Brown, p. 284.

51. Cramer (2000), op. cit., pp. 324*ff.*

52. Ashe and Deford (1993), op. cit., pp. 78–79.

53. Parr (1976), op. cit., p. 148.

54. Sokolove, M. (1990), *Hustle: The Myth, Life and Lies of Pete Rose,* New York: Simon & Schuster, pp. 182–86.

55. Edmonds (1973), op. cit., pp. 67–68.

56. Ibid.

57. Cramer, R. (1999), "What Do You Think of Ted Williams Now?" In Halberstam, D. (Ed.), *The Best American Sports Writing of the Century,* Boston: Houghton Mifflin, pp. 83–89.

58. Knox and Plaschke (1988), op. cit., pp. 64–65.

59. Berger, P. (1998), *Mickey Mantle,* New York: Park Lane Press, pp. 67, 134.

60. Ibid., p. 110.

61. Sokolove (1990), op. cit., pp. 74–75, 187, 197.

62. Cramer (2000), op. cit., pp. 192–93.

63. Morris (1971); Howe (1989), op. cit., p. 141.

64. Messner (1993), op. cit., pp. 415–17.

65. Parr (1976), op. cit., pp. 15–16.

66. Smith, M. (1987), *Life after Hockey,* Lynx, CT: Codner Books, 1987, pp. 145*ff.*

67. In Parr (1976), op. cit., p. 140.

68. Messing, S. with Hirshey, D. (1978), *The Education of an American Soccer Player,* New York: Dodd, Mead & Co., pp. 167–68.

69. Armstrong and Jenkins (2000), op. cit., pp. 224–25.

70. Bouton (1970), op. cit., *passim.*

71. Sampson, C. (1996), *Hogan,* New York: Broadway Books, pp. 61, 118.

72. Piersall, J. and Hirshberg, A. (1955), *Fear Strikes Out: The Jim Piersall Story,* New York: Grosset & Dunlap, pp. 182*ff.*

73. Ashe, A. and Rampersad, A. (1993), *Days of Grace: A Memoir,* New York: Knopf, pp. 261–62.

74. Stafford, T. (1990), *Dave Dravecky: Comeback,* New York: HarperCollins, pp. 142*ff,* 215.

75. Ibid., pp. 146, 255–56.

76. Merson, P. with Ridley, I. (2000), *Hero and Villain,* London: Collins Willow, pp. 278*ff.*

77. Bradley, B. (1995), *Life on the Run,* New York: Vintage Books, p. 70.

78. Sullivan, R. (2002), *Rocky Marciano: The Rock of His Times,* Urbana, IL: University of Illinois Press, p. 178.

79. Meggyesy (1970), op. cit., p. 169.

80. Romanowski, B. with Schefter, A. and Towle, P. (2005), *Romo: My Life on the Edge,* New York: William Morrow, p. 65.

81. Jordan, P. (1975), *A False Spring,* New York: Dodd, Mead & Co., pp. 180–81.

82. Cramer (2000), op. cit., p. 58.

83. Ashe and Deford (1975), op. cit., p. 77.

84. Bickley (1997), op. cit., p. 87.

85. Pryor, A. with Terrill, M. (1996), *Flight of the Hawk: The Aaron Pryor Story,* Sun Lake, AZ: Book World, Inc., pp. 130–31.

86. Cassidy, R. (1999), *Muhammad Ali: The Greatest of All Time,* Lincolnwood, IL: Publications International, p. 154.

87. Hauser, T. (1991), *Muhammad Ali: His Life and Times,* New York: Simon & Schuster, pp. 310–17.

88. Cramer (2000), op. cit., pp. 113*ff.*

89. Sokolove (1990), op. cit., pp. 62–63, 183–84.

90. In Creamer (1974), op. cit., p. 221.

91. Ibid., pp. 183, 221–22, 293, 302, 318.

92. Bouton (1970), op. cit., p. 275.

93. In Parr (1976), op. cit., p. 146.

94. Merson (2000), op. cit., p. 241.

95. Bradley (1995), op. cit., p. 111.

96. Ibid., p. 202.

97. In Morris (1997), op. cit., p. 43.

98. Kopay (1988), op. cit., p. 4.

99. Meggyesy (1970), op. cit., pp. 182–83.

100. Ibid.

101. Tosches, N. (2000), *The Devil and Sonny Liston,* New York: Little, Brown, pp. 135, 177–78, 193–94, 197.

102. In Heller (1995), op. cit., p. 386.

103. Ibid., *passim.*

104. Richards, R. with Ames, J. (1983), *Second Serve: The Renée Richards Story,* New York: Stein and Day, p. 42.

105. Parr (1976), op. cit., p. 225.

106. Richards (1983), op. cit., p. 77.

107. Hillenbrand, L. (2002), *Seabiscuit: An American Legend,* New York: Ballantine Books, pp. 99–100.

108. Tosches (2000), op. cit., pp. 134–35.

109. Meggyesy (1970), op. cit., pp. 299–301.

110. Kopay and Young (1988), op. cit., p. 126.

111. Ibid., p. 148.

112. Ibid.

113. "Composite U.S. Demographics" (2005), Adherents.com, from http://www.adherents.com/adh_dem.html.

Chapter 6: Team Colors: Sport and Race

1. Wiggins, D. (Ed.) (2004), *African Americans in Sports* [2 Vols.], Armonk, NY: M. E. Sharpe, Inc., pp. 160, 387.

2. Dizikes, J. (2000), *Yankee Doodle Dandy: The Life and Times of Tod Sloan,* New Haven, CT: Yale University Press, pp. 37–38.

3. Sullivan, R. (2002), *Rocky Marciano: The Rock of His Times,* Urbana, IL: University of Illinois Press, pp. 69–70; Wiggins (2004), op. cit., p. 43.

4. Betts, J. (1974), *America's Sporting Heritage: 1850–1950,* Reading, MA: Addison-Wesley, p. 168; Johnson, J. (1992), *Jack Johnson—in the Ring and Out,* reprint, New York: Citadel Press, pp. 2–10; Early, G. (Ed.) (1998), *The Muhammad Ali Reader,* New York: Rob Welch Books, p. 18.

5. Johnson (1992), op. cit., pp. 233–34.

6. Newcombe, J. (1975), *The Best of the Athletic Boys: The White Man's Impact on Jim Thorpe,* New York: Doubleday.

7. Ibid., pp. 116–17.

8. Stump, A. (1994), *Cobb: The Life and Times of the Meanest Man Who Ever Played Baseball,* Chapel Hill, NC: Algonquin Books, pp. 199–200.

9. Creamer, R. (1974), *Babe: The Legend Comes to Life,* New York. Simon & Schuster, p. 185*ff.*

10. Ibid., pp. 269–70.

11. Rampersad, A. (1997), *Jackie Robinson: A Biography,* New York: Knopf, p. 121.

12. Ibid., p. 115.

13. Brashler, W. (1978), *Josh Gibson: A Life in the Negro Leagues,* New York: Harper & Row, pp. 8, 31–33.

14. Ibid., pp. 14–15.

15. Oriard, M. (1993), *Reading Football: How the Popular Press Created an American Spectacle,* Chapel Hill, NC: Univ. of North Carolina Press, p. 232.

16. Gentry, T. (1990), *Jesse Owens: Champion Athlete,* New York: Chelsea House Publishers, pp. 43*ff.*

17. Rampersad (1997), op. cit., pp. 67–68.

18. Brashler (1978), op. cit., pp. 3–5.

19. Gentry (1990), op. cit., p. 65.

20. Ibid., pp. 67–68.

21. Ibid., 99–100.

22. Ibid., pp. 100–101.

23. Edmonds, A. (1973), *Joe Louis,* Grand Rapids, MI: Wm. B. Eerdmans, pp. 32–42.

24. Ibid., p. 104.

25. Tygiel, J. (1997), *Baseball's Great Experiment: Jackie Robinson and His Legacy,* New York: Oxford University Press, p. 335.

26. Sullivan (2002), op. cit., pp. 73–75, 79.

27. In Rampersad (1997), op. cit., p. 179.

28. Tygiel (1997), op. cit., pp. 336, 344–47.

29. Ibid., pp. 63, 344.

30. Rampersad (1997), op. cit., pp. 163–65, 171.

31. Ibid., pp. 170, 179.

32. Ibid., p. 178.

33. Ibid.

34. Ibid., pp. 172–73.

35. Wagenheim, K. (1973), *Clemente!,* New York: Praeger Publishers, pp. 10–11.

36. Stump (1994), op. cit., pp. 199–200.

37. James, C. (1983), *Beyond a Boundary,* New York: Pantheon Books, pp. 55–57, 60.

38. Cramer, R. (2000), *Joe DiMaggio: The Hero's Life,* New York: Simon & Schuster, pp. 40–41.

39. Wagenheim (1973), op. cit., p. 39*ff.*

40. Ibid., pp. 86–89.

41. Ibid., pp. 89–90.

42. Ibid., p. 132.

43. Ibid., pp. 45–46, 91.

44. Ibid., pp. 91–92.

45. Ibid., p. 99.

46. Ibid., pp. 138–39, 187, 252.

47. Tygiel (1997), op. cit., p. 335.

48. Bradley, B. (1995), *Life on the Run,* New York: Vintage Books, pp. 18–19.

49. Ibid.

50. Knox, C. and Plaschke, B. (1988), *Hard Knox: The Life of an NFL Coach,* San Diego: Harcourt Brace Jovanovich, pp. 152–55.

51. Cohen, J. (1971), *Big A: The Story of Lew Alcindor,* New York: Scholastic Books.

52. Plimpton, G. (1966), *Paper Lion,* New York: Pocket Books, pp. 156–57.

53. Ibid.

54. Morris, J. (1971), *Brian Piccolo: A Short Season,* Chicago: Rand, McNally, pp. 130–31.

55. Ibid.

56. Sokolove, M. (1990), *Hustle: The Myth, Life and Lies of Pete Rose,* New York: Simon & Schuster, pp. 55–57.

57. Ibid., pp. 58, 61.

58. Stravinsky, J. (1997), *Muhammad Ali,* New York: Park Lane Press, pp. 9–10.

59. Cassidy, R. (1999), *Muhammad Ali: The Greatest of All Time,* Lincolnwood, IL: Publications International, pp. 46–47.

60. Hauser, T. (1991), *Muhammad Ali: His Life and Times,* New York: Simon & Schuster, p. 81.

61. In Early (1998), op. cit., p. 140.

62. Ibid., p. 135.

63. Roberts, R. and Olson, J. (1989), *Winning Is the Only Thing: Sports in America since 1945,* Baltimore: Johns Hopkins Univ. Press, pp. 169–70.

64. Tosches, N. (2000), *The Devil and Sonny Liston,* New York: Little, Brown, p. 136.

65. Ashe, A. and Rampersad, A. (1993), *Days of Grace: A Memoir,* New York: Knopf, p. 61.

66. Ibid. p. 103; Weissberg, T. (1992), *Arthur Ashe: Tennis Great,* New York: Chelsea House, 1992, pp. 40–42, 77–78.

67. Ashe, A. with Deford, F. (1993), *Arthur Ashe: Portrait in Motion,* New York: Carroll & Graf, p. 173.

68. Green, T. (1996), *The Dark Side of the Game: My Life in the NFL,* New York: Warner Books, pp. 46–47.

69. Ibid., pp. 56–57.

70. Sanders, D. with Black, J. (1998), *Power, Money & Sex: How Success Almost Ruined My Life,* Nashville: Word Publishing, pp. 19–20.

71. Ibid., pp. 31–32.

72. Ibid.

73. Bickley, D. (1997), *No Bull: The Unauthorized Biography of Dennis Rodman,* New York: St. Martins, pp. 42–44.

74. Sands, R. (1999), *Gutcheck!,* Carpinteria, CA: Rincon Hill Books, pp. 207–8.

75. Early (1998), op. cit., p. 14.

76. Rosaforte, T. (1997), *Tiger Woods: The Makings of a Champion,* New York: St. Martin's.

77. Ibid., pp. 14–15*ff.*

78. Halberstam, D. (1999), *Playing for Keeps: Michael Jordan and the World He Made,* New York: Random House, pp. 17–18.

79. Andrews, D. (1998), "Excavating Michael Jordan: Notes on a Critical Pedagogy of Sporting Representation," In Rail, G. (Ed.), *Sport and Postmodern Times,* Albany, NY: SUNY Press, pp. 201–14.

80. Early (1996), op. cit., p. xv.

81. In Roberts and Olson (1989), op. cit., p. 163.

82. Cole, C. and King, S. (1998), "Representing Black Masculinity and Urban Possibilities: Racism, Realism, and Hoop Dreams," In Rail, G. (Ed.), *Sport and Postmodern Times,* Albany, NY: SUNY Press, p. 52.

83. Cole, C. (1998), "Addiction, Exercise, and Cyborgs: Technologies of Deviant Bodies," In Rail, G. (Ed.), *Sport and Postmodern Times,* Albany, NY: SUNY Press, p. 262.

84. Roberts and Olson (1989), op. cit., pp. 179–87.

CHAPTER 7: THE ATHLETE AND HIS BODY

1. Sparkes, A. (2002), *Telling Tales in Sports and Physical Activity: A Qualitative Journey,* Champaign, IL: Human Kinetics, p. 99; MacNeill, Margaret (1998), "Sex, Lies and Videotape: The Political and Cultural Economies of Celebrity Fitness Videos," In Rail, G. (Ed.), *Sport and Postmodern Times,* Albany, NY: SUNY Press, p. 175.

2. Kopay, D. and Young, P. (1988), *The David Kopay Story,* New York: Primus, p. 48.

3. Higgs, R. (1981), *Laurel & Thorn: The Athlete in American Literature,* Lexington, KY: The University Press of Kentucky, pp. 1–2.

4. Synnott, A. (1992, March), "Tomb, Temple, Machine, and Self: The Social Construction of the Body," *British Journal of Sociology,* 43(1), p. 79.

5. Solotaroff, P. (1999), "The Power and the Glory," In Halberstam, D. (Ed.), *The Best American Sports Writing of the Century,* Boston: Houghton Mifflin, p. 582.

6. Stuart, O. (1995), *Perpetual Motion: The Public and Private Lives of Rudolf Nureyev,* New York: Simon & Schuster, p. 109.

7. Sparkes, A. and Smith, B. (2002), "Sport, Spinal Cord Injury, Embodied Masculinities, and the Dilemmas of Narrative Identity," *Men and Masculinities,* 4(3), pp. 258–85.

8. Oriard, M. (1982), *The End of Autumn: Reflections on My Life in Football,* New York: Doubleday, pp. 18–19.

9. Dryden, K. (1983), *The Game,* Toronto: Macmillan, p. 141.

10. Romanowski, B. with Schefter, A. and Towle, P. (2005), *Romo: My Life on the Edge,* New York: William Morrow, p. 194.

11. Heller, P. (1995), *Bad Intentions: The Mike Tyson Story,* New York: De Capo Press, p. 157.

12. Patterson, F. and Talese, G. (1998), "In Defense of Cassius Clay," in Early, G. (Ed.), *The Muhammad Ali Reader,* New York: Rob Welch Books, p. 65.

13. Berger, P. (1998), *Mickey Mantle,* New York: Park Lane Press.

14. Gergen, M. and Gergen, K. (1993), "Narrative of the Gendered Body in Popular Autobiography," In Josselson, R. and Lieblich, A. (Eds.) *The Narrative Study of Live,* Newbury Park: Sage Publications, p. 204.

15. Romanowski (2005), op. cit., p. 6.

16. Kretchmer, A. (1999), "Butkus," In Halberstam, D. (Ed.), *The Best American Sports Writing of the Century,* Boston: Houghton Mifflin, p. 401.

17. Bouton, J. (1970), *Ball Four: My Life and Hard Times Throwing the Knuckleball in the Big Leagues,* New York: World Publishing Co.

18. Howe, S. with Greenfield, J. (1989), *Between the Lines: One Athlete's Struggle to Escape the Nightmare of Addiction,* Grand Rapids, MI: Masters Press, p. 183.

19. Oriard (1982), op. cit., p. 18.

20. Merson, P. with Ridley, I. (2000), *Hero and Villain,* London: Collins Willow, p. 126.

21. Patterson and Talese (1998), op. cit., p. 65.

22. Oriard (1982), op. cit., p. 218.

23. Jordan, P. (1975), *A False Spring,* New York: Dodd, Mead & Co.

24. Weiss, P. (1969), *Sport: A Philosophic Inquiry,* Carbondale: Southern Illinois Univ. Press, p. 23.

25. Sokolove, M. (1990), *Hustle: The Myth, Life and Lies of Pete Rose,* New York: Simon & Schuster, p. 66.

26. Ibid.

27. Armstrong, L. with Jenkins, S. (2000), *It's Not About the Bike: My Journey Back to Life,* New York: Putnam's Sons, pp. 3–4.

28. Halberstam, D. (1999), *Playing for Keeps: Michael Jordan and the World He Made,* New York: Random House, p. 11.

29. Smith, B. and Sparkes, A. (2002), "Men, Sport Spinal Cord Injury and the Construction of Coherence: Narrative Practice in Action," *Qualitative Research,* 2(2), p. 150, following van Manen.

30. Oates, J. (1987), *On Boxing,* London: Pan Books, pp. 25–26.

31. Messing, S. with Hirshey, D. (1978), *The Education of an American Soccer Player,* New York: Dodd, Mead & Co., p. 68.

32. In Romanowski (2005), op. cit., p. 14.

33. Cassidy, R. (1999), *Muhammad Ali: The Greatest of All Time,* Lincolnwood, IL: Publications International, p. 12.

34. Sokolove (1990), op. cit., pp. 69–70.

35. Ibid., p. 88.

36. Romanowski (2005), op. cit.

37. Ibid., pp. 90–251 *passim.*

38. In Holtzman, J. (1995), *No Cheering in the Press Box,* New York: Henry Holt, p. 247.

39. Heller (1995), op. cit., p. 94.

40. Smith. M. (1987), *Life after Hockey,* Lynx, CT: Codner Books, p. 284.

41. Green, T. (1996), *The Dark Side of the Game: My Life in the NFL,* New York: Warner Books, p. 21.

42. Kramer, J. (1968), *Instant Replay: The Green Bay Diary of Jerry Kramer,* Edited by Dick Schaap, New York: New American Library, p. 20.

43. Ibid., pp. 33–34.

44. Ibid.

45. Kopay (1977), op. cit., p. 61.

46. Meggyesy, D. (1970), *Out of Their League,* Berkeley, CA: Ramparts Press, pp. 151–52.

47. Green, T. (1996), *The Dark Side of the Game: My Life in the NFL,* New York: Warner Books, pp. 36–38.

48. Knox, C. and Plaschke, B. (1988), *Hard Knox: The Life of an NFL Coach,* San Diego: Harcourt Brace Jovanovich, pp. 91–92.

49. Hillenbrand, L. (2002), *Seabiscuit: An American Legend,* New York: Ballantine Books, pp. 82–83.

50. Armstrong and Jenkins (2000), op. cit., pp. 65, 219–20.

51. Messing (1978), op. cit., p. 69.

52. Ibid., p. 51.

53. Bradley, B. (1995), *Life on the Run,* New York: Vintage Books, p. 132.

54. Sullivan, R. (2002), *Rocky Marciano: The Rock of His Times,* Urbana, IL: University of Illinois Press, p. 131.

55. Schollander, D. and Savage, D. (1971), *Deep Water,* New York: Crown Publishers, pp. 14–15.

56. Lear, C. (2000), *Running with the Buffaloes,* Guilford, CT: The Lyons Press, pp. 4–5, 9, 30, 35.

57. Salvino, C. with Klein, F. (1988), *Fast Lanes,* Chicago: Bonus Books, pp. xii–xvii, 91.

58. Sampson, C. (1996), *Hogan,* New York: Broadway Books, pp. xi, 67–68.

59. Rosaforte, T. (1997), *Tiger Woods: The Makings of a Champion,* New York: St. Martin's, p. 193.

60. Sands, R. (1999), *Gutcheck!,* Carpinteria, CA: Rincon Hill Books, p. 157.

61. Morris, J. (1971), *Brian Piccolo: A Short Season,* Chicago: Rand, McNally, pp. 126, 129.

62. Roberts, A. (accessed May 2006), "Steroids in Baseball and Sports," Steroid.com, available from http://www.steroid.com/steroids-in-sports.php.

63. Meggyesy (1970), op. cit., p. 83.

64. Sokolove (1990), op. cit., pp. 78–80, 168; Bouton (1970), op. cit. *passim.*

65. Romanowski (2005), op. cit., pp. 60–120 *passim.*

66. Ibid., pp. 134–36, 188–89, 226.

67. The NFL banned steroids and started testing for them in 1987; major league baseball didn't ban steroids until September, 2002.

68. Green (1996), op. cit., p. 78.

69. Bradlye (1995), op. cit., p. 132.

70. Halberstam (1999), op. cit., p. 167.

71. Sokolove (1990), op. cit., pp. 70, 85.

72. Creamer, R. (1974), *Babe: The Legend Comes to Life,* New York: Simon & Schuster, pp. 232, 241, 289, 323.

73. DeGregorio, G. (1981), *Joe Dimaggio: An Informal Biography,* Princeton, NJ: Townhouse Publishers, pp. 38–233 *passim.*

74. Wagenheim, K. (1973), *Clemente!,* New York: Praeger Publishers, pp. 65–69.

75. Brashler, W. (1978), *Josh Gibson: A Life in the Negro Leagues,* New York: Harper & Row, pp. 51–54.

76. Romanowski (2005), op. cit., pp. 246, 302–10.

77. Oriard (1982), op. cit., p. 221.

78. Berger (1998), op. cit., pp. 64–67, 135.

79. Stump, A. (1994), *Cobb: The Life and Times of the Meanest Man Who Ever Played Baseball,* Chapel Hill, NC: Algonquin Books, pp. 141, 152, 201, 294–95, 310, 343.

80. Messing (1978), op. cit., p. 144.

81. Ibid.

82. Cramer, R. (2000), *Joe DiMaggio: The Hero's Life,* New York: Simon & Schuster, p. 110.

83. Dryden (1983), op. cit., pp. 121–22.

84. Green (1996), op. cit., p. 45.

85. Salvino and Klein (1988), op. cit., pp. xiv, 120.

86. Fleischer, N. (1931), *Gene Tunney—enigma of the Ring,* Springfield, MA: The Ring, Inc.; Sullivan (2002), op. cit., pp. 21–22.

87. Meggyesy (1970), op. cit., p. 82.

88. Parr, J. (1976), *The Superwives,* New York: Coward, McCann & Geoghegan, p. 230.

89. Dryden (1983), op. cit., pp. 116–17.

90. Deford, F. (1999), "The Boxer and the Blonde," In Halberstam, D. (Ed.), *The Best American Sports Writing of the Century,* Boston: Houghton Mifflin, p. 523.

91. Oates (1987), op. cit., pp. 88, 93.

92. Hauser, T. (1991), *Muhammad Ali: His Life and Times,* New York: Simon & Schuster, p. 14.

93. Cassidy (1999), op. cit., pp. 144–45.

94. Armstrong and Jenkins (2000), op. cit., p. 47.

95. Hillenbrand (2002), op. cit., pp. 88–89.

96. Ibid., pp. 197, 238–39, 258–61, 297.

97. Conner, B. with Ziert, P. (1985), *Winning the Gold,* New York: Warner Books, pp. 58–60.

98. Ibid., p. 97.

99. Meggyesy (1970), op. cit., pp. 83–84, 152.

100. Romanowski (2005), op. cit., p. 74.

101. Graham, F. (1942), *Lou Gehrig: A Quiet Hero,* Eau Claire, WI: E.M. Hale & Co.

102. Ashe, A. and Rampersad, A. (1993), *Days of Grace: A Memoir,* New York: Knopf, pp. 1–33.

103. Stafford, T. (1990), *Dave Dravecky: Comeback,* New York: HarperCollins.

104. Dizikes, J. (2000), *Yankee Doodle Dandy: The Life and Times of Tod Sloan,* New Haven, CT: Yale University Press, p. 54.

105. Cramer (2000), op. cit., p. 94.

106. Oriard (1982), op. cit., p. 283.

107. Knox and Plaschke (1988), op. cit., p. 129.

108. Conner (1985), op. cit., pp. 58–60.

109. In Bradley (1995), op. cit., p. 226.

110. Ibid., p. 131.

111. Cramer (2000), op. cit., pp. 41, 56.

112. Creamer (1974), op. cit., pp. 346–47.

113. Holtzman (1995), op. cit., p. 329.

114. Cramer (2000), op. cit., p. 85.

115. Holtzman (1995), op. cit., p. 152.

116. Cramer (2000), op. cit., p. 226.

117. Meggyesy (1970), op. cit., p. 80.

118. Berger (1998), op. cit., pp. 131–32.

119. Wagenheim (1973), op. cit., pp. 113–14.

120. Cramer (2000), op. cit., pp. 256–57, 283.

121. Berger (1998), op. cit., p. 101.

122. Green (1996), op. cit., pp. 28, 30.

123. Rail, G. (1998), "Seismography of the Postmodern Condition: Three Theses on the Implosion of Sport," In Rail, G. (Ed.), *Sport and Postmodern Times,* Albany, NY: SUNY Press, pp. 148–49.

124. Oriard (1982), op. cit., pp. 223–24.

125. Ibid.

126. Green (1996), op. cit., pp. 127–28.

127. Ibid., pp. 128–29.

128. Howe (1989), op. cit., pp. 5, 190.

129. Stafford (1990), op. cit., pp. 142–43, 150.

130. Sampson (1996), p. 139.
131. Conner (1985), op. cit., pp. 62–65.
132. Ibid., p. 66.
133. Messing (1978), op. cit., p. 130.
134. Conner (1985), op. cit., pp. 66–67.
135. Dryden (1983), op. cit., pp. 116–17.
136. Boswell, T. (1999), "Pain," In Halberstam, D. (Ed.), *The Best American Sports Writing of the Century,* Boston: Houghton Mifflin, p. 457.
137. Sands (1999), op. cit., pp. 159, 164.
138. Oriard (1982), op. cit., p. 217.
139. Romanowski (2005), op. cit., p. 24.
140. Oriard (1982), op. cit., pp. 217–18.
141. Armstrong and Jenkins (2000), op. cit., pp. 5, 88, 220.
142. Schollander and Savage (1971), op. cit., pp. 14–15.
143. Ibid.
144. Conner (1985), op. cit., p. 52.
145. Messing (1978), op. cit., pp. 130, 192.
146. Stump (1994), op. cit., p. 395.

CHAPTER 8: RETIRING FROM SPORT

1. Cramer, R. (2000), *Joe DiMaggio: The Hero's Life,* New York: Simon & Schuster, p. 314.
2. Ibid.
3. Schollander, D. and Savage, D. (1971), *Deep Water,* New York: Crown Publishers, pp. 90, 227, 246.
4. Dizikes, J. (2000), *Yankee Doodle Dandy: The Life and Times of Tod Sloan,* New Haven, CT: Yale University Press.
5. Oriard, M. (1982), *The End of Autumn: Reflections on My Life in Football,* New York: Doubleday.
6. See Cashmore, E. (Ed.) (2000), *Sports Culture: An A–Z Guide,* London: Routledge, pp. 6–8, 58–60.
7. Romanowski, B. with Schefter, A. and Towle, P. (2005), *Romo: My Life on the Edge,* New York: William Morrow, p. 56.
8. See Messner, M. (1992), *Power at Play: Sports and the Problem of Masculinity,* Boston: Beacon Press, chapters 6, 7.
9. Wagenheim, K. (1973), *Clemente!,* New York: Praeger Publishers, p. 51.
10. Jordan, Pat (1975), *A False Spring,* New York: Dodd, Mead & Co., p. 263.
11. Ibid., p. 264.
12. Oriard (1982), op. cit., p. 289.
13. Ibid., p. 311.
14. Smith, M. (1987), *Life after Hockey,* Lynx, CT: Codner Books, pp. 7–8.
15. Ibid., p. 208.
16. Oriard (1982), op. cit., p. 130.
17. Meggyesy, D. (1970), *Out of Their League,* Berkeley, CA: Ramparts Press, p. 191.
18. Smith (1987), op. cit., pp. 173–86.
19. Howard, J. (1999), "The Making of a Goon," In Halberstam, D. (Ed.), *American Sports Writing of the Century,* Boston: Houghton Mifflin, p. 572.

20. Dryden, K. (1983), *The Game,* Toronto: Macmillan, p. 14.

21. Schollander and Savage (1971), op. cit.

22. Gordon, S. (1995), "Career Transitions in Competitive Sport," In Morris, T. and Summers, J. (Eds.), *Sport Psychology: Theory, Applications and Issues,* Brisbane, Australia: Jacaranda Wiley, pp. 474–501.

23. In Fortunato, V. and Marchant, D. (1999), "Forced Retirement from Elite Football in Australia," *Journal of Personal & Interpersonal Loss,* 4(3), pp. 269–80.

24. In Smith (1987), op. cit., p. 94.

25. Wagenheim (1973), op. cit., p. 204.

26. Oriard (1982), op. cit., pp. 316–17.

27. Brashler, W. (1978), *Josh Gibson: A Life in the Negro Leagues,* New York: Harper & Row, pp. 145-46.

28. Sands, R. (1999), *Gutcheck!,* Carpinteria, CA: Rincon Hill Books, p. 235.

29. Berger, P. (1998), *Mickey Mantle,* New York: Park Lane Press, p. 139.

30. Ibid., pp. 141–44.

31. Creamer, R. (1974), *Babe: The Legend Comes to Life,* New York. Simon & Schuster, pp. 392–95.

32. Heller, P. (1995), *Bad Intentions: The Mike Tyson Story,* New York: De Capo Press, pp. 188–89.

33. Deford, F. (1976), *Big Bill Tilden: The Triumphs and the Tragedy,* New York: Simon & Schuster, pp. 273–75.

34. Salvino, C. with Klein, F. (1988), *Fast Lanes,* Chicago: Bonus Books, p. 98.

35. Stafford, T. (1990), *Dave Dravecky: Comeback,* New York: HarperCollins.

36. Sampson, C. (1996), *Hogan,* New York: Broadway Books, pp. 115*ff.*

37. In Holtzman, J. (1995), *No Cheering in the Press Box,* New York: Henry Holt, p. 293.

38. Edmonds, A. (1973), *Joe Louis,* Grand Rapids, MI: Wm. B. Eerdmans, pp. 103–6.

39. Evensen, B. (1996), *When Dempsey Fought Tunney: Heroes, Hokum, and Storytelling in the Jazz Age,* Knoxville: Univ. of Tennessee Press, pp. 98, 121.

40. Isaacs, N. (1995), *Batboys and the World of Baseball,* Jackson, MS: Univ. of Mississippi Press, p. 185.

41. Bradley, B. (1995), *Life on the Run,* New York: Vintage Books, pp. 190–92.

42. Dryden (1983), op. cit., p. 14.

43. Fortunato and Marchant (1999), op. cit.

44. Messner (1992), op. cit., pp. 111–14.

45. In Smith (1987), op. cit., pp. 228–29.

46. Dryden (1983), op. cit., p. 246.

47. Green, T. (1996), *The Dark Side of the Game: My Life in the NFL,* New York: Warner Books, p. 261.

48. Sands (1999), op. cit., p. 235.

49. In Holtzman (1995), op. cit., p. 275.

50. Fortunato and Marchant (1999), op. cit.

51. Bradley (1995), op. cit., pp. 190–92.

52. Creamer (1974), op. cit., pp. 400*ff.*

53. In Smith (1987), op. cit., p. 219.

54. Ibid., p. 229.

55. Fortunato and Marchant (1999), op. cit.

56. Oriard (1982), op. cit., p. 249.

57. In Messner (1992), op. cit., p. 126.

58. Hauser, T. (1991), *Muhammad Ali: His Life and Times,* New York: Simon & Schuster, pp. 473–74.

59. Ashe, A. and Rampersad, A. (1993), *Days of Grace: A Memoir,* New York: Knopf, p. 45.

60. In Smith (1987), op. cit., p. 212.

61. Berger (1998), op. cit., pp. 146–55.

62. Stafford (1990), op. cit., pp. 261–62.

63. In Smith (1987), op. cit., p. 219.

64. Berger (1998), op. cit., pp. 154–63.

65. Smith (1987), op. cit., pp. 18–20.

66. Ibid., p. 106.

67. Ibid., p. 208.

68. Ibid., pp. 136–38.

69. Messner (1992), op. cit., p. 135.

70. Brashler (1978), op. cit., p. 185.

71. Smith (1987), op. cit., p. 274.

72. Meggyesy (1970), op. cit., p. 95.

73. Updike, J. (1996), *Rabbit Run,* New York: Ballantine Books.

74. Messing, S. with Hirshey, D. (1978), *The Education of an American Soccer Player,* New York: Dodd, Mead & Co., p. 13.

75. Green (1996), op. cit., pp. 260–61.

76. Ibid., pp. 263–64.

77. Jordan (1975), op. cit., p. 11.

78. Sokolove, M. (1990), *Hustle: The Myth, Life and Lies of Pete Rose,* New York: Simon & Schuster, pp. 105, 112, 180.

79. Messner, M. (1993), "The Meaning of Success: The Athletic Experience and the Development of Male Identity," In Eitzen, D.S. (Ed.), *Sport in Contemporary Society,* New York: St. Martin's Press, p. 414.

80. Conroy, P. (2002), *My Losing Season,* New York: Doubleday, p. 379.

81. Ashe and Rampersad (1993), op. cit.

82. Stump, A. (1994), *Cobb: The Life and Times of the Meanest Man Who Ever Played Baseball,* Chapel Hill, NC: Algonquin Books.

83. Smith (1987), op. cit.

84. Edmonds (1973), op. cit., pp. 103–6.

85. Newcombe, J. (1975), *The Best of the Athletic Boys: The White Man's Impact on Jim Thorpe,* New York: Doubleday.

86. Ibid., pp. 235. 241–46.

87. Gentry, T. (1990), *Jesse Owens: Champion Athlete,* New York: Chelsea House Publishers, pp. 78–83.

88. Ibid.

89. Ibid., pp. 85–96.

90. Creamer (1974), op. cit., pp. 395–96, 401–3.

91. Ibid., pp. 403–8.

92. Ibid., pp. 302, 404–5, 408*ff.*

93. Graham, F. (1942), *Lou Gehrig: A Quiet Hero,* Eau Claire, WI: E.M. Hale & Co., pp. 227–28, 236, 247.

94. Cramer (2000), op. cit., 426, 446; DeGregorio, G. (1981), *Joe DiMaggio: An Informal Biography*, Princeton, NJ: Townhouse Publishers, p. 249.

95. Dizikes (2000), op. cit., pp. 162*ff.*

96. Berger (1998), op. cit., p. 149.

97. Stump (1994), op. cit., p. 23.

98. Ibid., pp. 5–7, 408.

99. Brashler (1978), op. cit., pp. 175, 190.

100. Ibid., pp. 184–85.

101. Smith (1987), op. cit., p. 299.

102. Oriard (1982), op. cit., pp. 302–3.

103. Rampersad, A. (1997), *Jackie Robinson: A Biography*, New York: Knopf, pp. 303*ff.*

104. Johnson, J. (1992), *Jack Johnson—in the Ring and Out*, reprint, New York: Citadel Press, pp. 244–45.

105. Evensen (1996), op. cit., pp. 121*ff.*

106. Fleischer, N. (1931), *Gene Tunney—enigma of the Ring*, Springfield, MA: The Ring, Inc.

107. Cassidy, R. (1999), *Muhammad Ali: The Greatest of All Time*, Lincolnwood, IL: Publications International, pp. 146–49.

108. Mailer, N. (1998), "Ego," in Early, G. (Ed.), *The Muhmmad Ali Reader*, New York: Rob Welch Books, p. 107.

109. Ashe and Rampersad (1993), op. cit.

110. Sampson (1996), op. cit., pp. 236–37.

111. Morris, T. (1997), *Making the Team: The Cultural Work of Baseball Fiction*, Urbana: University of Illinois Press, p. 3.

112. Brashler (1978), op. cit., p. 171.

113. Graham (1942), op. cit.

114. Higgs, R. (1981), *Laurel & Thorn: The Athlete in American Literature*, Lexington, KY: The University Press of Kentucky, p. 5.

CHAPTER 9: CONCLUSIONS

1. Quoted in Tygiel, J. (1997), *Baseball's Great Experiment: Jackie Robinson and His Legacy*, New York: Oxford University Press, p. 53.

2. Gutman, Bill (1991), *Bo Jackson: A Biography*, New York: Pocket Books, p. 70.

3. Boorstin, D. (1962), *The Image, or What Happened to the American Dream*, New York: Atheneum.

4. Koppett, L. (1994), *Sports Illusion, Sports Reality: A Reporter's View of Sports, Journalism, and Society*, 2nd ed. Champaign, IL: University of Illinois Press, pp. 239–40.

5. Asimov, S. (1996), *Yours, Isaac Asimov: A Life in Letters*, New York: Main Street Books; Brodie, F. (1977), *The Devil Drives: A Life of Sir Richard Burton*, New York: W. W. Norton; Stuart, O. (1995), *Perpetual motion: The Public and Private Lives of Rudolf Nureyev*, New York: Simon & Schuster.

6. Gregory, R. (1993), *Diz: The Story of Dizzy Dean and Baseball during the Great Depression*, New York: Penguin Books; Creamer, R. (1974), *Babe: The Legend Comes to Life*, New York. Simon & Schuster.

INDEX

37–38, 49, 53–54, 70, 73–81 passim, 106, 113–14, 133, 146, 164, 167, 169, 174–75, 182; and Brother Matthias, 18–19; early life, 5, 18–19, 31; and wives, 98, 106
Ryun, Jim, 82

Saleski, Don, 169
Salvino, Carmen, xvii, 5–6, 19, 49, 54, 69, 72, 75–76, 98, 143, 149; early life, 8, 20; wife Ginny, 69, 98
Sanctuary, sport as, 16, 21–24, 28–29
Sanders, Deion, xix, xxi, 27, 46, 73, 81, 87, 129, 170; and coach Dave Capel, 17, 19; early life, 4, 6–10 passim, 16–17, 20
Sands, Robert, xxiv, 25–26, 28, 35, 84, 97, 130, 143, 157, 163, 166; *Gutcheck!*, xxiv
San Francisco (CA), 50, 87
Sanguillen, Manny, 2
Sayers, Gale, 15, 83, 125
Schaap, Dick, xx, 49
Schecter, Leonard, xxi
Schmeling, Max, 45, 48, 173
Schollander, Don, xxiv, 10, 40, 45, 47, 62, 69, 71–72, 85, 87, 89, 96, 142, 157–62 passim; *Deep Water*, xxi; early life, 3, 5, 14, 16, 19–20
Schulz, Joe, 95
Scouts, talent, 2, 6, 8, 33, 46, 162, 169; Pedrin Zorila, 6
Seabiscuit (Hillenbrand), xxiii
Season of competition, schedule, xv, xix–xx, 12, 30, 61–62, 64–74 passim, 78, 84, 88, 99, 103–4, 108, 122, 139, 142–43, 146–48, 153, 161, 168
Sex (coitus), 105–8, 182; abstinence, 104; aggressive, 97, 107; casual, 104–9, 182; group, 107–9; as performance, 107–8; with prostitutes, 105–6, 108–9
Shakespeare, William, 158
Shell, Todd, 160
Sifford, Charlie, 117
Simms, Willie, 111
Sisyphus (myth of), 61

Sloan, Tod, xxii, 46, 48, 51, 68, 71, 73, 76, 80, 86, 112, 159, 175, 183; and Broadway musical "Yankee Doodle Dandy," xxii, 46early life, 46;
Smith, Ed, 39
Smith, Gary, 101
Smith, Michael, 172; *Life After Hockey*, xxiii, 172
Smith, Tommy (sprinter), 116
Smith, W. W. "Red," 31
Snider, Edwin "Duke," 119
Soccer, xxiii–xxiv, 3, 5, 8, 11, 15, 25, 55, 61–62, 71–73, 82–83, 102, 142, 148, 170; NASL, xxiii, 72; New York Cosmos, 15, 48, 83, 102; World Cup, 71
Social class of athletes, 3–4, 8, 15, 17, 19–20, 81–82, 116, 120; social mobility, 4, 20, 112
Sokolove, Michael, xx, 44
Soul on Ice (Cleaver), 117
South African apartheid, 128, 179
Speaker, Tris, 76
Spiller, Bill, 117
Sportsman v. athlete, xxiii–xxiv
Sports writers. *See* Journalists
Stadiums, arenas, and ballparks: Balch Gym (Boulder, CO), 142; Bennett Park (Detroit), 68; Boston Garden, 12; Busch Stadium, 79; Fenway Park, 12; Forbes Field, 48, 114; Madison Square Garden, 49, 178; Polo Grounds, 119; Queen's Park Club (Trinidad), 120; Riverfront Stadium (Cincinnati), 86; Sesquicentennial Stadium (Philadelphia), 45; Yankee stadium, 99, 148, 180
Starr, Larry, 146, 171
Stereotypes: African American, 128, 132; American Indian, 113, 173; athlete's father, 10; black athlete, 129–30; child athlete, 3; failed black family, 19, 128; jock, 74, 183; women (within male sport culture), 98
Stewart, Bobby, 18
Stovall, J. C., 115
Stram, Hank, 36